SPORTSMAN'S BEST

BOOK & DVD SERIES

FS Books:
Sportsman's Best: Boats
Sportsman's Best: Inshore Fishing
Sportsman's Best: Offshore Fishing
Sportsman's Best: Kayak Fishing
Sportsman's Best: Sight Fishing
Sportsman's Best: Surf Fishing
Sportsman's Best: Snapper & Grouper
Sportsman's Best: Sailfish
Sportsman's Best: Trout
Sportsman's Best: Redfish
Sportsman's Best: Dolphin
Sportsman's Best: Snook

Sport Fish of Florida
Sport Fish of the Gulf of Mexico
Sport Fish of the Atlantic
Sport Fish of Fresh Water
Sport Fish of the Pacific

Baits, Rigs & Tackle
Annual Fishing Planner
The Angler's Cookbook
Florida Sportsman Magazine

Florida Sportsman Fishing Charts
Lawsticks
Law Boatstickers
Field GuideID Lawsticks

Authors, James Crounse, Dave East
Photo Credits, James Crounse, Florida Sportsman, Eric Wickstrom Photography
Edited by Florida Sportsman Editors
Graphic Design by Mark Naumovitz, Drew Wickstrom
Graphic Illustrations by Jeff Macharyras

First Printing
Copyright ©2014 by Florida Sportsman
2700 S. Kanner Hwy., Stuart, FL 34994
All Rights Reserved
Printed in the United States of America

ISBN-13: 978-1-934622-24-7
ISBN-10: 1-934622-24-9

www.floridasportsman.com

Find us on
Facebook

BOATS

HOW TO CHOOSE, RIG AND HANDLE YOUR NEW BOAT

Boating Know-How ■ Tips From the Pros ■ Catch More Fish

CONTENTS

**SPORTSMAN'S BEST
BOATS**

10

104

Twenty years from now you will be more disappointed by the things that you didn't do than by the ones you did do. So throw off the bowlines. Sail away from the safe harbor. Catch the trade winds in your sails. Explore. Dream. Discover.

— Mark Twain (unconfirmed)

Fishing at Sebastian Inlet State Park in Florida, looking forward to the day of owning a boat.

Foreword
Your Day Has Come

If you're dreaming of owning your first boat, or looking to buy a new boat that better fits your needs, your day has come. Americans are taking to the water in record numbers: Of the 241.9 million adults in the US in 2013, 36.6%, or 88.5 million, participated in recreational boating at least once during 2013. And unlike any time in our history, boat manufacturers are building – and rigging – boats to fit your very specific need or activity.

So with this in mind, buying the right boat, the best boat for you, means more about choosing the boat based on how you're going to use it rather than who builds it. *SPORTSMAN'S BEST: BOATS,* author Dave East sums it up when he says "be realistic" with your boating plans when considering what boat to buy.

Once you have the right boat all the rest will fall into place, but to help you in the process, *SPORTSMAN'S BEST: BOATS* author James Crounse has some very straightforward and practical advice on making your days on the water stress free and enjoyable.

I've owned seven boats, from 14 feet to 40 feet, over the last 29 years, and without a doubt boating is easier today than ever before. Outboard power is as dependable as your car. Incredibly user-friendly electronics make navigation much easier. Cell phones solve much of the old communication issues, and boats are simply built with better, longer lasting materials.

So, what are you waiting for? Your day has come.

Happy Boating,
Blair Wickstrom
Publisher, Florida Sportsman Magazine

Introduction
The Allure of Boating

Boats are an endless source of good times... family fun, camaraderie, adventure, relaxation and even delicious and nutritious seafood.

There you were, standing on the shoreline, fishing for hours to little or no avail. Boats and the lucky ones aboard them could be seen off in the distance fishing the same waters, but they had a distinct advantage. Be it as a wide-eyed kid or as a retired grandfather, you soon began to wish that you too could just step onto a boat, turn the key, and venture out to explore for your own secret honey hole.

The tactical advantages gained by fishing from a boat, as opposed to fishing from land, are exactly why any avid angler simply needs to own a fishing boat. And with today's high-tech electronics and fishing equipment, catching fish is more fun and less work than ever before.

There are plenty of other compelling reasons for owning a boat. Just being out on the water can be therapeutic and relaxing. When the weather and water conditions are just right, there's really nothing quite like it. It's an extraordinary way to temporarily escape the stress and pressures of life.

There's also a sense of pride that comes along with owning a boat... the type that one owns says a lot about who they are.

Boating opens up endless opportunities to explore new waterways, ports and islands. It's a great way to gain a fresh appreciation for our planet's natural, beautiful scenery from a new perspective.

Going fishing, participating in watersports and cruising to points of interest in a boat with family or friends is a fun way to enjoy quality time together, while at the same time connecting with nature and experiencing unforgettable adventures. And the possibility of bringing home some fresh fish, as well as the probability for some cherishable photo and video opportunities are certainly gratifying bonuses.

Whether you're new to the world of fishing boats and boating, or just looking for guidance to help you get back on the water and after the fish, you've landed the best resource available anywhere.

SPORTSMAN'S BEST: BOATS is your comprehensive guide to recreational fishing boats in the trailerable, 14' to 38' range. This insightful and current book offers boatloads of useful information and tips, helpful how-to's, and practical advice relevant to the most popular types of fishing and family-friendly boats.

Need help choosing your ideal boat? Which type of motor and accessories will best meet your specific fishing and boating needs? Should you opt for a new boat or a used one? Have you considered the transportation and storage requirements for your new boat?

There are several important questions that need to be considered prior to making such a major purchasing decision. Where to search, what to look for, and what to know before negotiating are all crucial to achieving what should be your ultimate goal – to land the most practical and ideal boat for you and your locale.

Presented on the pages ahead are boating safety guidelines and precautions, checklists of what you'll need onboard to boat and fish trouble-free, and much more.

We'll help take the stress out of trailering, launching and loading your boat, and guide you in the right direction so that you won't turn any heads at your local boat ramp.

We'll cover boat operating and handling, along with guidance for navigation to keep you on course.

Did you know that in certain conditions, anchoring a boat incorrectly can actually capsize it in a matter of seconds? You'll learn how to prevent that, and how to securely anchor your vessel every time.

Docking a boat well is probably the one aspect of boating that beginners tend to struggle with the most. We'll go over step-by-step docking procedures that will help you learn to dock like a pro.

And of course, stealthily getting to where the fish are is covered as well.

We also advise wise ways to avoid a variety of costly problems with excellent maintenance tips, and offer recommendations for boat storage and winterizing to help you protect your investment.

Last but not least, the final chapter provides the legal requirements and responsibilities pertaining to boat ownership, along with lists of some great resources we recommend.

Welcome aboard, it's time to show you the ropes!

James Crounse, Author

Author James Crounse has been immersed in the marine industry since 1998, including a decade owning and managing a year-round powerboat rental business on the Intracoastal Waterway in Brevard County, Florida. Over the course of 10-plus years and thousands of rentals and charters of various types of powerboats, he developed the skills and gained the expertise that he conveys and shares in *SPORTSMAN'S BEST: BOATS.*

James is also the author of *BOATING SAVVY: What KNOT To Do™ – Often-overlooked & Lesser-known Keys To Safe & Smart Power Boating.* He continues to enjoy working in, writing about and

photographing the incomparable world of boating.

Author Dave East is the Boating Editor for Florida Sportsman magazine and host of the Florida Sportsman Best Boat TV series. His love for boating started at a very early age and eventually became his livelihood, working as a boat manufacturer for over 23 years. In that time Dave has seen more than one person purchase a boat out of impulse only to find out later that it wasn't the best boat for their needs. Now through the Best Boat TV series, magazine and book he hopes to assist you in making a more informed buying decision.

CHAPTER 1

Choosing the Best Boat for You

Browse around at a boat show and take in all of the marine industry's new product developments and design improvements. Compared to what was being displayed just ten years ago, there are some very prominent and welcome changes. One change that may jump out and grab your attention is in the ultra-modern, sleek design features of many of the latest boat models. SB

Which type of the latest boat designs will be ideal for you and your boating needs?

The Miami
International Boat
Show is one of the
world's largest
venues of its kind.

Get Started

Outboard-powered boats are the most popular, making up about 82 percent of the new boat market.

Remember back in the '90s when you would always see artists' renderings of those awesome-looking concept cars and boats in the magazines, and you looked forward to seeing them in traffic or out on the water? And then... nothing. They never seemed to make it to mass production, at least not looking a whole lot like those concept illustrations. Well those days are over. Thanks to technological advancements in computer-aided design and manufacturing processes, marine (and car) manufacturers are now much better-equipped to make their concept designs a reality, and it's really beginning to show.

You also can't help but notice all of the enticing, new, cutting-edge equipment that can be seen from bow to stern on every type of new boat. Companies that produce boat and fishing accessories and electronics are currently on a roll of outdoing themselves by continually coming up with exciting new inventions and high-tech toys that didn't exist just a few years ago. Most of them are really quite impressive, and they'll be covered in Chapter 5.

Another recent change across the board in the recreational boating industry is an increase in the percentage of new boats sold that are outboard powered, as opposed to stern drive (I/O) or inboard engine powered. Outboard-powered boats are now the most popular type, making up about 82 percent of the new boat market. For recreational fishing boats, that percentage is even higher.

Outboard motor manufacturers continue to raise the bar on horsepower output, reliability, and improved fuel economy, as well as reduced emissions and engine noise levels. Much more about outboard motors is coming up in Chapter 4.

A versatile bay boat, above, is an increasingly popular choice for people who enjoy cruising and fishing.

Many newer bay boats are designed and equipped to ride and fish offshore in moderate seas, though always know your limits.

Companies that produce boat and fishing gear and electronics are continually coming up with exciting new innovations.

Big center consoles, like this one roaring out of Hillsboro Inlet in Florida, are made for handling a variety of sea conditions.

New Boats vs. Used Boats

As when shopping for vehicles, there are pros and cons of buying new versus used that should be weighed out in order to decide which option best suits your principles and financial situation.

So which is better, new or used? Will your spouse be onboard with your decision to bring home a brand new boat? Do the savings of buying used, outweigh the potential risk?

Only you can decide... here are some key points to consider that should help you choose what is best for you:

New Boat Pros:

• Factory Warranties: (Peace of mind)
Outboard Motors: 3- to 6-year limited warranty.
Boat Components: 1- to 5-year limited warranty.
Boat Hulls: 3 years to lifetime warranty.
(No boat warranty covers everything. Be sure to read the fine print.)
• Availability of the latest, most advanced and powerful, fuel-efficient, reliable, quietest, low-emission outboard motors ever produced. (Although used boats can be repowered with new outboard motors.)
• Availability of the latest, most advanced high-tech electronics, equipment and accessories ever produced. (Although used boats can be retrofitted and equipped with new components.)
• None of the used boat concerns, such as undetected mechanical or electrical problems, or underlying structural issues.
• A shiny, brand new boat runs like a dream, looks great, and makes you proud to own it.

New Boat Cons:

• You take the initial depreciation hit. Once a boat has been used, it is worth substantially less than the original retail price.
• All of the recent technology and quality improvements come at premium, raising the cost of many new boats considerably.
• Deluxe model boats or adding on multiple upgrade options, significantly increases the cost of a boat from its base price.
• Even new boats can have mechanical, electrical or fiberglass problems, such as factory wiring issues or gelcoat voids.
(Covered by warranty, but inconvenient)
• Keeping a new boat running and looking like new requires plenty of time, energy and/or money.

Brand new boats look great, run like a dream, and offer peace of mind.

A used boat can be a less expensive starter option for those new to boating, with plans to eventually transition from a smaller class to a larger one.

Used Boat Pros:

• The original buyer already took the initial depreciation hit for you. A good used boat can cost as little as one third of its original retail price.
• Buying used may make your ideal dream boat affordable, without settling for a smaller or lesser one. The same amount of money can buy a lot more used boat than new.
• Used boats can be a less expensive starter option for those new to boating, with plans to eventually transition from a smaller boat to a larger one.
• Low-quality parts and materials are easier to detect on used boats. Rapid corrosion and low-grade gelcoat that turns chalky, begin to reveal themselves after the first few years.
• A 5-year-old, top-tier brand boat can outlast a new, low-tier brand boat.
• Used boats are more likely than new boats to already be fully equipped with the fishing accessories, gear and extras that you would otherwise need to purchase separately.

Used Boat Cons:

• Possibility of buying someone else's existing and/or soon-to-arise problems, such as underlying structural issues, fuel system troubles caused by ethanol gas, undetected mechanical or electrical problems or various motor problems caused by neglect.
• Used boats invariably require more maintenance and part replacements than new boats.
• Usually As-Is with no warranty (unless the original owner purchased an extended, transferable warranty that's still in effect, or unless it's still a nearly new boat).
• The older a boat is, the less fuel-efficient it is likely to be.
• Used boats aren't new. For some people, that alone is worth the price difference.

Aluminum or Fiberglass

Certain models of aluminum boats are now as stylish, capable and well-equipped as their fiberglass counterparts.

If you're in the market for any type of freshwater fishing boat under 25 feet, you should include aluminum-hulled boats in your boat shopping quest.

Aluminum fishing boats have come a long way in recent years and certain models are now just as stylish, capable and well-equipped as their fiberglass counterparts, but cost substantially less. Thanks in part to advances in computer-aided, aluminum fabrication processes, aluminum boat hulls can now be efficiently manufactured with stronger and more complex hull shapes than ever before.

Aluminum boats have increased in popularity and sales recently throughout freshwater fishing regions of the U.S. With aluminum being lighter and less-expensive than fiberglass, they not only cost less to purchase up front than comparable fiberglass boats, but also cost slightly less to own, since they require less horsepower and fuel to run and to tow.

Have you seen the modern, aluminum fishing boats lately? If not, it's possible that you actually have, but didn't recognize them as being made of aluminum.

Many new aluminum boats offer a more affordable alternative to fiberglass boats.

Aluminum: Welded vs. Riveted

There's some debate about welded versus riveted aluminum boats, in terms of construction. Rivets can loosen, and welds can fail, causing leaks. It's probably more common for a riveted boat to eventually require a leak repair than a welded boat. But it's also more difficult to correctly repair broken welds than rivets.

The good news is, the majority of owners of either build type will get decades of reliable use out of their aluminum boat without a single leak. As long as excessive stresses on the hull are avoided, such as impacts against rocks or stumps, and hard poundings on rough waters, both riveted and welded aluminum boats offer a low-maintenance, durable alternative to small to mid-size fiberglass boats.

Many fiberglass boat builders produce hulls, transoms and decks that are wood-free, using stronger and lighter materials that won't rot.

The majority of boats are built of fiberglass. Modern design and manufacturing techniques allow virtually any conceivable hull shape to be fiberglass molded. This allows for boat builders to design and produce high-strength, heavy-duty hulls that meet the performance requirements for a wide variety of boating activities, water conditions and depths.

Although fiberglass is strong, durable and fairly low-maintenance, it does require some long-term maintenance and protection from the elements. Shiny, new gelcoat, which is the smooth, hard surface layer applied to the hull and most exposed surface areas on fiberglass boats (made from polyester resin or epoxy), will fade, chalk and stain over time if not kept clean and protected from the sun, weather and contaminants.

Another concern with some fiberglass boats is internal: There is the potential for structural wood rot in any boat constructed with wood in the hull, transom, or deck. Wood and fiberglass cannot chemically bond, and even fiberglass-laminated, marine-grade plywood can expand and contract over time, which can eventually cause delamination and/or wood rot, leading to structural weakness or failures. Also, wood softens when wet, allowing mounting screws and fasteners to fail and pull loose.

Many builders produce boats with hulls, transoms and decks that are wood-free, using stronger and lighter structural materials that won't delaminate or rot.

The majority of medium to large size recreational boats are constructed of fiberglass because of its moldability, strength and durability. Below, modern manufacturing techniques allow virtually any conceivable hull shape to be fiberglass molded.

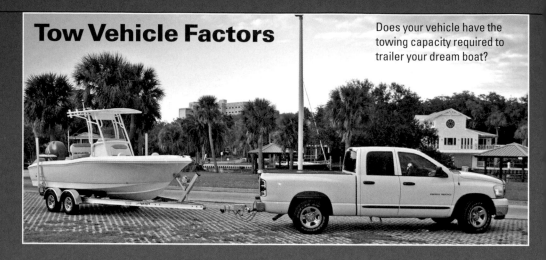

Tow Vehicle Factors

Does your vehicle have the towing capacity required to trailer your dream boat?

Unless you're able to keep your boat on a dry storage rack at a marina, or on its own boat lift at your private dock, then – like the majority of boat owners – you'll be keeping your new boat on its trailer and having to tow it behind your vehicle.

As a very basic guideline, 3,500 pounds is the general dividing line between light-duty and heavy-duty towing requirements. For any boat/motor/trailer combination weighing less than 3,500 pounds (including a full tank of fuel in the boat and all loaded equipment and gear), a medium-sized truck or SUV will suffice for towing on relatively flat terrain. This can include certain 4-cylinder trucks if, and only if rated by the manufacturer for towing up to 3,500 pounds. If you're in the market for a smaller, lighter boat (typically under 21 feet) and already own a vehicle rated accordingly, then the only additional equipment you might need to purchase and install on your vehicle, is a frame-mounted trailer hitch package, unless of course it already has one.

However, for most boats that are around 21 feet and larger, a full-sized truck or SUV is needed, along with a boat trailer equipped with a brake system and two or more axles. Naturally, the heavier a boat is, the more heavy-duty of a tow vehicle is needed to haul it. The largest of trailerable boats can only be properly towed with the most powerful line of heavy-duty dually trucks, which are expensive to purchase and keep fueled up.

So prior to beginning your boat shopping mis-sion, it will be necessary to check your vehicle owner's manual or manufacturer's website for the maximum trailering capability. Then, for each boat you have serious interest in, be sure to find out what the combined weight of the boat (full of gas, gear, and any stored water), motor(s), and trailer are, in order to determine whether or not it can be safely and legally towed by your vehicle.

Is it really that big of a deal? Absolutely, and it's also an aspect of boating that's sometimes

3,500 lbs. is the dividing line between light- and heavy-duty boat-towing requirements.

disregarded or overlooked, despite the inherent safety hazards. Exceeding the towing capacity of a vehicle can be the cause of problems ranging from an expensive traffic citation, to a major highway accident. And even if you're fortunate enough to avoid either from happening, hauling an excessive load can still result in engine and transmission damage to the tow vehicle. Also, in the case of a related accident, you'd face the possibility of being denied by your insurance company for any accident claim. Much more about trailering and towing capacities will be explained in Chapter 7.

Boat Ownership is Both a Financial and Time Commitment

Besides the initial cost of purchasing or putting a down payment on a boat, there are ongoing, long-term costs associated with boat ownership. So not only is it necessary to ask yourself if you can afford the boat itself, you also need to be sure you'll be able to take on all of the unavoidable, additional expenses too. Here's a basic table to help you tally up the usual expenses and to track your annual costs:

EXPENSE	ANNUAL COST
Monthly Payment x 12 (if financed)	$
Boat & Trailer Registration Fees	$
Insurance Premium	$
Fuel	$
Maintenance & Repairs	$
Depreciation (ask your CPA)	$
Storage Fees (if applicable)	$
2-cycle Oil (2-stroke motors only)	$
Miscellaneous	$
TOTAL	$

There's no shortage of boat owners who have added up the total annual outlay of owning their boat, only to realize that it's costing them thousands of dollars *per boat trip* – simply because they're using the boat so much less than they had hoped to when it was purchased. And a cruelly ironic side-effect of letting a boat sit unused is that it only exacerbates this economic frustration by costing even more for the inevitable repairs that are typically required after long periods of non-use.

So think it through to be sure that boat ownership really is right for you, and that you have no doubts about being able to find the time to use your new boat enough to justify the overall and ongoing costs. If you do have any reservations about these long-term commitments, you may want to consider boat renting or a membership club as an alternative.

Renting is a great way to get your feet wet and help you decide which type of boat is right for you.

Renting Before Buying

A great way to get a lengthy, on-the-water demo in the type of boat(s) you're interested in, is to rent one for a day. If you have access to a rental facility that happens to rent the same type of boat you're leaning towards, this can be a much more telling way to really get a feel for it than the short trial runs offered by boat dealerships, without any of the high-pressure sales tactics you sometimes encounter from salesmen. Some boat dealers don't allow their new boats to hit the water until the sale is signed and delivered (which is reasonable for new boats sold in saltwater market areas). Any used boat should be allowed to go out for a trial run, and if not – be leery.

Renting or a membership club are alternatives to owning a boat.

Provided that you live within driving distance of an outfit offering rentals or a boat club, renting or a membership plan can be a less-expensive, relatively hassle-free alternative to boat ownership. If there are any doubts that you would be able to find the time and/or energy to take a new boat out more than just a few times per year, as is the case for too many boat owners, this can be a very viable option.

Renting can still be beneficial for boat owners too. For example, owners of vessels such as large sportfishing boats sometimes need a smaller, more practical boat for taking the grandkids out for a day of tubing and casual fishing. Or, owners of bass boats or flats boats might sometimes need a larger, family-style boat to take visiting friends out for a tour of the local waters. A half or full day rental of a boat, such as a deck boat, is the perfect solution to entertain family or friends for the occasional change of boating needs.

Fuel Expenses and GPH

Fuel is of course a major factor in the cost of boat ownership. The larger and heavier a boat is, the more horsepower it will require to run, and the more vehicle towing capacity it will require to tow, which naturally will require more fuel for both – the higher up the boat size scale you go. To get an idea of how much you're likely to spend on fuel per year is more complicated than figuring the miles per gallon of an automobile, which is much more constant. Gallons per hour is a better representation of boating fuel consumption. There are more variables involved in GPH factors, and the GPH that a boat will actually burn can fluctuate signifi-

The price of marina fuel is higher than on the road, due to the marina's extra costs.

cantly from one boating trip to the next, based on wind and water conditions, how hard the boat is run, and the loads it is subjected to.

If you ask the dealership or person selling a boat to you, what you can expect GPH-wise, likely you'll get only a rough estimate. They don't really know what your boating activities will entail or how conservative you'll be on the throttle lever.

Most new boats equipped with digital gauges also have integrated fuel-flow sensor electronics that display a GPH reading. But for boats that don't have this feature, the best way to get an accurate average GPH for your boat, is to first top

Manufacturers have met the demand for a greater variety of all-purpose boat types.

off the fuel tank(s) to completely full. Then when you go out boating, log the total number of hours that the boat was running, including idle speed. When you refuel, completely top it off again to see how many gallons it takes to refill. To calculate the GPH, just divide the number of gallons it took to refill, by the total number of hours the boat ran, and you'll have your GPH average. Example: 43.75 Gallons ÷ 6.25 Hours = 7.0 GPH Average. You can later figure an overall average of your typical fuel usage, after a few more top-offs are calculated.

Family Fun with Watersports

Watersports are ever popular, with new types of boards and water toys appearing all the time, and watersports that require a tow boat are no exception. Wakeboarding has become the boating watersport of choice for anyone who's into board sports, especially the younger generations. Tubing has come a long way from the old days when truck tire inner tubes were actually used. The variety of tubes on the market now includes any design you can imagine, and then some. Tubing is fun way to cool off for people of all ages, and is almost as entertaining to watch from the boat, as it is for the rider. Plus, anyone of any skill level can do it since it all you have to do is hold onto the handles for dear life.

Fish & ski boats, bay boats, deck boats, dual console boats and even pontoon boats are widely available with plenty of horsepower and every option needed to enjoy water-skiing and other activities on the same day trip. So unless your boating activities will be strictly limited to serious fishing, choosing a fishing boat that's perfect for you and that can also accommodate your family needs and wants is very much within reach.

Tubing has come a long way from the old days when truck tire inner tubes were actually used.

Be Prepared to Be Prepared

Once you've decided exactly which type and size of boat and motor will be best for you, and whether to focus your boat shopping efforts toward new or pre-owned, you'll be ready to start comparing the specific boats for sale in your market area.

But first, before beginning to narrow down your potential choices to the one boat that will become your pride and joy, you need to know the best, most time-efficient ways to start your search, and what to know and look for before negotiating. The next few chapters will get you primed and prepared to make your best choice.

Wakeboarding has become the boating watersport of choice for anyone who's into skateboarding, snowboarding or surfing.

CHAPTER 2

Types of Fishing Boats

Fishing is one of America's most popular nature-based, outdoor recreational activities. It draws many millions of participants of all ages to lakes, rivers, bays and waterways of all kinds, from coast to coast, even out into our vast oceans. So it's no coincidence that watercraft that can be classified as recreational fishing boats constitute the largest category of boats manufactured and sold in the USA.

The most popular fishing boats range in size from 14 feet to 38 feet. About the only attributes they all have in common across the board are: They're designed for fishing, they're propelled by a motor of one kind or another, and they can be trailered. But that's basically where the similarities end. SB

Watercraft that can be classified as recreational fishing boats constitute the largest category of boats manufactured and sold in the USA.

A boat's hull shape – more than anything else – is what determines which type of boat it actually is, and which type of waters and fishing it's built and best suited for.

Boat Design

In a comparison of the various fishing boat types, design elements such as the hull shape, structural framework, deck and helm station layout, and the overall size and weight – as well as the specific types of construction materials used to build any particular boat – are all major factors in a boat's realistic practicality and capabilities.

There are now more available choices than ever of exceptionally versatile boat types that are well-equipped for fishing, watersports and pleasure cruising alike. Manufacturers have also adapted certain boats to be suitable for both freshwater and saltwater for maximum usability and fishability.

The conveniences offered by these versatile boat options should make choosing a fishing boat that's best for you, and that can also accommodate your family needs and wants, a lot less difficult.

For the most devoted anglers who are willing to pay a premium for the ultimate, loaded, specialty fishing boat – geared precisely for their favorite kind of fishing – some of the choices may be very expensive, but they're also very impressive.

In this chapter we'll cover the more important details of the most popular, trailerable fishing boat types on the market today. But first, there are some key points to keep in mind that apply to these boats in general.

Hull Types

There are three main hull types: displacement, semi-displacement, and planing. Each has advantages and drawbacks, and the variables that affect these can get quite complex. Let's keep it simple and just focus on the hull design basics relevant to the boat types covered in this book.

Displacement hulls are mostly round-bottomed, and are much more common to sailboats and larger, heavier boats, yachts and ships. Most trailerable fishing boats belong to the planing hull category.

Planing hulls are designed to plane out and ride on the water's surface, rather than plowing or pushing through water, as displacement hulls do. A plan-

ing hull takes advantage of hydrodynamic lift, which is produced by the combination of forward speed and surface force, and is enhanced by the chines and strakes that are molded into the hull. The resulting advantage over a displacement hull is reduced drag and increased speed. But the drawbacks, which multiply exponentially the more a boat weighs, are a

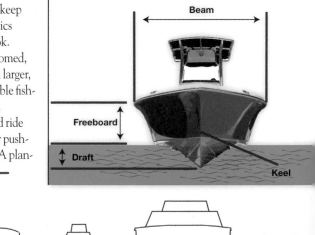

Skiff   Center Console   Bay Boat   Catamaran

Shown are a few of the most prevalent types of popular recreational fishing boats. The design of the hull determines what waters the boat is appropriate for and what performance characteristics, like stability, handling, seaworthiness and speed, the boat will display.

demanding power-to-weight ratio (it takes a lot of horsepower and fuel to get a heavy boat up on plane), and relative inefficiency when running below planing speeds.

Again, these are the three most basic hull shapes. There are several more combinations or hybrids of these basic hull shapes that have been developed to produce more complex, multi-faceted hull shapes that are designed into the majority of modern boats.

The 3 Basic Hull Shapes	Advantages	Disadvantages
Flat	Very stable at rest. Very shallow draft. Requires less hp to plane.	Limited to calm waters. Harsh ride in chop. Not seaworthy.
Vee	Best for high speed. Tracks well. Cuts through chop & waves.	Requires more hp to plane out. Deep draft. Less lateral stability at rest.
Round (Displacement Only)	Efficient at low speeds. Requires less hp to propel.	Limited speed. Tends to rock laterally at rest.

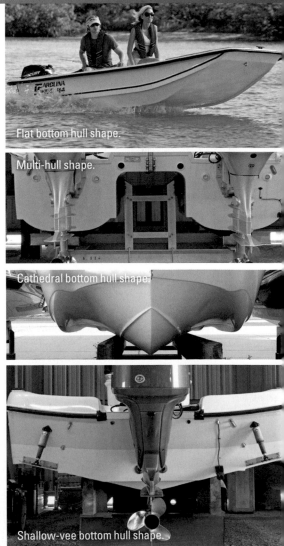

Flat bottom hull shape.

Multi-hull shape.

Cathedral bottom hull shape.

Modified-vee bottom hull shape: deep-vee at the bow (above), transitioning to a shallow-vee at the stern (below).

Shallow-vee bottom hull shape.

The boat types featured in this book will have one of the following hull shapes: flat, shallow-vee, cathedral or tri-hull, modified-vee, deep-vee, tunnel-hull, multi-hull or pontoons. These are all either defined in the glossary, or explained in the appropriate boat description.

The marine industry continues its quest to design and build hulls that fulfill the requirements and desires of the widest possible variety of boaters.

Why? Because significantly different hull types and shapes produce such radical differences in overall stability, motor power necessity, efficiency, ride quality, handling characteristics, top speed capability and seaworthiness. And since there is no universal, all-purpose hull shape that can deliver every possible hull design advantage, the challenge continues. For many anglers, the ultimate fishing boat would have no problem poling through a foot of water without running aground, on Saturday, and then be able to handle 6-foot seas without knocking out any teeth, on Sunday. So far, no such boat exists. For the fisherman who wants it all in a fishing boat, there has to be some compromise one way or the other.

Deep-vee bottom hull shape:
a bow view (above),
a stern view (below).

The Center Console Clarified

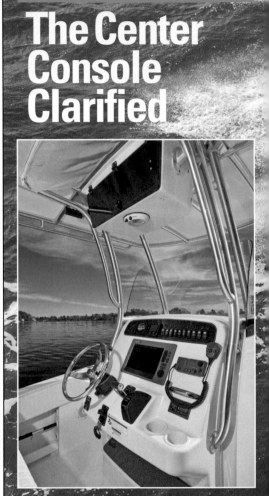

The term "center console" is somewhat imprecise and overused in reference to certain types of fishing boats, though there's a reason for the common misnomer.

There are at least four different types of fishing boats built with the ever-popular and distinctive center helm station configuration. Fishing skiffs, flats boats, bay boats and the actual center console boats – long called called "open fisherman" – all have similar deck and seating layouts, and share many of the same surface finishes, utility features, fishing equipment and metalwork.

What's the best way to differentiate between center console boats that look so much alike? Just look at the shape of the hull from bow to

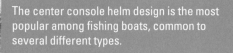

The center console helm design is the most popular among fishing boats, common to several different types.

Most boat builders designate a center console as a seaworthy fishing boat with a deep-vee hull, designed and constructed for offshore use.

stern. A boat's hull shape – more than anything else – is what determines which type of boat it actually is, and which type of waters and fishing it's best suited for. Once you become familiar with the different hull shapes and what they're designed for, you'll be able to quickly ascertain exactly which type of boat you're looking at. The same principle of course applies to other boat types that can also look so similar to each other, such as dual consoles and fish and ski boats.

A few manufacturers may refer to certain boats as a center console model, in reference to an optional helm station configuration. So it's not exactly egregious to call any boat with a center console, a "center console." But most boat builders designate a center console boat as a seaworthy fishing boat with a deep-vee hull, designed and constructed for both inshore saltwater and offshore ocean or large lake use. None of the other three aforementioned boats have deep-vee hulls built for seaworthiness, so aren't designed to handle and endure rough offshore seas. We'll get to what they are designed for, boat by boat.

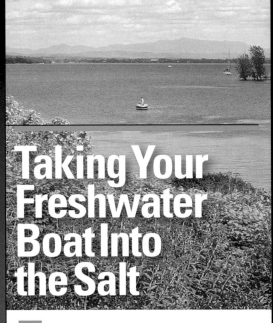

The center console design allows for full 360-degree visibility around the boat.

There are four good reasons for the popularity of the center console helm station design. First, it allows for the boat to be comfortably-operated from a standing position with a good handhold, which is often advantageous for the best overall view of the water – and for riding through rough seas. Second, it allows for 360 degree, unobstructed access to the water from the boat, which is of course very advantageous for fishing. Third, it centralizes all of a boat's controls, electronics and gauges, and places at least one dry-storage compartment within arm's reach of the captain. And fourth, the T-top – a favorite option on center console boats and bay boats – provides shade and additional rod storage overhead without compromising access to the gunwales.

T-tops are a favorite option for center console boats.

The center console helm design allows for the boat to be comfortably operated from a standing position with a good handhold.

Taking Your Freshwater Boat Into the Salt

For the most part, freshwater boats rigged and outfitted for use in freshwater, are best kept in freshwater. This is primarily because when these boats are assembled, they aren't rigged and wired with marine-grade, corrosion-resistant components such as stainless steel hardware and tinned copper wiring, as saltwater boats are. The saltwater environment – both water and air – causes rapid corrosion and pitting, damaging the unprotected components and accessories. Exceptions obviously are certain freshwater boats, such as some aluminum jon boat and bass boat models that are rigged with marine-grade wiring and stainless or plastic hardware.

Fresh water angler with a nice lake trout.

15

Left: Freshwater fishing at Lake Champlain, Plattsburgh, New York. Right: Quality aluminum boats generally associated with freshwater, can be rigged for the saltwater environment as well.

Specs of the Most Popular Fishing Boats in the Trailerable, 14' to 38' range.

Boat Type Category:	Waters Made For:	Primary Fishing Use:	Boat Size Range:	Persons Capacity:	Outboard Motor Range:
Aluminum Jon Boat & Utility Boat	Fresh or Inshore	Multi-Purpose Freshwater Fish	10-21'	2-6	2.5-115 hp
Fishing Skiff	Fresh or Inshore	Multi-Purpose Fresh / Saltwater Fish	14-24'	2-8	5-200 hp
Multi-Species or Walleye Boat	Fresh	Walleye, Crappie, Musky, Smallmouth, Bass, etc.	16-22'	4-6	60-300 hp
Bass Boat	Fresh	Bass, Crappie, Bream, Redfish, Seatrout, Snook, Tarpon, etc.	16-24'	2-4	60-300 hp
Flats Boat / Flats Skiff	Inshore / Nearshore	Redfish, Seatrout, Snook, Tarpon, etc	15-22'	2-4	40-300 hp
Bay Boat	Inshore / Nearshore	Multi-Purpose, Saltwater Fish	16-26'	4-8	50-350 hp
Fish & Ski / Crossover	Fresh / Inshore	Multi-Purpose, Saltwater Fish	17-22'	4-8	115-300 hp
Deck Boat	Fresh / Inshore	Multi-Purpose Fresh / Saltwater Fish	18-26'	6-12	150-300 hp (1 to 2 motors)
Pontoon Boat	Fresh / Inshore	Multi-Purpose Fresh / Saltwater Fish	16-30'	6-16	40-350 hp (1 to 2 motors)
Catamaran or Multihull	Inshore / Offshore	Multi-Purpose, Saltwater Fish	14-35'	3-12	40-350 hp (1 to 2 motors)
Dual Console	Inshore / Offshore	Multi-Purpose, Saltwater Fish	17-37'	6-12	75-350 hp (1 to 3 motors)
Center Console or Open Fisherman	Inshore / Offshore	Multi-Purpose, Saltwater Fish	15-38'	3-12	50-350 hp (1 to 3 motors)
Walkaround Boat	Fresh / Inshore / Offshore	Multi-Purpose, Fresh or Saltwater Fish	20-38'	6-12	150-350 hp (1 to 3 motors)

What's the best boat for you?

For an online boat selecting tool based on where and how you want to fish, visit: http://www.floridasportsman.com/boating/

Aluminum Jon Boats

Aluminum jon boats can range from just the basics to the surprisingly-well outfitted.

Jon boats are basic but durable, low-maintenance, 2 to 6 person boats, between 10' and 21' in length, and are versatile for fishing, hunting or utility purposes. Although they can be constructed of fiberglass, plastic or wood, the vast majority are made of marine aluminum alloy because of its strength to weight ratio, durability, and relatively low cost. Smaller models are also easily portable due to their light weight.

These handy boats have a flat or mostly flat hull shape, which is very stable, and allows for access to shallow waters. The rough ride quality of flat-bottomed boats in choppy waters limits their practical use to calm, sheltered waters. This is because flat-shaped hulls fully bear the brunt of any chop or waves, rather than slicing through the water like vee-hull boats do.

Jon boats have a fairly rectangular outline shape, typically with nearly the same width from bow to stern. They usually have one to three integrated benches for seating, or for mounting comfortable swivel or pedestal seats.

Smaller jon boats are usually powered by a lightweight, portable, tiller-steered outboard motor of between 2.5 and 20 hp, and utilize a portable fuel tank. On larger or more elaborate models, the motors are often permanently-mounted, and range from 20 to 115 hp. Jet drive outboard motors can be a good option for jon boats that run in shallow, rocky rivers, where protruding lower units and propellers wouldn't stand a chance.

Jon boats are used mainly in calm, sheltered fresh waters, but 15- to 21-footers are sometimes used in brackish or inshore saltwater on calm days.

The entry level and the least expensive of powerboat types, jon boats can be simply a bare-bones open hull, or fully-customized and literally decked out. The larger, more loaded and expensive models can be equipped with all sorts of upgrades. Options such as a helm console with remote steering and motor controls, Bimini top, cooler seats, pedestal seats, raised decks with built-in storage compartments, trolling motor, livewell, rod holders, push pole, poling platform, bilge pump, built-in fuel tank, floatation pods, kayak racks and more, can all be had to make these boats much more than just an aluminum shell.

The unmatched, minimal draft of jon boats allows them to fish the shallowest of shallows, for an extensive variety of fish of all kinds, in both sheltered freshwater and sheltered saltwater.

The least expensive of all fishing boat types, jon boats are a very affordable option for accessing shallow, sheltered waters.

Aluminum utility boats are an economical option for fishing and camping trips.

Aluminum Utility Boat

Utility boats offer a comparable alternative to jon boats, with the ability to negotiate moderately choppy conditions.

Aluminum utility boats are similar to jon boats in many ways. They offer some of the same advantages, and can be accessorized and upgraded with the same options, but have a significantly different bow and hull shape. Utility boats have a pointed bow and modified vee-hull, which opens up their practical use to more than just calm, sheltered waters, but also requires a bit more water depth. Also, the pointed bow shape doesn't provide quite the same lateral stability and bow area space that a jon boat's square bow does.

Utility boats offer a comparable alternative to traditional jon boats: low cost, light weight with the ability to negotiate moderately choppy conditions, which of course broadens the types of waters they're practical for and the kinds fishing they're capable of.

Many first-time boat owners have started off with a basic-but-functional, aluminum utility boat.

Multi-Species Boat

Multi-species fishing boats, which are also commonly called either walleye boats or all-purpose fishing boats, are used in rivers and lakes of all sizes to pursue walleye, crappie, musky, smallmouth bass, and many other kinds of freshwater fish. These versatile and sturdy, 16' to 22' boats are made of aluminum, fiberglass, or polyethylene, with a deep-vee hull at the bow, wide beam, high freeboard and tall windshields – all designed to deal with the rough conditions of large, coldwater lakes and rivers.

Depending on the size and model, they can seat 4 to 6 people comfortably, but for serious fishing it's best to bring along no more than four.

Multi-species boats can be rigged with a single outboard motor ranging from 60 to 300 hp. The larger, higher horsepower models are often rigged with an additional, transom-mounted, low-hp kicker motor for trolling.

Multi-species or Walleye Boat.

Walleye boats, like this fully-loaded model, feature a tall, protective windshield.

Fishing Skiff

Fishing skiffs are 2 to 8 person, 14' to 24', fiberglass or polyethylene boats, used in both freshwater and inshore saltwater. They have a mostly flat hull bottom, and some have either a modified-vee or tri-hull entry shape at the stem to take on light chop. Their flat bottom hull shape is great for stability and access to water depths as shallow as 6 inches (with the motor tilted up). But as with jon boats, the rough ride quality of flat-bottomed boats in choppy waters limits their practical use to calmer, naturally-sheltered waters.

The smallest and most basic, bare-bones fishing skiffs are similar to basic jon boats, only made of fiberglass rather than aluminum. They're typically powered by a lightweight, portable, tiller-steered outboard motor of between 5 and 20 hp and utilize a portable fuel tank.

The larger and more elaborate models will have a permanently-mounted outboard motor ranging between 20 and 200 hp, and can be equipped with plenty of upgrades. They'll usually have a center console or side console helm station configuration, with remote steering and motor controls. Option such as Bimini top, cooler seats, pedestal seats, raised decks with built-in stowage lockers, trolling motor, livewell,

The super-shallow draft of fishing skiffs allows them to fish practically any shallows, marshes or flats.

rod holders, push pole, poling platform, bilge pump, stereo system, built-in fuel tank and more are common to the more loaded fishing skiffs.

The shallow draft of fishing skiffs allows them to fish in marshes, flats, or just about any other fish habitat with sheltered waters, for a variety of fish in freshwater, brackish water and saltwater.

Tri-hull entry shape at the stem, designed for light chop.

Like tournament bass boats, tournament-quality walleye boats can be geared up with an arsenal of the latest high-tech electronics, downriggers, rod holders, livewells, trolling motor, and everything else needed to out-fish the competition.

Aluminum multi-species boats have spiked in popularity and sales in recent years throughout freshwater fishing regions of the U.S. With aluminum being considerably lighter and less-expensive

Multi-species or walleye boats have a vee hull at the bow, but the transition to the stern varies by model, from nearly flat-bottomed to a deep-vee shape.

than fiberglass, they not only cost less to purchase up front than comparable fiberglass boats, but are also a bit more economical since they require less horsepower and fuel to run and to tow.

Bass Boat

These bass boats are purpose-built for all the demands of tournament bass fishing.

Bass boats are made primarily for catching freshwater bass, though they're perfectly suited for catching various panfish and catfish, too. They're designed for 2 to 4 anglers to fish simultaneously, and are ideal for rivers and lakes, in smooth to light chop water conditions. These sleek, feature-rich fishing machines range from 16' to 24' long, and are available in both fiberglass and aluminum.

The latest tournament-quality bass boat models are built to be extra-wide, and often come standard with every state-of-the-art option needed to compete at a high level, including a powerful outboard motor of up to 300 horses. The aluminum versions are typically lighter and less expensive and require a little less horsepower.

Bass boats have either a modified-vee or shallow-vee hull, designed for both high speeds for tournament purposes, and minimal draft for accessing shallows and marshes. They also offer excellent stability at rest, thanks to their low profile, wide beam, and hull shape.

Bass boats can be rigged with a single outboard motor ranging from 60 to 300 hp, depending on the size and weight of the boat, personal preference and whether or not it will be used for competitive bass fishing. Why do tournament bass fishermen feel the need for speed? Because during a competition they often need to be able to quickly reach several distant fishing spots that can be located far apart, and then hurry back in to beat the deadline for the contest's weigh-in.

Today's bass boats are well-designed and can be equipped with an impressive array of features and accessories. A high capacity, built-in gas tank can hold plenty of fuel. Elevated casting decks, fore and aft, provide a good view for sight fishing and help to make casting easy and accurate. Swiveling pedestal chairs allow anglers to sit comfortably while fishing

Some boats have sportscar-like cockpits, designed for their high performance.

Modern bass boats include plenty of tackle space, like rod lockers, right . They also sport bait and release wells, below.

Sleek and feature-rich, bass boats are available in both fiberglass and aluminum.

and waiting for a bite. Multiple deck hatches secure built-in supply lockers, livewells, coolers, and rod and tackle lockers, keeping everything well-organized and stowed neatly out of the way. Onboard electronics often include a depth/fish finder, underwater imaging system, and GPS chartplotter with satellite weather-tracking. And options like a retractable, bow-mounted trolling motor, jack plate, shallow water anchor, and stereo system are additional accessories available to outfit the modern bass boat.

Stylish, matching trailers are an option with some bass boat models.

For bass boat owners, this is what it's all about.

Bass boats offer excellent stability at rest, thanks to their low profile, wide beam and hull shape.

Wide casting decks and walkable gunnels on flats boats allow anglers to easily step around the boat.

Flats fishing with a vantage point to survey the crystal clear shallows.

Flats Boat or Flats Skiff

Flats boats are 2 to 4 person, 15' to 22', fiberglass boats with a shallow-vee, modified-vee or tunnel-hull. They're built for a combination of stealth (by quietly push-poling), skinny-water access, all-around stability, unobstructed casting, and for certain models – speed. Several boat builders refer to them simply as skiffs, while others call them fishing skiffs, poling skiffs, technical poling skiffs, light tackle boats, shallow water skiffs, shallow water fishing boats or other combinations of these terms.

Most people involved in the world of flats fishing, call them "flats boats." These specialized fishing boats can definitely put you right at the top of the food chain in coastal, inshore or nearshore saltwater flats, where redfish, seatrout, snook, flounder, permit, tarpon, bonefish, ladyfish, and other estuarine species thrive.

Their hulls are designed to have a high strength-to-weight ratio, and for a minimal draft of just a foot or less. They're also designed to minimize the sound of small waves slapping against the hull, for quiet movement through the water while push-poling. Flats boats are best kept in calm coastal waters, rivers and lakes, although their hull shapes are also designed to offer a dry ride in moderately choppy conditions, by deflecting spray out and away.

Flats boats are distinguished by their deck configuration, featuring wide, flat, fore and aft casting decks that are flush and level with the extra-wide, walkable gunnels. This allows anglers to easily step all around the boat while fishing. Typically, all or most of the hatch handles and deck cleats will be recessed or flush-mounted to facilitate a flat and unencumbered surface.

The most common helm setup is a center console configuration, situated close enough to the rear casting deck to sit there and operate the boat. Also available are flats boats with an elevated center console or ones with a side console helm location.

A raised, forward casting platform, shown here on the bow, is an optional add-on.

Cruising into a mangrove tunnel, heading for the saltwater flats.

These boats aren't exactly designed for comfy, leisurely cruising. We're talking serious, shallow water fishing platforms built for one purpose, so some of the creature comforts common to similar types of fishing boats, such as a Bimini top, T-top or cushy bow seating, aren't likely to be found onboard. On a flats boat, unobstructed casting space takes priority over these things, so shade isn't an option. This is why people fishing from a flats boat are usually seen covered head-to-toe in lightweight, breathable clothing that provides protection from the blazing sun.

Nearly all flats boats have a poling platform mounted over the motor, along with a long push pole which is attached to one of the gunnels with quick-release holders. The ability to silently push-pole through the flats while standing at a higher vantage point, is one of the key advantages of a flats boat.

They're rigged with a single outboard motor, ranging widely from 40 to 300 hp, depending on the size of the boat and personal preference. Other options include a raised, forward casting platform, removable console seat/cooler, jack plate, trim tabs, shallow water anchor, lighted livewells, depth/fish finder, GPS chartplotter with satellite weather-tracking, stereo system, and an LED package of deck and underwater lights.

Some flats boat anglers opt for a trolling motor, preferring not to engage in the "work" involved with push-poling, especially on hot and humid,

Line-up of various, differently equipped flats boats.

The poling platform standard to most flats boats is very advantageous for a stealthy approach to sight fishing.

summer days. Others keep onboard and utilize both options, while some choose to use only a push pole when in fish-stalking mode.

There are plenty of ardent fishermen willing to spend the big bucks on a top-quality flats boat. Such is the appeal of high-end, specialty fishing boats.

Bay Boat

Bay boats provide a versatile compromise between a flats boat and a center console.

A bay boat is a 4 to 8 person, 16' to 26' fishing boat, designed to be somewhat of a hybrid between a shallow water flats boat and a seaworthy center console boat. They can't quite sneak into the ultra-shallow flats the way that jons, skiffs and flats boats can, and they're not quite built for the pounding of high, offshore seas, but they do offer a great compromise.

Most bay boats are fiberglass-constructed. Hull shape is most commonly a modified-vee, but can also be a modified-vee with a stepped hull, a tunnel-hull, or a catamaran hull. They're designed to provide that elusive combination of a shallow draft and a smooth ride through choppy waters.

Bay boats are a great option for fishing brackish or inshore saltwater estuaries, as well as for nearshore fishing in the gulf or ocean, in pursuit of a huge variety of estuarine and nearshore fish species like snapper, drum, jack, mackerel, striper and so many more.

A well-equipped bay boat, sporting a T-top rigged with a sight-fishing chair, combining practicality with comfort.

All bay boats have a center console configuration, with either a cooler/bench seat or twin chairs at the helm station, and most also have seating directly in front of the console, which doubles as either a cooler or a livewell. Depending on the size and model, they can have additional, cushioned seating in the bow and stern areas, or none at all. A bow casting deck, built-in dry-storage, deck lockers, insulated fish boxes, large coolers, and a high capacity fuel tank are fairly standard in the mid to large-sized bay boats.

A flotilla of bay boats, moving on to the next rendezvous point.

Bay boats are available in models to suit various needs, styles and budgets.

Cushioned bow seating is available in many bay boat models.

Livewells with an aquarium-like view are an alluring, trendy upgrade.

Outboard motor options range from 50 hp all the way up to 350 hp, depending of course on the size, weight and intended use for the boat. Other options include a console tower (elevated, second helm station for sight fishing), sliding windshield, T-top, Bimini top, swim platform and ladder, raw water washdown, jack plate, trim tabs, shallow water anchor, trolling motor, lighted livewells, and high-tech toys such as a depth/fish finder, underwater imaging system, GPS chartplotter with satellite weather-tracking, DSC-VHF radio, stereo system, and an LED light package.

Bay boats are available in a variety of models to suit every need, style, and budget, from simple economy models to the super-upscale, many designed with the whole family in mind.

This high-end bay boat features a second helm station, or console tower-equipped T-top, which provides a high vantage point to operate the boat from.

Outboard power options for bay boats range from 50 hp all the way up to 350 hp.

Cruising bay boats, on the Intracoastal Waterway.

Bay boats are a great option for fishing brackish or inshore saltwater estuaries, as well as for nearshore fishing in the gulf or ocean.

Bimini tops and ski tow pylons are popular, inexpensive options on bay boats.

Fish & Ski Boat

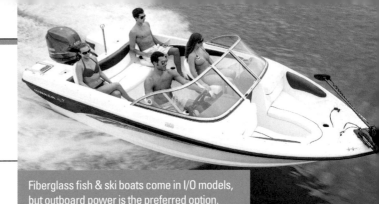

Fiberglass fish & ski boats come in I/O models, but outboard power is the preferred option.

Cross a bay boat with a bowrider, and you get a fish and ski boat. That's the idea behind these 4 to 8 person, 17' to 22', fiberglass, aluminum or polyethylene, dual-purpose boats designed to please the whole family. With the hull and fishing features of a bay or bass boat, and the side console helm station, walk-thru windshield, and additional bow and stern seating closer to that of a bowrider, fish and ski boats offer the best of both worlds.

Bowriders are popular family boats, but they're not the best choice for serious fishing because they're not really equipped for it, and their soft, vinyl upholstery and carpet-covered decks don't hold up well to the rigors of fishing. That's why many fish & ski models have less vinyl and carpet to tear up, and more easy-to-clean, hard surface materials throughout their interiors than most bowriders. Fish and ski boats offer just enough comfortable seating to serve as a family-friendly watersports and fishing boat.

> **Fish & ski boats, or crossovers, offer enough comfortable seating to serve as a family-friendly watersports and fishing boat.**

The outboard motor options vary between 115 and 300 hp, although a minimum of a 150 hp motor is definitely recommended if you want to be able to pull up an adult skier or rider with a boat full of passengers and gear.

These boats typically come standard with amenities like a swim platform and ladder, in-floor ski locker, a livewell, one or two removable, pedestal fishing seats, rod holders and slide-out tackle boxes. Add-on options include a removable trolling motor, depth/fish finder, stereo system, raw water washdown, and a removable, collapsible, or permanently-mounted ski tow pylon or wakeboard tower.

If you plan to use a fish & ski boat in brackish water or inshore saltwater, be sure to purchase one with parts, hardware, and wiring made specifically for saltwater use. If the marketing materials of a particular boat model don't disclose a clear indication that it's a saltwater-compatible model, then you can safely assume that it's best kept in freshwater.

Aluminum fish & ski models are popular dual-purpose boats for freshwater use.

Deck Boat

If the dual-purpose versatility of a fish and ski boat interests you, but you'd prefer a larger option with more capacity and more seating, then a deck boat could be the perfect choice. These 18' to 26', fiberglass or aluminum boats offer a heck-of-a-lot more than their name would seem to indicate. The boating version of a family SUV, deck boats are widely available in models that are factory-equipped for both fishing and watersports, with enough comfy seating for up to three families of four.

Deck boats are another one of the types of boats available in both freshwater and saltwater versions, though not necessarily from all of their manufacturers. For regular use in brackish water or inshore saltwater, only purchase one specifically made for saltwater, with parts, hardware and wiring that are all saltwater-compatible.

Outboard motors on deck boats will range between 150 hp and 300 hp, and some of the larger, heavier models can be rigged with twin outboards. If you plan to pull up and tow adult skiers or riders while loaded to capacity with passengers and gear, then you should definitely opt for the maximum recommended horse-

Deck boats are ideal for a fun-filled day of casual fishing, exciting watersports, and pleasure cruising for the whole family and then some.

power for the particular boat that you choose.

Fishing model deck boats commonly come standard with amenities such as removable, pedestal fishing seats, a livewell, rod holders, slide-out tackle boxes, in-floor ski locker, ample under-seat stowage space, swim platform, bow and stern retractable swim ladders, potable water system, raw water washdown, built-in sink, cooler, trash bin, removable table, docking headlights, stereo system, and a Bimini top. Upgrade options would include an enclosed portapotti/dry storage compartment, recessed pull-up cleats, removable, snap-in carpet, removable trolling motor, depth/fish finder, GPS chartplotter with satellite weather-tracking, transom stereo remote, LED light package, collapsible or permanently-mounted ski tow pylon or wakeboard tower and more.

Deck boats can have a modified-vee hull, tri-hull, tunnel-hull, or catamaran hull, designed for a smooth, dry and controlled ride in up to moderately choppy conditions. Although they can be up to 26 feet long with twin motors, they're not designed and built for offshore seas. What they are ideal for is a fun-filled day of casual fishing, exciting watersports and pleasure cruising for one, two, or even three families, without ever needing to go back to the dock until the day is done.

Accessory-loaded deck boats like these offer a lot more than their name would seem to indicate.

Power cats, as they're known, are also a favorite of scuba divers.

Catamaran or Multihull

Power catamaran (or multihull) boats may have either twin planing hulls or twin, high-speed displacement hulls on some of the larger sized sportfishing catamarans. Displacement-hulled boats are not normally associated with high speeds, but a mid-sized, high-speed displacement-hulled power catamaran can efficiently cruise at planing-like speeds of up to 30 mph because their twin hulls are narrow enough to escape the inherent limitations of a wider, displacement monohull.

The advantages gained with any type of catamaran hull, compared to a vee-shaped monohull, are a softer ride in conditions ranging from choppy to white-knuckle seas, less roll (with the planing hulls) and greater stability at rest and better fuel economy. These qualities are primarily attributed to the weight and buoyancy being distributed between the two hulls and to the boat's outer edges, which also contributes to a shallower draft.

Catamarans can have either a center console or dual (side) console helm station applications, or can be a walkaround cabin model. They range from 14' to 35' in length, carry from 3 to 12 people onboard, and are powered by 40 to 350 hp motors, with a twin outboard rigging being by far the most common. Of course the smaller sizes are bay boat models and aren't meant for heading out into the ocean. For that – the bigger the boat, the better and safer it is.

A drawback of smaller catamarans is the lack of below-deck space in their narrow hulls, although there's plenty of space above deck. The rectangular shape of a catamaran's deck allows for more usable deck space than monohull boats, so it's a fair tradeoff. The smaller, bay boat style catamarans are rigged and equipped just as monohull bay boats are, but the larger, seafaring, sportfishing cats can be fully-outfitted and accessorized for tournament offshore fishing and semi-long distance island hopping. An array of options such as state-of-the-art, high-tech electronics like a joystick control system, depth/fish finder, underwater imaging system, GPS chartplotter with satellite weather-tracking, DSC-VHF radio, stereo system, and an LED light package are just some of the extras common to power catamarans.

The ability to handle rough conditions, combined with a shallow draft, makes power catamarans extremely versatile for fishing all sorts of waters. From the Great Lakes to the Intracoastal Waterway, to the teeming oceans, practically any species of fish can be caught from these very capable fishing vessels.

Cat hulls can offer a softer ride in rough seas, less roll, more stability at rest and fuel economy.

Catamarans have recently become more in-demand by open ocean anglers who venture far offshore for bluewater fishing.

Pontoon Boat

Pontoon boats are no longer just slow, casual-cruising party boats. They're now attainable in innovative, head-turning editions with curved, sexy lines. They can also now be classified as fast, versatile, impressively-equipped and extremely comfortable, making them a viable option for fishing and watersports enthusiasts alike, as well as for those who demand plenty of cozy lounge seating.

The wide, rectangular contour of pontoon boats provides seating and deck space for anywhere from 6 to 16 people, and they range from 16' to 30' in length. The horsepower requirements vary from one extreme to the other, starting at 40 hp for the smallest, lightest models all the way up to 350 hp for the largest tri-tubes.

The majority of the actual pontoons are made of marine aluminum alloy, but there are a few manufacturers making fiberglass pontoon versions. Pontoon boats are available in ether twin or tri-tube models, with the latter being designed for higher weight and horsepower capacities.

Some of the newest, most-innovative tri-tube designs have greatly improved the acceleration, planing (yes, planing), top speeds, and handling abilities of these advanced pontoon boats to performance levels that weren't previously possible. If you haven't yet, you'll eventually see one of these high-performance, tri-tube models fly by you and then bank into a hard turn as if on rails. They track very well at all speeds and offer unprecedented ride quality, handling semi-choppy conditions fairly well.

Pontoon boats are best kept in rivers, estuaries and lakes. They're very popular in both freshwater and brackish waterways nationwide. But as with any boat, if you intend to use it in brackish water, be sure to shop around for one built with saltwater-compatible components.

For anyone in the market for a pontoon boat who's not super-skilled at docking, there are a few distinct advantages and disadvantages to consider. For their overall size, they're probably the easiest type of boat to maneuver and dock in confined areas because they track well in the water and tend to steer a little more precisely than most monohull boats. They're also relatively lightweight for their size, and less weight means less momentum to have to control. But – as with any high-sided boat – a strong wind, or being fully-loaded to weight capacity will substantially offset these advantages.

One benefit of any pontoon boat... they have no bilge or bilge pump to worry about.

Until recently, the words "performance" and "pontoon boat" did not belong in the same sentence, but that's no longer the case. The 50 mph pontoon boats are here.

One of the benefits of any pontoon boat is shallow draft, allowing access to waters two feet deep or less. Another plus – they don't have a bilge to worry about filling up with water, and no bilge means no bilge pump to worry about failing either. It could rain for forty days and forty nights, and a pontoon boat won't sink unless both pontoons happen to get punctured, which, while not impossible, is an unlikely scenario.

One advantage of an outboard-powered boat is always being able to see the direction of the motor with no guesswork as to which way you're directing thrust. But on some pontoon boats, the driver's view of the motor is completely blocked by upholstery. This can be somewhat of a problem when slow-maneuvering in close quarters. The good news is that if you do find this to be a problem, in most cases the piece of upholstery covering the motor can be detached, opening up a line of sight to the motor.

Most pontoon boats have thin aluminum panel siding, which is easy to scratch and dent. So although it's fairly easy to avoid any impact with docks or anything that could damage the siding, even the most experienced boaters can struggle to completely prevent dings and dents while docking in high winds. More and more pontoon boat companies are now using sleek, lower-profile, stronger, molded fiberglass on one or more of their models for the front corner panels, and on some models, the rear corners too.

If you're looking for a casual fishing platform that also happens to be a veritable entertainment room on the water, a pontoon boat just might be your ticket.

Pontoon boats are available in scores of different floor plans, and often come standard with removable pedestal fishing seats, a livewell, rod holders, slide-out tackle boxes, ample under-seat stowage space, cooler, removable table, docking headlights, stereo system, Bimini top, and a swim ladder. Upgrade options are plentiful: a bar, refrigerator, enclosed portapotti, depth/fish finder, LED light package, freshwater wash-down system, ski tow pylon or tower, choice of carpet or easy-to-clean, non-skid surface flooring (a smart choice for anyone with kids or for the serious anglers) and much more.

Dual Console Boat

Dual Console boats are available in a wide variety of sizes, from 17' to 37'.

The dual console boat, also referred to as a DC, combines the deep-vee, heavy-duty, seaworthy hull of a center console boat with the deck and additional seating layout, the side console helm station setup and the walk-thru windshield of a fish and ski boat. Boat manufacturers often use the same hull for both their center console and dual console boat models of the same size. Some boaters like the DC's combination of bow seating for guests, along with a full windshield for protection from the elements at the helm.

These 6 to 12 person, 17' to 37' fiberglass or polyethylene boats are designed for family-style cruising and fishing, capable of handling choppy lake waters or rough seas.

Dual consoles are certainly capable of doubling as a watersports boat, but the larger models over 21' or so aren't really the best choice for it—their weight and deep-vee hull, combined with the tow load of a skier or rider, produce a confluence of fuel-burning inefficiency that can be unkind to your wallet. However, those DC boats do generate a tantalizing wake: big and steep. For wakeboarding, a bigger wake means bigger aerial maneuvers and more surfing-like fun. Be careful, though, the higher you fly... the harder you fall!

Designed for family-style cruising and fishing.

With the smaller DCs under 23', it's safer to stay inshore, nearshore or on mid-sized lakes. Some of the larger dual console boats, however, are suitable for offshore sportfishing. Motors range from a single 75 hp motor, up to triple 350s as an option on the biggest DC, for a total of 1,050 horses.

Dual console boats can look a lot like a fish & ski boat or bowrider, but the major difference is in the DC's deep-vee, heavy-duty hull.

The smaller of the dual console boats are rigged and equipped pretty-much the same as fish & ski boats are, but the larger ones can be geared up for tournament offshore fishing and comfortable entertainment. Options such as a tower, a hardtop, a head, and the latest, greatest electronics like a joystick control system, depth/fish finder, underwater imaging system, GPS chartplotter with satellite weather-tracking, DSC-VHF radio, stereo system, and an LED light package are just a sampling of the many upgrades available on DC's.

Dual console boats are a good, durable choice for fishing open waters that tend to get rough – fresh or saltwater. If you need the extra seating and stowage that they offer compared to center console boats, and if you don't mind occasionally having to work around the windshields when you have a fish on the line, then DC boats are worth a close look.

Dual console boats are a good, durable choice for fishing open waters that tend to get rough – fresh or saltwater.

Dual consoles can be equipped just enough for a day's fishing, with few bells and whistles, or can be loaded with amenities.

Center Console Boat

Center console boats are built to handle rough, offshore conditions.

Center console boats vary very widely in size, from 15' to over 40'.

The center console, or open fisherman, is the boat of choice for dedicated anglers who enjoy offshore or big lake fishing. Its fiberglass, deep-vee or stepped deep-vee hull is shaped and constructed specifically for cutting through and holding up to the choppy conditions or rough seas that regularly occur on expansive, open waters. Its centrally located helm station allows for unobstructed, 360-degree access to the water, making the task of following a hooked fish around the boat as easy as possible.

Center console boats vary widely in size and horsepower, carrying between 3 and 12 passengers. Those in the 15' to 22' range are typically reserved for inshore, nearshore or mid-sized lake use. Models from 23' on up to 40' (+) are excellent performers offshore, ranging as far as fuel capacity and sea conditions will allow. Frequent targets include mahi-mahi (dolphinfish), tuna, billfish, king mackerel, wahoo, cobia, grouper and snapper.

Outboard power applications on center console boats start at a single 50 hp motor for the lightest 15-footer and shoot all the way up to triple 350 hp outboards, rigged onto some of the largest models.

Big center consoles with tower helm stations are well-equipped to find fish.

Open fisherman boats can run fast, a favorable attribute for trips to distant waypoints.

Equipment and feature-wise, open fisherman boats vary from the bare necessities, to a full assortment of the latest electronics and gadgetry.

On the smaller models, the space inside of the console serves as a dry (or at least semi-dry) stowage area, but the larger sizes – 23' and up – will often have a head located down inside of the console. A few of the largest luxury class center console boats feature a forward cabin built into the bow area and are labeled as a cuddy cabin model (not to be confused with cuddy cabin cruisers which are seldom designed for fishing).

The most basic center console fishing boats will come factory-equipped with at least an anchor locker, deck locker(s), livewell, rod holders, a cooler/bench seat, twin chairs, or a leaning post at the helm station, and most have a seat directly in front of the console, doubling as either a cooler or a livewell. Many additional accessories and equipment options are available with upgrade packages or dealership add-ons. These can include extras such as a T-top, a console tower (elevated, second helm station for sight fishing), joystick docking system, a windlass, outriggers, downriggers, sliding windshield, Bimini top, lighted livewell(s), built-in insulated fish boxes, extra-large coolers, swim platform and ladder, potable water system, raw water washdown, trim tabs, depth/fish finder, underwater imaging system, GPS chartplotter with satellite weather-tracking, DSC-VHF radio, stereo system, LED light package, radar and a whole lot more.

Luxury-class center consoles feature onboard heads and other amenities.

This twin outboard CC displays impressive power and handling.

Express or Walkaround Boat

A walkaround is great for heading out on overnight fishing trips.

Walkaround boats combine the creature comforts of a cuddy cabin cruiser with the fishability of an offshore sportfishing boat. They're named for the narrow walkway that's used to literally walk around the perimeter of the forward, upper deck, in order to access the bow lines and the anchor, and also to follow hooked fish around the boat. This walkway is complemented by a tall hand rail for safety.

Below the upper deck is the cabin, used to duck out of inclement weather, for dry storage, and in most walkarounds as a sleeping berth. The cabins on these boats can vary from being just a dry storage area with bench seating and a removable table to luxury-class cabins with all the amenities of a loaded RV. Galley equipment such as a refrigerator, stovetop, microwave oven, sink, and a countertop on one side, with an enclosed head and shower on the other, all fit surprisingly well within relatively tight quarters. Entertainment components like an HDTV, DVD player, and a stereo system are some of the available "icing on the cake" upgrades. Cuddy cabins can be unexpectedly comfortable to relax in, and are especially beneficial to parents with young children.

If you do most of your boating in regions that remain hot and humid throughout the peak boating season, consider purchasing a walkaround boat with air conditioning in the cabin. Many of the smaller sizes don't have A/C since it requires considerably more battery power or even an onboard generator.

Walkaround boats are named for the narrow walkway used to walk around the perimeter of the forward, upper deck.

Walkaround boats are a viable option for serious offshore fishing.

outboard motor. The largest, heaviest models may be powered by as many as three 350 hp outboards. The combined heavy weight and deep-vee hull shape of this particular type of fishing boat makes them less practical for double-duty as a watersports boat than other types of boats.

Walkaround boats can be just as well-equipped for tournament-level fishing as any center console or catamaran sportfishing boat. Most models feature fold-away seating at the stern to make room for fighting fish, from freshwater species like lake trout and salmon to saltwater fish of all kinds.

In places such as Florida, without A/C, these cabins can become quite hot during the long summers.

Conversely, in colder climates with shorter, milder summers, these same boats are very popular since they provide a good deal of protection from chilly winds during the early spring and late fall months. Walkaround boats are quite popular throughout the Great Lakes for this reason, and because they're built to handle the ocean-like conditions of massive lakes.

Sized between 20' and 38', and suitable for between 6 and 10 passengers (fewer, for serious fishing), walkaround boats are primarily constructed of fiberglass and have the same, deep-vee hull shapes as center and dual console boats. Catamaran hulls are also available. This makes them just as capable as other open water fishing boats for large lake chop and rough seas.

Even the smallest walkaround boats are relatively heavy, so they're rigged with at least one 150 hp

Super heavy-duty towing capacity is required to trailer the largest express boats.

Walkaround cabins vary from a basic storage area with bench seats and a removable table, to a luxury-class cabin with all the amenities of a nice RV.

CHAPTER 3

Boat Shopping Wisdom

What type of boat are you looking for? A boat show is a great place to see a large selection of new boats all on the same day or weekend.

Depending on where you live, boat shows can range from a few dozen boats being displayed by two or three local boat dealerships to literally thousands of boats being displayed by boat dealerships and manufacturers from all over the world. SB

Before getting caught up in the excitement of boat shopping, take time to evaluate plenty of different boat options.

Boat shows, like The Southeast U.S. Boat Show, in Jacksonville, Florida, above, Miami International Boat Show, right, offer one-stop shopping, lots of variety, and deals for new boats to get you on the water.

Boat Buying

Major boat shows display all kinds of the marine industry's new, innovative products.

Online research can surely save you lots of time and money.

Online research is an obvious option, though it can be tough to find all of the websites of all of the boat brands being sold in your state or locale. You'd think that an internet search for a specific type of boat would result in scores of different brands, but that's rarely the case. As an example, if you search for "bay boat," you'll find that only a very small fraction of the number of companies making bay boats will be listed. This is partially because there are so many different boat brands that make each type of boat, and many of them are only sold regionally.

So then how can you find which brands are regionally available to you? Just do an internet search for "boat dealers _____" with your county and state, which will result in a list of your local boat dealerships. As you click around on the different dealer websites, you'll be able to make a list of the particular brands of boats that are carried within your target segments. Then you'll be able to go directly to each brand's website to get detailed and comprehensive information about each different boat model. You'll find that many of the local dealership websites contain less-detailed info than what you'll find on the manufacturers' websites, where you'll find each individual boat model's specs, standard equip-

ment, special features, upgrade options, motor options, warranty info, etc.

Online Boat Shopping Rescources

It's fairly common for private sellers to advertise their used boat for sale with the hopes of selling it for enough to pay off its loan balance, which is sometimes more than the current retail value of the boat. When you see late-model, used boats for sale that are priced practically the same as the equivalent, brand new boat, this is often the reason why.

As with any major purchase, it's important to have a reasonably accurate idea of the market value before beginning any sort of serious inquiring. A good online resource for looking up the approximate retail values of used boats and outboard motors, as well as new boat retail prices, is NADA Guides at nadaguides.com/boats.

Keep in mind that the retail values and prices you'll find there can sometimes be off by 10 to 15 percent or more of the actual, current value. This is mostly due to depreciating boat values, and because of due discrepancies in the estimated values assigned to the numerous accessory and component options listed for each boat, which are subject to widely-varying actual values. Also, the bottom line in terms of a used boat value... it is ultimately worth what a willing seller and a willing buyer can agree to.

The following websites are excellent resources for finding pre-owned (and new) boats for sale by both private individual sellers and boat dealerships:

» boattrader.com
» boats.com
» boatstore.floridasportsman.com
» craigslist.org
» ebay.com
» thehulltruth.com

The SeaTrial

It is wise and advisable to try out a boat in the water before you buy it. This may sound obvious... you certainly wouldn't buy a car without test driving it first, right? But you'd be surprised how often boats are sold without a trial run out on the water by the buyer. Some dealerships won't allow their new boats to hit the water until after the sale transaction is complete (a reasonable policy for new boats sold in saltwater market areas). Used boats, however, should always be made available for a trial run, and if not you should be leery.

If possible, a trial run on a moderately windy and choppy day is strongly recommended (not really applicable to flat-bottomed boats). This is the only way to know how dry and smooth of a ride the boat will actually provide when the wind kicks up. For any boat that's supposed to be designed for light to moderate chop, such as a bay boat for example, slightly choppy water conditions and small waves (under a foot) shouldn't cause the boat to pound on the water while at cruising speed.

Tip: If possible, charter a fishing trip with a captain running the same boat. You'll get a chance to see how the boat handles, learn some new fishing spots, and you might catch a few fish.

You'd be surprised how often boats are sold without a trial run out on the water.

Used Boat Mechanical Checklist

❏ Hull Exterior
1) Keel damage
2) Gelcoat finish/fading/voids, major cracks
3) Rubrail – components, condition
4) Thru hull fittings – material, sealed
5) Transom strength
6) Hull to deck joint

❏ Hull Interior
1) Soft spots in deck
2) Gelcoat/carpet/non-skid
3) Seat cushions
   – comfort, construction, condition
4) Deck hardware
5) Watertightness, hatches,doors,ports
6) Bilge – access, cleanliness, water, oil, debris

❏ Electrical System
1) Nav/anchor lights
2) Bilge pump/s - auto/manual
3) Baitwell pump/s – auto/manual
4) Switch panel
5) Gauges – fully functional
6) Fuse/breaker panel
7) Additional equipment operation (VHF, depth/
   fish finder, stereo, radar, trolling motor,etc)
8) Battery/s – connections and access
9) Overall condition of wiring

❏ Mechanical
1) Steering
2) Shift and throttle movement
3) Seat sliders/height adjustment
4) Hatches/hinges/latches
5) Fasteners/snaps
6) Hose connections
7) Thru hull fittings/seacocks
8) Fuel lines
9) Fuel filter/water separator
10) Fuel tank
11) Water tank
12) Holding tank
13) Head

❏ Misc
1) Canvas
2) Isinglass
3) Windscreen
4) Trim tabs

❏ Motor/s
1) Cylinder compressions

2) Oil
   – level, condition, presence of water (4 stroke)
3) Oil tank/s – access, condition, lines (2 stroke)
4) Lower unit/oil – condition, presence of water
5) Powerhead/block – corrosion, leaks
6) Wiring harnesses, plug wires
7) Zincs
8) Propeller/s
9) Crank, smoke
10) Smoothness at idle
11) Shifting – forward/reverse
12) Trim & tilt function

❏ Test Drive (a.k.a. Sea Trial)
1) Stability at rest
2) Time to plane
3) Ride – chop handling, bow spray deflection
4) Maneuverability
5) Stability on plane
6) Wide open throttle – stability/RPMs
7) Bilge - leaks

❏ Additional Equipment Included
1) Coast Guard kit
2) Fishing accessories and gear
3) Skis/boards/tubes
4) Anchor/rode
5) Dock lines
6) Compass
7) Trailer lock

❏ Overall Condition and Value
1) N.A.D.A. listed value
2) Remaining warranties
3) Maintenance history/requirements

❏ Trailer
1) Corrosion
2) Coupler
3) U-Bolts/welds
4) Axle/s and springs
5) Hubs – seals leaking grease
6) Safety chains
7) Wiring – plug and harness
8) Brakes (if equipped) actuator, lines, calipers,
   pads
9) Tires/spare
10) Lights
11) Bunks – supports, material
12) Guides

Crucial Mechanical Checks for Used Boats

When test-running a used boat, take note of how easy or how hard the steering wheel is to turn. Tight steering is usually a sign that a steering cable needs to be replaced. Loose steering with too much play and a lack of immediate response indicates that either air is trapped in the lines and needs to be bled out, or that there's a hydraulic steering fluid leak.

Never judge a used motor's mechanical condition without running it under load.

Check how smoothly the motor shifts into and out of gear. If the gear resists being shifted back into neutral, the problem could be as simple as a few cable adjustments, or as severe as internal gear damage.

Keep in mind that what may sound loud and clunky to the "untrained ear," may actually be fairly normal for certain outboard motors, even when new. The best way to be sure is to have an experienced marine mechanic listen to and check the boat's gear shifting.

Also lift off the motor cowling (cover) and look for any signs of corrosion or fluid leaks, and any evidence of maintenance neglect. For any 4-stroke motor, be sure to check the oil. If it's milky-colored or you see water droplets along with the oil, that's bad news for the seller because you won't be buying his boat (unless you're willing to negotiate the value of his blown motor out of the deal.) If the oil feels gritty between your fingertips or is super-black, those are signs of neglected maintenance. It is also a good idea to ask for any maintenance and repair records the seller may have to check for any recurring problems. Walk all around on the deck to feel for any soft spots, which could be structural decay or damage. For any boat

with a cabin, a strong, musty or moldy smell could be from leakage or water damage.

These are a few of the things you can initially check for yourself, but these and several more mechanical and electrical checks need to be thoroughly made on any used boat you have serious interest in buying. Consider hiring a qualified, factory-certified marine mechanic to perform a complete systems inspection of the boat, motor(s) and trailer, as well as his own trial run out on the water to make sure that all is OK with the boat and motor while under load. Many problems don't present at all unless the motor is running under load or at speed.

A poorly-sealed electrical compartment that doesn't stay dry is a fairly common design flaw that will eventually result in corroded wiring harnesses and components.

Electrical wiring in disrepair is a clear indicator of maintenance neglect.

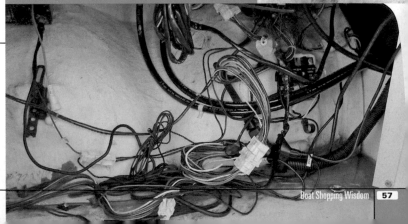

Some dealerships sell select used boats with a short-term warranty.

unsound and unreliable, even if it's been kept covered and inside of a garage. Because it's so common for boats to sit unused for months or even years at a time, they can and will develop all kinds of problems simply by sitting and not being run. Rubber seals and lines dry up and crack, electrical wiring terminals and harnesses corrode, internal metal surfaces corrode and seize, plastic components become brittle and fragile, etc. Plus, if ethanol fuel sits stagnant in a boat's fuel system and gas tank for even six months, it will inevitably cause costly fuel system problems that must be fixed before the motor can be expected to run well at all. (Ethanol fuel issues will be covered in Chapter 13.)

Sometimes people will decide to sell their boat, but for one reason or another they don't bother to get it mechanically up to par for the next owner. They may just clean it up to look nice, hoping that someone will base its overall condition on how shiny it is. Don't assume anything based on looks alone. A used boat can look brand new, but actually be very mechanically

Some design flaws can only be observed when the boat is afloat, and some only while at cruising speed.

Often-overlooked Design Issues: New and Used Boats

For any boat that makes it into your final qualifying round, while it's in the water, be sure to sit down at the helm for a while and think about how it's going to feel throughout a full day of boating. Is there comfortable legroom and reach to the steering wheel and controls at both the sitting and standing positions? Is the seat positioned high enough at its highest adjustment for you to always have good forward vantage point of the water in front of the bow? Does the helm station feel too confined and likely to be stuffy on hot days? These are all important considerations that affect both comfort and safety.

When evaluating and comparing different boats, while in the water, look for the following important-to-consider design features. Look closely throughout the boat and scrutinize it for any annoying design flaws, which can be found even on new boats. Some design flaws can only be observed when the boat is afloat, and some only while at cruising speed. These

Part of your decision process should include sitting down at the helm for a while, considering whether or not it's a good, comfortable fit for you.

would include, but are not limited to:

» Poorly-designed self-bailing deck drainage systems that keep water puddles in corners of the deck while the boat is afloat and at rest. (More about this issue coming up.)

» Captain's chairs that sit too low for good visibility over the bow.

» Boats that list (lean) to port or starboard at

Quality Checking New Boats

The fit and finish of a boat tells a lot about its overall quality. There are QC (quality control) procedures in place at every boat factory, but since they are assembled almost entirely by human hands, no boat can be completely flawless. Some brands are built with more precision and are closer to flawless than others, as you can image, based on some of the huge price gaps between them. Still, even some of the highest-end boats can leave the factory in need of some improvements or corrections.

The following list outlines the most common quality deviations or oversights that can be found on new boats. Some are minor, attention-to-detail concerns, while others are valid reasons to leave a particular brand off of your potential boat candidates list.

» Look closely along the sides of the hull to see if there are visible, wavy ripples that can also be felt as you walk along and run your hand along the hull surface. At the same time, look down the rubrail to see whether it's straight or unevenly attached. These would be a fair reason to steer clear of that boat brand.

» Check the hull for visible fiberglass patterns, which are a sign of a poor-quality fiberglass construction technique and a reason you wouldn't want a boat from that particular factory.

»Lower-quality parts and components typically have a cheap look and feel to them. Anything that logically seems like it should be strong and sturdy, such as windshield frames and supports or door and hatch hinges, should be just that.

» Look and feel around the boat for any protruding, sharp corners or rough edges, and also check the edges of compartment openings for sharp or jagged fiberglass edges. These are surprisingly not that uncommon, but are obviously unsafe and could cause injury while boating.

» Inspect the upholstery for crooked or highly-stressed seams, protruding staples, or snaps that are flimsily attached to thin, lightweight vinyl. These won't last for very long at all.

» Look down into the bilge area and the bottom of the compartments and lockers. If there's a good amount of left-behind boat construction debris (which could clog up a bilge pump), it could be a sign that the boat was rushed out of the factory without a thorough final QC inspection.

rest (even without anyone or any gear onboard); caused by being built with unbalanced weight distribution, or by a single, large-capacity fuel tank installed far to one side.

» Poorly-sealed electrical panel compartments and dry storage compartments that don't stay dry.

» Difficult-to-access bilge or battery/switch compartments.

» Insufficient motor well space to allow the outboard motor to be tilted all the way up without crimping the rigging cable/hose assembly.

» Storage compartments that can only be accessed by unsnapping multiple seat cushions, and then having to be re-snapped every time they're opened, in order to keep the cushions from blowing out of the boat while underway.

» Boats sold in saltwater market areas that are incompatible for saltwater use because they were assembled using low-grade stainless steel parts, chrome-plated zinc hardware and untinned copper wiring that are prone to rapid corrosion when exposed to a saltwater environment.

» Underpowered boats that lack the horsepower to plane out when the boat is loaded to its weight capacity with passengers, gear and fuel. (More about this is coming right up in Chapter 4.)

New Boat Quality Checklist

❏ Hull Exterior
1) Smooth, even surface – not wavy
2) Straight, even keel
3) Gelcoat finish – free of bubbles/voids, cracks
4) Rubrail – components, straightness
5) Thru hull fittings – material, sealed

❏ Hull Interior
1) Fit and finish throughout
2) Gelcoat/Carpet/Non-Skid
3) Seat cushions – comfort, construction
4) Deck hardware
5) Watertightness, hatches, doors, ports
6) Bilge – access, routing of wiring/hoses

❏ Electrical System
1) Bilge pump/s - auto/manual
2) Baitwell pump/s – auto/manual
3) Switch panel
   – number of open switches for options
4) Gauges – features, interface
5) Fuse/Breaker panel
   – number of open switches for options
6) Additional equipment (VHF, depth/fish finder, stereo, radar, trolling motor, etc)
7) Battery/s – connections and access
8) Installation of wiring

❏ Mechanical/Functional Design
1) Steering
2) Shift and throttle movement
3) Seat sliders/ height adjustment
4) Hatches/Hinges/Latches
5) Fasteners/Snaps
6) Installation of motor rigging cable/hose assembly
7) Hose connections
8) Thru hull fittings/Seacocks
9) Fuel lines
10) Fuel filter/Water separator
11) Fuel tank
12) Water tank
13) Holding tank
14) Head

❏ Misc
1) Canvas
2) Isinglass
3) Windscreen
4) Trim tabs

❏ Motor/s
1) Factory recommended horsepower
2) Oil tank/s – location/access (2 stroke)
3) Installation of wiring harnesses
4) Propeller/s – size, pitch, material

❏ Test Drive (a.k.a. Sea Trial)
1) Stability at rest
2) Smoothness at idle
3) Shifting – forward/reverse
4) Gauges – function
5) Time to plane
6) Ride – chop handling, bow spray deflection
7) Maneuverability
8) Stability on plane
9) Wide open throttle – stability/RPMs

❏ Additional Equipment Included
1) Coast Guard kit
2) Anchor/rode
3) Dock lines
4) Compass

❏ Overall Value
1) N.A.D.A. listed value
2) Warranties
3) Maintenance requirements

❏ Trailer
1) Steel or aluminum
2) Max capacity – sized to the boat with full load, fuel and gear
3) Coupler size
4) Hubs – grease fittings
5) Wiring – type of plug and harness
6) Brakes (if equipped) actuator
   – hydraulic or elect. over hydraulic
7) Spare tire
8) Lights (quality)
9) Bunks – supports, materials
10) Guides

Boat Floatation Requirements

Even the largest sizes of trailerable boats are available from manufacturers that proudly boast their unsinkable products.

"But this ship can't sink!"

Did you know that level floatation requirements (unsinkability) for outboard-powered, monohull (and certain catamaran) boats, rated for motors of more than 2 hp, apply only to boats that are less than 20 feet in length? Level floatation is defined by the USCG as, "*A floatation system that will keep a swamped boat and a specified quantity of the weights of its motor, equipment and passengers floating in an approximately level attitude. Sufficient stability is provided to prevent the swamped craft from capsizing in calm water when one-half of the passengers are evenly distributed at one side of the passenger carrying area and as low as possible in the boat. Level Floatation does not provide a self-righting capability.*"

That last sentence is important. No recreational power boat is self-righting, which is a capability possible only by specialized, offshore rescue vessels and industrial life boats that are designed to automatically roll back to an upright position when flipped over by high seas.

Another requirement, Basic Floatation, applies specifically to the manufacture of monohull, inboard or I/O-powered boats and airboats less of than 20 feet. This is simply, "*A floatation system which will keep a swamped boat from sinking when its passengers are in the water clinging to it, provided that the aggregate weight of the motor, passengers and equipment carried in or attached to the boat does not exceed the boat's maximum weight capacity. With Basic Floatation,* the swamped boat may float at any attitude. It does not require that the boat remain in an upright or any specific position. It may float, and usually does, in a 'spar' position, with the bow sticking up and the stern sunk.*"

(None of these federal floatation requirements apply to any sailboats, canoes, kayaks, inflatables, amphibious vessels, certain multi-hull boats or race boats.)

This information may very-well factor into your ultimate choice if you're in the market for a boat over 20 feet long. Fortunately, several – but certainly not all boat manufacturers build foam-filled, unsinkable boats that are longer than 20 feet, and advertise them accordingly. However, they aren't all necessarily built to provide level floatation in the event of a swamping. Since these requirements apply only to boats under 20 feet, any of the manufacturers that do offer boats larger than this with built-in floatation, do so by choice, whether as incentive to safety-conscious boaters, to meet

At this rescue scene, the boat's floatation more than likely saved the life of the man clinging to the engine.

their own safety standards, or both.

If you decide to purchase an unsinkable boat, just keep in mind that it could still roll over and "turtle" hull-up if swamped in turbulent waters or foul weather conditions with rough to high seas. In these or other crisis situations, having only the bottom of a boat's hull or bow to (try to) cling to, might not be always be feasible. But then again, having something to cling to is definitely better than nothing, especially out on large bodies of water where rescue can be far away.

An automatic bilge pump, with its own monitoring system for water level.

Self-Bailing Decks

For boats that aren't unsinkable, the next-best feature to have is a self-bailing deck. There are three differently-designed types of self-bailing systems that all abate rainwater and washdown water, but the first one of these is a better option than the last.

1. The most effective self-bailing deck uses a system of gravity-fed drainage holes and conduits, without the assistance of a pump. It simply allows water to drain from the deck and directly out of the boat, pouring down into the water. This precludes water from filling up the boat, although a bilge pump is still required to pump out the water that will inevitably find its way down into the bilge. Unfortunately, this simple but very effective design can only work in boats that have a higher profile with a main deck that sits high enough above the boat's water line, so that the exterior drain outlets can be located lower than the deck, but still above the waterline. Many deep-vee-hulled boats around 19 feet and larger have this type of self-bailing system that is literally self-bailing.

2. In another common deck drainage system,

> For boats that aren't unsinkable, the next-best feature to have is a self-bailing deck.

the water exits the boat through conduits that are connected to scuppers located below the waterline, which in many boats is a necessary, but less-than-desirable design. This type is often found on low-profile boats, and it generally does what it's supposed to do, but not without presenting an annoying problem on certain boats. If the main deck sits either at or below the waterline, there is no downhill water flow, and because the scuppers are located underwater, they tend to allow water to flow back into the boat when it's at rest. Boats with this type are prone to having a constant puddle of water at the drain holes in their aft deck area... not usually something you'd want in your boat, unless you're a duck or a frog.

3. The third and least-loved type of deck drainage system is designed to drain water off of the deck and down into the bilge, which then puts all of the responsibility of preventing the boat from swamping or sinking on the boat's bilge pump and battery power. Since no bilge pump or battery charging system can be 100 percent reliable, 100

percent of the time, it wouldn't be wise to take a sinkable boat with this type very far away from the nearest shore. This type of drainage system also results in the accumulation of sand and small pieces of food, bait and fishing line in the lowest point of the bilge, which can eventually clog up the bilge pump and cause it to fail.

A water-filled bilge can – at the very least (in unsinkable boats) – cause major handling problems, and wreak havoc with any electrical wiring and components if not dealt with immediately, especially in saltwater. And at worst – depending on the boat and the size of its bilge space – a water-filled bilge can quickly capsize or sink a boat.

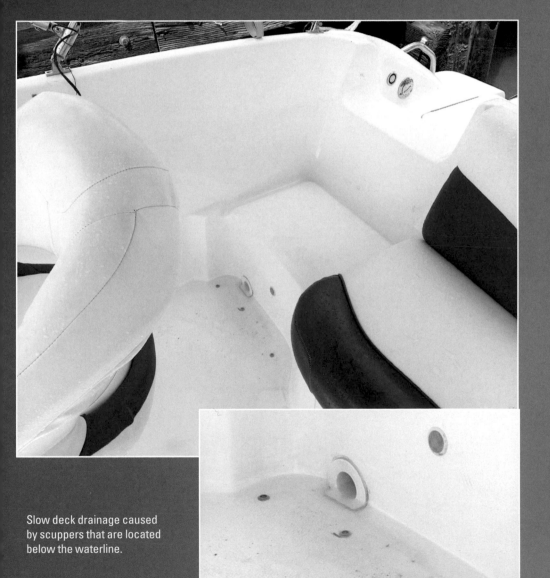

Slow deck drainage caused by scuppers that are located below the waterline.

Other Important Boat Feature Considerations

Having plenty of stowage capacity will definitely help to keep your boat well-organized.

Stowage Capacity

Check each boat's storage areas and compartments to make sure there's enough room to stow everything that you plan to keep onboard.

Beamier is Better

A boat with a wide beam tends to be roomier and more stable than a narrower boat. For some fishing boat types, such as bass and flats boats, a wide beam is also better because the wider they are, the less water they tend to draw, allowing access to shallower waters.

Fuel Capacity

The more outboard horsepower that's strapped to a boat, the larger the fuel tank should be in order to make it through a full day of boating without the inconvenience of needing to refuel before being ready to call it a day. As a very basic guideline, any boat with 150 hp or more should have a built-in fuel tank with a capacity of at least 40 gallons.

The Trailer

New boat packages often come with an inexpensive, painted or galvanized steel trailer of average quality, which helps to keep the price down. In most freshwater regions, these base model trailers will hold up for years to come if properly maintained. But in coastal, saltwater areas, aluminum trailers last a lot longer. If it's within your budget to do so, it's a good idea to pay the difference to upgrade to an aluminum trailer with a surge brake system.

Towing weight regulations that require boat trailers to have a brake system, vary from state to state, and apply to any boat-motor-trailer combinations above specific, set weights. But even if your combined boat weight is below your state's requirement for trailer brakes, for all but maybe the smallest, lightest aluminum boats, having a trailer equipped with surge brakes for safety's sake is well worth the extra cost, and may reduce your insurance premium.

A word of caution about used boat trailers – when negotiating the purchase of a used boat and trailer combo, if the trailer looks old and rusty with corroded framework or rust holes, worn out tires, and wiring in disrepair, then it almost surely also has worn out wheel bearings and corroded brake parts too (if equipped).

A boat trailer in bad shape could be more trouble than it's worth to refurbish back into safely usable condition.

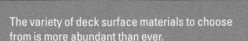

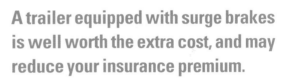

The variety of deck surface materials to choose from is more abundant than ever.

All these can be fixed, but not without money, material and work – yours or someone's whom you pay. It's not at all unusual to see used boats for sale that are in good condition, sitting atop a trailer in very poor condition that would be unsafe and illegal to tow a boat with. If you come across a trailer in bad shape like this, it may be more trouble than it's worth to refurbish back into a safely usable condition. In such cases, if you decide to buy the boat you should negotiate the value of the repair work on the trailer or the entire trailer out of the deal.

A trailer equipped with surge brakes is well worth the extra cost, and may reduce your insurance premium.

Deck Surface

For boats with a fiberglass/gelcoat deck, a smooth, non-slip surface is the more user-friendly option than a diamond deck surface. Diamond deck is a good non-slip surface, but it's more difficult to clean and keep clean, and it can also be rough on the skin of your feet and knees.

Carpeted decks may be the most comfortable, but they also tend to collect lots of sand and anything else that makes its way to the deck, such as dirt, food crumbs, bait, fish slime and small leaves. Even marine-grade carpet will eventually wear out and begin to break down after regular exposure to the elements and foot traffic. This is why carpeted boat decks aren't as common as they once were. There are now more deck-covering material choices that are comfortable, durable and easy to keep clean. Different boat brands offer different types of deck materials, depending on the boat type.

Boat Financing

If your new (or used) boat will be financed, the first thing you should do is review all three of your credit reports as far in advance of the purchase as possible. Check them for any score-affecting errors or omissions that would need to be corrected prior to applying for your boat loan. Doing this is in your best interest (literally) because boat loan qualification requirements are more stringent than for auto loans, since boats aren't a necessity. Most minor credit report discrepancies can be cleared up in just a few weeks. But some corrections involve a lengthy process that starts with having to convince the creditor of their error, and requesting for it to be rectified. Since it can take months for these issues get resolved and reflect accordingly on your updated credit file, the sooner you do this the better.

Everyone is entitled to receive one free credit report per year from each of the 3 main credit bureaus: Equifax, Experian and TransUnion. The official website for consumer access is: annualcreditreport.com Or call: 877-322-8228. You should also find out in advance what your current credit score is. Creditkarma.com is a reputable website that provides free credit scores and monitoring. The score you see there may differ from your FICO score, but it will give you a good indicator of where you stand in terms of creditworthiness.

Friends get together on the water at a meeting spot where boats can anchor near each other in the shallows.

Just as it is for auto financing, the wisest way to get your best/lowest possible interest rate, terms and monthly payments on a boat loan is to get pre-approved prior to any sales negotiations. If you take the time to check around and compare your financing options, and then get pre-approved by the lender with the best rates, you'll be well-prepared to start your boat shopping and ready to negotiate for your best deal, with the least amount of stress.

If you dive head-first into your boat shopping foray without first knowing what your credit score is and what your own financing sources would offer, you could risk paying thousands more over the life of the loan than you really had to. Accepting a higher APR, longer loan term, and higher monthly payments than you could've pre-qualified for, is an easy trap to get caught in if you rush into a dealership and get lured in by a tempting deal that supposedly "ends today."

Dealerships can receive back-end compensation (kickbacks) called "dealer reserves" from lenders, as incentive to "sell" (manipulate the terms in favor of the lender) loans with higher interest rates, even if the borrower can actually qualify for a lower rate... unethical but legal. Dealers that employ this dishonest tactic will downplay a borrower's credit score as "unfortunate news" that they don't qualify for the low APR they'd

Financing takes a bit of work and a monthly nut to crack, but the boater's lifestyle opens a world of new adventures for the boat owner.

hoped for, and try to pressure him into a higher APR loan, often with additional loan fees. This may involve an offer to "offset" the higher APR by extending the loan out to a longer term (adding more months or years) as a way to lower the monthly payment. But this will of course cost much more over time.

Never let a sales person negotiate your deal by trying to focus your attention toward the monthly payment, and away from the all-important bottom-line price, APR and term (months). Tell them that your monthly payment will work itself out, if and when all of the other factors are negotiated to your liking.

By no means is this to say that anytime a buyer has to be told that their lower credit score will cost them a higher rate or longer term, they're automatically being manipulated. Boat loans do require fairly good credit for approval, and higher risk borrowers should expect to pay higher rates. Most boat industry dealers and sales reps are good, honest people who will gladly help their customers get a loan they'll be happy with, afterall it's good for business. But sadly there are some unscrupulous dealers who may try to take advantage of uninformed or overeager customers, especially if they happen to have mediocre credit.

Boat and outboard manufacturers occasionally advertise very attractive rebates or special financing programs, such as a zero down payment loan with an incomparably-low APR in the low single digits. These loan offers are truly great... if you can get them. Problem is, only borrowers in the highest tier of credit scores can qualify for them. If you get approved for one of these factory offers, the dealer shouldn't use it as a reason to resist discounting the price, pointing out the great financing deal as your

Local banks and credit unions can provide loans for boat purchases.

Many boat dealerships offer both new and used vessels and service as well.

savings. Those savings are between you and the manufacturer's lender, not the dealership. Most dealers have room to negotiate the sale price of boats, and to a lesser extent outboards.

Credit unions consistently offer some of the lowest loan interest rates, with little or no additional loan fees, although some banks can offer competitive rates as well. Down payment requirements vary among different lenders and range from $0 to 30 percent, based on credit approval criteria. Unless you have a top-tier credit score and qualify for one of the manufacturer's occasional, special financing programs, with average credit you can expect to pay a 2 to 9 percent higher APR on a boat loan than you'd pay for an auto loan. Boat loan terms can be up to 180 months (15 years), but the shorter your loan term is, the less interest you'll pay overall.

If trading in a boat, you can look up its approximate value online at nadaguides.com/boats before all the fun begins. There aren't any trade-in or wholesale values listed there, it only shows the low and high retail averages. But at least you'll be able to guesstimate your trade value by figuring it'll definitely be less than the low retail value. Of course you can almost always get more by selling your used boat than you'll get for trade-in credit.

Full coverage boat insurance is required for any financed boat, but should be carried for paid-for boats as well. It's best to have and not need, than to need and not have. Whether cruising out on the water or hauling down the highway... you never know what may be around the next turn.

Boat loans do require fairly good credit for approval, or at least for a good APR.

Boat and Motor Warranties

Boat warranties are a little more complicated than vehicle warranties. There are various different warranty coverages for several different components of a boat, motor and trailer. When comparing different product brands, it's important to also compare their warranties. The time period and the extent of the coverages for different boat and outboard motor warranties can vary widely from brand to brand. The more crucial warranty coverages are for the hull and deck structures, and the outboard motor(s), since they are by far the two most expensive components of a boat to repair or replace.

You may find it necessary to contact the boat manufacturers directly, or at least check their websites for clarification of what some of their warranty coverages actually cover and what they don't. Unfortunately, there are a few salesmen out there with a propensity to exaggerate or tell you more of what you'd want to hear, than some of the not-so-great facts about certain warranties.

When evaluating and comparing any type of warranties, whether the original, factory warranty or an extended service plan that you might purchase, be on the lookout for the words "prorated schedule" and "declining scale." These are wise to avoid. Warranties that express either of these terms stipulate a continually-reducing percentage of coverage for a particular element of the product (such as hull blisters or gelcoat defects), and protect you less and less throughout the warranty period. Preferably, opt for non-prorated or non-declining warranties, which mean that the coverage is the same on the last day of the warranty as it is on the first.

Nearly all boat and outboard motor warranties are transferable, allowing any remaining coverage to be assigned to a subsequent owner. If you decide to sell your boat before the warranty expires, that's an attractive selling point. Just be sure to check on the manufacturer's transfer requirements and fees. Certain outboard motor companies require for warrantied motors to be taken in to a factory-authorized dealer to be inspected in order to qualify for the warranty transfer, which will usually involve a service fee.

Once you've purchased your boat, you're ready to live the boater's lifestyle, both at home and on vacation, wherever your dreams lead you.

CHAPTER 4

Outboard Motors

T oday, the majority of new, recreational, trailerable boats are powered by an outboard motor, as opposed to a stern drive (I/O) motor or inboard motor. Outboards are more versatile and user-friendly overall, and are the best power choice for fishing boats especially. Hooked fish will sometimes entangle fishing line around the boat's propeller, and it's so much easier to untangle or cut the line from around the prop when you can tilt it up and out of the water. (Caution: always pull the key out of the ignition switch before anyone gets anywhere near the boat propeller for any reason at all.) SB

The majority of new, recreational boats are powered by outboard motors.

Being able to fully tilt outboard motors up – completely out of the water – is a significant advantage, especially for fishing boats.

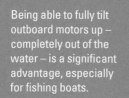

Get in Gear

The following list of comparisons outlines the primary reasons for the preference and widespread popularity of outboard motors:

Outboard vs. Inboard/Outboard Motors

» Outboard motors can be fully tilted up and completely out of the water, which is very handy for trolling or pushing-poling the boat through shallows, or inspecting the prop for any fouling (obstruction) or damage. I/O outdrives (Inboard/Outboard sterndrive) remain partially – if not mostly submerged, even when fully tilted up.

» Outboard boats have more usable space in the boat since the motor is externally mounted to the transom, rather than inside of the boat.

» Many modern outboards motors are more fuel-efficient than comparable I/Os.

» Unlike I/O's, outboard motors are usually visible from the helm, taking the guesswork out of which way the prop is aimed when docking and backing down in Reverse for maneuvering.

» Maintenance and repair costs can be lower on outboard motors, attributable mainly to the ease of access, which requires less labor time. Working on an I/O motor often involves reaching down into a cramped engine compartment. For an outboard, you just stand comfortably on your feet working at about chest level. Also I/O boats have considerably more components and parts to maintain, repair and replace than outboard boats do.

» With I/O boats, there are the concerns of both deadly carbon monoxide and potentially-explosive gasoline vapor accumulation. They're equipped with built-in exhaust blowers for this, but then you also have the additional concern of that not working. These issues are much less of a worry with outboard boats because they don't have an engine compartment.

» I/O boats will eventually leak water into the bilge because there are several possible leak points and their seals can deteriorate and fail over time. This problem can't occur in outboard boats because the entire motor and gear case are externally mounted to the boat's transom, as opposed to through the boat's hull and below the waterline.

Outboards are more versatile and user-friendly overall.

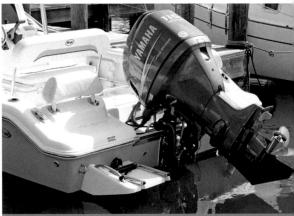

Fully tilted outboard motor (above). Inboard/outboard motor (below) is much less accessible.

Two-Stroke Outboard Motors vs. Four-stroke Outboard Motors:

Two-stroke outboard motors have been around for over 100 years and have a long-standing reputation for providing high-performing acceleration and top-end speeds. Accompanied by this raw power, though, are some characteristics that aren't/weren't so user-friendly.

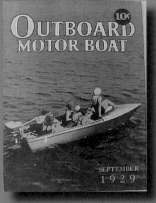

Two-stroke outboard motors have been in use for more than a century.

The most recent EPA emission standards require outboard motor manufacturers to produce a much cleaner and more efficient generation of outboards than in previous years. Prior to these changes, most 2-stroke motors were smoky at idle and low speeds (caused by the 2-cycle oil they burn), annoyingly loud at high speeds and considerably-less fuel-efficient than the latest lines of progressively engineered 2-stroke outboards.

A few of the major outboard manufacturers have accepted and met the challenge by making significant technological improvements to their lines of 2-stroke motors, engineering them to be much cleaner, quieter, and more efficient. These innovations have also been spurred on by competition from quickly-advancing developments in the 4-stroke outboard market sector. In fact, some of the new 2-stroke outboard motors can now offer fuel efficiency, low emissions and noise levels that are comparable to that of 4-stroke motors, which have always been inherently at or above EPA standards in all of these performance categories.

Other manufacturers have already phased out nearly all of their 2-stroke products, and have instead made the transition to producing mainly 4-stroke outboard motors.

Despite the welcome improvements, all 2-stroke outboard-powered boats – even the newest, most advanced ones – still have one inherent drawback... they require the extra expense and inconveniences involved with needing 2-cycle oil added, usually upon refueling. All 2-stroke motors require a gasoline and 2-cycle oil mixture to burn together within the fuel system. Fortunately, most modern 2-stroke motors have an oil injection or blending system that automatically delivers the correct 2-cycle oil ratio while the motor is running. With these systems, an oil reservoir is either attached directly to the motor or mounted inside of the boat, requiring only that an adequate oil level be maintained. (Old 2-stroke motors and small – 2 to 30 hp – 2-stroke motors require 2-cycle oil to be pre-mixed, or pre-measured and manually poured into the gas tank at a specific fuel-to-oil ratio... typically either 50:1 or 100:1.)

As consumers, we benefit more and more from ongoing competition among outboard manufacturers to out-design and out-sell each other.

There is one benefit that somewhat offsets the extra oil costs, inconveniences and environmental concerns of 2-stroke outboards... there's no periodic oil and filter change to pay for and deal with, as there is with 4-stroke motors.

Four-stroke outboard motors are more like your truck or car motor, in terms of oil requirements. Four-cycle motor oil and filter need to be replaced once or twice per year (typically every 100 hours), but the fuel systems don't require any 2-cycle oil to be consumed along with the gasoline.

If you're wondering how 2-stroke and 4-stroke motors compare cost-wise in terms of oil to burn versus oil to change, it really depends on a few factors.

by a factory-authorized service center in order to keep any warranty from being voided.) If turning wrenches isn't your thing, and if you spend an average amount of time boating just seasonally, then on average you'll spend roughly the same amount per year whether regularly pouring 2-cycle oil into a 2-stroke-powered boat, or routinely taking in a 4-stroke-powered boat to be professionally serviced.

Four-stroke outboard motors are now widely available from most brands.

For boats that are run frequently – such as offshore fishing boats that go out on long-distance, full-day trips throughout the year – 4-stroke motors can provide annual savings well into the thousands of dollars, simply by not requiring any need for 2-cycle oil.

Four-stroke outboards have a much shorter history than 2-strokes, with most of the larger horsepower models being developed just in the past decade or so. Ten years ago, 4-stroke outboard motors lacked the raw power of comparable 2-stroke motors, but today's 4-stroke outboards have caught up in that category and are now engineered to respond and perform just as well.

Although 2-stroke outboards must burn 2-cycle oil, there are no oil and filter changes to deal with.

If you're mechanically-inclined and have the desire and time to do your own oil and filter changes, with a 4-stroke motor, you can save at least $100 or more per scheduled maintenance by doing the work yourself, rather than paying a marine repair service outfit. (Keep in mind that certain scheduled maintenances are required to be performed

Although 2-stroke motor technology has made impressive strides recently and continues to retain a large following of loyal users, 4-strokes outboards continue to gain widespread popularity for their exceptional fuel economy, quietness, ultra-low emissions and oil cost savings.

The bottom line is both 2-stroke and

4-stroke outboard motors are now being engineered and built to be more reliable, durable, and better-performing than at any time in the past. As consumers, we benefit more and more every year from the ongoing competition among outboard manufacturers to out-design and out-sell each other.

Pre-rigged, boat-motor-trailer packages are usually the best deals for new boats.

Outboard Motor Options for New Boats

Dealerships commonly sell new boats that are already rigged with an outboard motor, and ready-to-launch with a trailer as a discounted package deal. These complete packages are almost always priced lower than custom-ordering the same boat model with a specific motor of your choice and optional accessories. More often than not, the motor included with these factory or dealer packages is appropriately matched to the boat, in terms of horsepower.

When shopping around for new boats, you'll notice that certain brands are available only with one particular brand of outboard motor. This is because some boat manufacturers have exclusivity agreements with specific motor manufacturers. These contracts are mutually-beneficial for the companies, but they obviously limit the consumers' choice to the one brand. Fortunately for all of us, thanks to modern technology and market share competition, the few outboard motor brands that used to be wise to avoid are now much more reliable than they used to be, so there's really no single brand that should be considered a major compromise.

Other boat brands are sold with a choice of two or more outboard brands, allowing buyers to choose, and opt for motors up to the boat's max horsepower rating. In some cases, custom-ordered boats are rigged with the customer's chosen outboard motor(s) at the boat factory, and delivered to the dealership ready to go. Or the motor rigging is done by the dealership's service department after the customer chooses a specific outboard brand and model.

Outboard motors range in horsepower from 2.5 hp portable "kicker" motors to 350 hp work horses.

The recent, substantial increases in available horsepower now allow large sportfishing boats to be outboard powered, too.

Outboard warranty periods of between three and six years, unheard of a decade ago, are now the norm.

If you're wondering how to decide among all of the different choices of outboard motors to choose from, it often starts with first deciding on the boat type and specific model you want, which in itself will narrow down the choices for you, based on what the manufacturer's and dealership's available options are. Tell your dealership what you expect performance-wise from your new boat, what your preferences are in regards to 2-stroke or 4-stroke motors, and ask them to explain all of your outboard options.

Otherwise, for new boat brands that offer wide-open choices, it's best to start with comparing different warranty coverage details of the outboard brands that are available to you. This is another area of recent improvement in the world of outboard motors that benefits the consumer. Warranty periods of between three and six years, unheard of a decade ago, are now the norm. Just be sure to read the fine print... no warranty covers everything, and some cover more than others.

As for which brands of outboard motors are the best, ask four people and there's a good chance you'll get four different opinions. The current generation of outboards can all be considered quality-built, dependable motors, as is indicated by the warranties now being offered by their manufacturers.

Outboard Motor Requirements

If purchasing a boat and outboard motor separately, it's important to get an outboard that is correctly matched to the boat hull, in terms of horsepower and shaft length.

A boat's USCG Maximum Capacities Plate (or decal) indicates the maximum safe horsepower for the boat. Conversely, an underpowered boat can be inadequate for its intended purpose. An outboard motor rated at less than 75 percent of a boat's maximum

Twins

Any boat that travels miles offshore and into oceans or the large lakes has an added measure of reliability if it has twin motors so that one can serve as a backup motor if the other one fails. Still, plenty of anglers with fishing boats powered by a single outboard motor are seen fishing well beyond the sight of land. They might choose to carry an additional kicker motor with enough horsepower to limp back to port, should the need arise.

Certain boats are rigged with twin or triple outboard motors for the additional power needed by larger, heavier boats, especially offshore fishing boats with deep-vee hulls. It takes a lot of horsepower to get them up on plane and cruising along.

A new, very intriguing component available for twin outboard-powered boats is joystick steering control systems. These automated systems make boat docking amazingly easy, requiring the boat operator to simply point the joy stick toward the desired direction. We'll explain more of the interesting details in the next chapter.

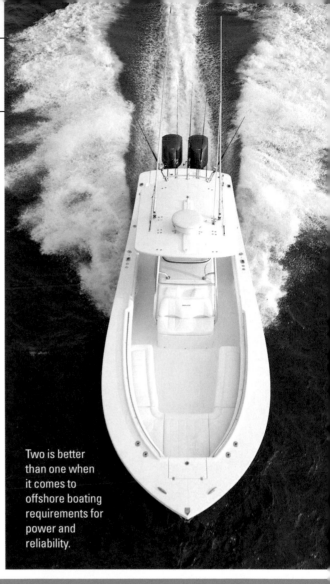

Two is better than one when it comes to offshore boating requirements for power and reliability.

hp capacity will typically lack the necessary power for the boat's weight and hull shape. Example: if a boat's max hp capacity is 175 hp, and it has a 115 hp outboard motor attached to it; 75 percent of 175 = 131. So it would be underpowered since the motor is only 115 hp, and is most-likely not powerful enough for the boat to be used to its full potential.

Outboard motor shaft lengths are standardized to correctly fit boat transoms of various, specific heights. A motor shaft that is too long will extend too far down into the water, creating excessive drag which hinders performance and fuel ef-

ficiency. A motor shaft that is too short will result in ventilation, and also potentially cause damaging overheating of the motor due to the raw water intakes not being completely submerged.

An outboard motor should also be mounted onto the transom at just the right height for optimal performance. Ideally, it needs to be set as high as possible without raising the raw water intakes above the waterline and without causing ventilation. The antiventilation plate (aka cavitation plate) most commonly will be nearly level with the keel, or up to 2 inches higher, with the motor set to neutral trim level.

Jet Drive Outboard Motors

An increasingly-popular option for boats that need to negotiate shallow, rocky-bottom rivers where protruding lower units and propellers would be frequently damaged, is jet drive outboard motors. These prop-free outboards can also be advantageous for anglers because four-stroke jet drives are very quiet-running

For propulsion, jet drive outboards turn an internal impeller, rather than an external propeller...problem solved.

motors. They're available in up to 150 hp, which also makes them an option for boat owners who'd prefer to avoid any of the concerns associated with propellers.

Jet drive outboards are most commonly matched to aluminum boats that are built for navigating through shallow, rocky waters, but can also be an option for small to medium-sized fishing boats that frequent any super-skinny shallows.

A great option for aluminum boats that need to access shallow, rocky-bottom rivers is jet drive outboards.

Underpowered Boat Package Deals

An underpowered boat is problematic because it lacks the horsepower to plane out when the boat is loaded up to its maximum weight capacity with passengers, gear, and fuel, etc. This usually results in the boat being either forced to plod along slowly, well below cruising speed, or to be pushed along at full throttle just to gain some semblance of planing, with the bow riding up at an unsafe attitude, often blocking the boat driver's view.

Avoid buying an underpowered boat. Not only will you be disappointed in its performance and end up with a good ol' case of buyer's remorse, you'll also be stuck with a boat that's difficult to sell or trade in.

If the size of the motor rigged onto a boat is the manufacturer's minimum-recommended horse-power model, be sure to take the boat out for a trial run on before agreeing to anything. Load up at least the average number of passengers and/or weight you would be having onboard, and run the boat to see if it struggles at all to plane out. If it does lag and takes more than 5 or 6 seconds to get on plane upon full throttle, or if the bow won't level off, then the boat is probably underpowered. This is assuming that it has the right propeller size and pitch, and that the correct trim adjustments were being made.

Twin outboard boats also can be underpowered for their size, depending on their loads.

Be cautious of special packages that include the boat's minimum-recommended hp motor.

For any boat rigged with the minimum-recommended hp motor, be sure to load it up and take it out for a trial run on the water to ensure that it's not underpowered.

Used Boat Outboard Motor Repowering

I f you buy a used boat with an old outboard motor that you'll be replacing, it's best to repower it with the same brand of motor. If you switch to a different motor brand, you'll also have to replace any of its connected, remote components because different brands of motors and components aren't compatible with each other. These would include the control box/shift lever assembly, the ignition key switch, the motor-connected gauges and the shift/throttle cables. Also, none of the associated mounting holes in the boat will line up the same. So while it's not at all unheard of to do, switching a boat's existing outboard motor from one brand to another is more expensive and labor-intensive than repowering it with the same brand.

Of course this concept doesn't necessarily apply if replacing a dinosaur-of-a-motor with a brand new one, since the old gauges and controls probably won't be compatible with a new, high-tech motor.

Choosing the Right Propeller

The complexities of boat propellers can be a bit baffling. Props are available in different materials; aluminum, stainless steel, composite metals and composite plastics. They're available in many different 3, 4 and even 5-blade designs (for most outboards). They come in many different diameter sizes, and with different blade pitch, rake, and cup. Plus there's straight, or constant pitch, and progressive pitch. Props are also available with different types of hubs, designed to minimize both prop and internal motor damage in the event of an impact. There are more aspects to boat propellers,

A stainless steel prop. On its stamp, diameter is the first number, and pitch is the second number.

but you get the point.

So how are you supposed to know which propeller is right for your motor, with so many different variable factors? Fortunately, general application recommendations for props are predetermined by motor manufacturers for each motor model, or – for boat and motor packages that are factory or dealer-rigged – the boat manufacturer or dealership. However, these are not intended to be an absolute recommendation, since boats, operating conditions and uses vary. Outboard motor manufacturer websites also post propeller charts that can be very helpful guidelines when trying to select or confirm which prop is right for your boat's hull type, size, weight and primary use.

How can you know which prop is right for your motor, with so many different variables?

Most new boat purchases will already include the appropriate propeller, often with the option to upgrade to a stainless steel or higher-performance prop. For a used boat purchase, it's usually safe to assume that the previous owner or the selling dealership has installed the right prop for the boat. But it's also a good idea to double-check it yourself.

If you plan to do any research or trial and error testing for the purpose of "dialing in" the optimal propeller option for your boat and motor combination, being familiar with the following terms and information will definitely help.

Diameter is the distance across the outer "circle" of a propeller. The diameter and pitch of most props are stamped on the prop. On the stamp, diameter is the first number, and pitch is the second number listed. For props with no stamp, or for props that have been reconditioned (which sometimes reduces diameter), you can check the diameter simply by measuring the radius and multiplying it by 2. (The radius is the distance from the hub center to the outermost tip of one of the blades.)

Pitch is the forward movement of a propeller for one revolution, assuming no prop slip. For example, a 15 pitch propeller will theoretically move 15 inches for every revolution. (Some prop slip occurs with every propeller, but the amount varies depending on prop design.)

A Reusable Hub System

Sometimes, when you run into a submerged object and spin a hub, your prop blades might not sustain damage on the impact, but your hub system will be down for the count and you'll need a tow to get back to port.

A few years ago, PowerTech! Propellers of Shreveport, LA, introduced a reusable hub system, the Safety Torque Hub. Upon impact, the Safety Torque is designed to disengage and act as a compact clutch that instantly absorbs the shock load. Then, it automatically re-engages to full torque capability once you've cleared the obstruction.

The Safety Torque hub system is designed to replace square-cavity, drop-in hubs (Mercury Flo-Torq, Michigan XHS, etc.) that fit into PowerTech! square hub cavity propellers, Mercury Flo-Torq propellers, Turbo/Stiletto square hub cavity propellers, and any other OEM/aftermarket propellers that accept these designs. The Safety Torque is available from any authorized PowerTech! dealer. At an MSRP of $399, it's more expensive than replacing a traditional sacrificial hub, but for boaters who travel deep into the backcountry or Bahamas, or who run tournament or charter vessels where down time is costly, it sounds like an attractive option. A similar system will be available for inboard drivelines. For more, visit www.ptprop.com and www.safetytorque.com

Changing out a prop at the dock (left). The Safety Torque hub system (right).

Rake is the degree that a propeller blade is angled in relation to the hub.

Cup refers to the curled lip at the trailing edge and/or tip of the prop blades. It improves the prop's "grip" in the water for better holding at high trim and through turns. Properly designed cupping can also increase propeller efficiency and provide higher top end speeds.

The best all-around outboard performance is achieved when wide open throttle (WOT, aka full throttle) motor operation occurs near the top of – but within – the WOT RPM operating range designated by the motor's manufacturer. For example, with a WOT range of 5000–6000 RPM, 5900 RPM would be ideal. Selecting the wrong propeller not only reduces performance, it can also damage the motor. A motor that doesn't reach the recommended RPM at WOT is "over-propped," resulting in "lugging." This high-torque operation puts a tremendous load on the pistons, crankshaft and bearings, and may cause motor damage. On the other hand, a motor that revs past the recommended RPM will have higher than normal wear and can also be damaged by fatigued parts breaking and passing through the engine. This is why it's essential that your motor is propped correctly for your boat/motor combo and your type of boating.

The best all-around outboard performance is achieved when WOT operation occurs near the top of the WOT RPM operating range.

Selecting the ideal option for your boat may require a few trial and error runs with different props.

Outboard Exterior

Terms and locations for various parts and features found on and around an outboard motor:

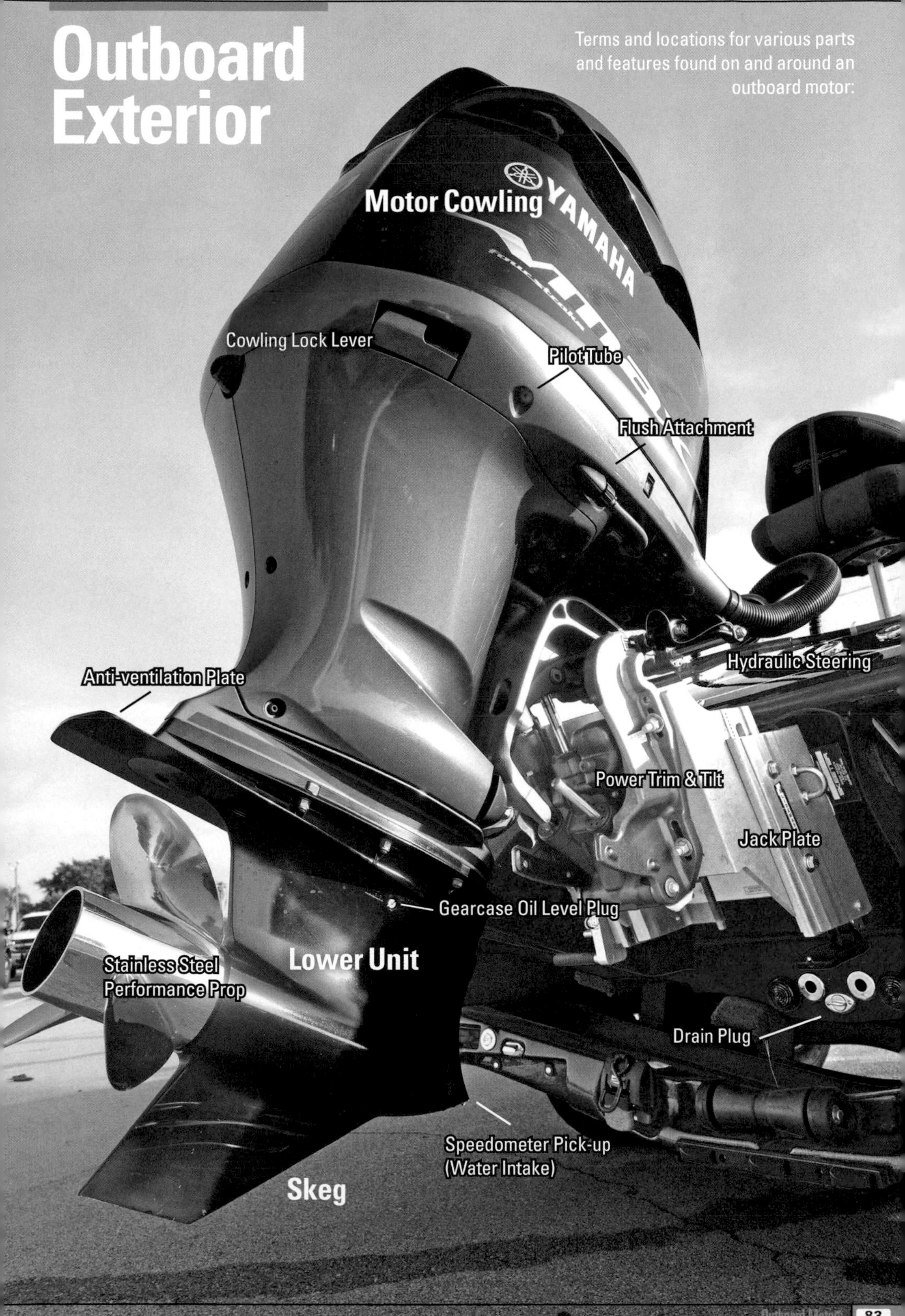

Motor Cowling

YAMAHA

Cowling Lock Lever

Pilot Tube

Flush Attachment

Anti-ventilation Plate

Hydraulic Steering

Power Trim & Tilt

Jack Plate

Gearcase Oil Level Plug

Lower Unit

Stainless Steel Performance Prop

Drain Plug

Speedometer Pick-up (Water Intake)

Skeg

Pitch Change Calculation

When in doubt, to easily calculate how much propeller pitch change may be required:

1. Check the specifications in your outboard motor manufacturer owner's manual for the recommended operating range at wide open throttle. A tachometer is necessary to determine the WOT RPM.

2. Run the boat at WOT to determine the maximum RPM. Be sure to adjust the motor trim angle for optimum performance.

3. If the WOT RPM is below the recommended RPM range of the engine, note the reading of the tachometer. Take that reading and subtract it from the top end of the operating range.

4. Example: operating range = 5000–6000 RPM
Top end of operating range = 6000 RPM
Tachometer reading = 5200 RPM
Difference = 800 RPM

5. For every 1 inch of pitch change, the effect will be approximately 200 RPM. The difference in this example of 800 divided by 200 = 4. So the next propeller to try would have 4 inches less pitch than the original prop. For a more conservative approach, you could instead try switching to a pitch reduction of 2 or 3 inches.

(Source: Reynolds Racing & Marine)

For loading a boat up to its maximum weight capacity or for water sports use, installing a prop with a pitch reduction of 2 inches or so less than factory-recommended specs, may help to compensate for the added weight and drag. It can also make a noticeable improvement in a boat's hole shot, fuel efficiency

Tachometer reading of 5,200 RPM at wide open throttle.

A severely damaged aluminum propeller.

and overall performance. But, remember to keep an eye on the RPM when running a lower pitch prop for these circumstances, since lowering pitch will increase motor RPM. Also be aware that the same pitch from different manufacturers will run slightly different RPM due to a difference in blade design. Speed

Never Run a Damaged Propeller

Continued use of a damaged propeller can lead to internal motor damage. When propeller blades have been bent or partially severed, the prop becomes very unbalanced and won't spin true. This causes excessive vibrations that transfer up into the motor. Also, a propeller that is even slightly damaged won't perform as well as a sound one because the damaged blades can degrade hydrodynamic efficiency.

(Source: Formula Propeller & Marine)

There are a few important factors to consider when choosing between aluminum and stainless steel props.

Aluminum vs. Stainless Steel Props

The main advantage of a stainless steel over an aluminum propeller is durability. Stainless steel props can withstand much more of the "oops moment" impacts with sand, small rocks or other objects. However, this strength can also be a drawback if the prop hits an object hard enough. Since there is minimal "give" in the blades, all of the energy from the impact has got to go somewhere, so the possibility of it transferring up into the lower unit and causing major damage is increased substantially, compared to aluminum. Another consideration is that they're as much as

Many inshore boaters opt for high performance stainless props (left) to both jump on plane quicker and run higher in the water.

3 to 4 times more expensive than the same size aluminum prop.

Aluminum props are a much less-expensive option. And although they're much less durable than stainless steel props, a significant advantage is that the blades will most likely sacrifice themselves before too much damaging energy is transferred up into to the lower unit.

CHAPTER 5

Rigging Your Boat to Help You Catch More Fish

To be a consistent boat angler, all you have to know is how to navigate, locate fish and position the craft properly to present an offering. Simple, right? But what if you're new to fishing and boats and don't have any experience? No problem, rigging your new boat with some of the latest technology can have you angling like a seasoned pro in no time. SB

Rigging your new boat with some of the latest technology can have you angling like a seasoned pro in no time.

A nice cobia makes this angler and his pals happy. Right, rocket launchers (rod holders) mounted on a T-top for quick access.

Latest Technology

GPS

With the advancements in global positioning system (GPS) units both in range of sizes and affordability, few boats don't have some form of moving map that includes marine charts with topography, navigation aids and details of channels plus structure. Many GPS units even have high resolution satellite imagery with aerial photography of ports, harbors and marinas. It's still a good idea to have paper charts onboard as a backup to the electronic software, but with a current GPS moving map, navigating is as simple as following your track on a screen to a pre-selected waypoint.

When choosing a GPS, take into consideration several things. First and foremost, display size. Will it fit in the space provided on your helm? Second choice will be mounting. Flush-mounted electronics are the most popular but where space won't allow it, using the gimbal mount provided with your unit will work. Third is choosing which manufacturer to go with. The best thing is to go to a marine supply store that has several brands on display that are powered up in simulator mode. Some units are very user intuitive, some are not and require use of the owner's manual. If you're going to be integrating the GPS with any other equipment like a fish finder, autopilot, VHF radio, etc., it may be better to keep all of the brands the same.

Small gimbal-mounted GPS units still pack a big punch when it comes to built-in features.

With a current GPS moving map, navigating is as simple as following your track on a screen.

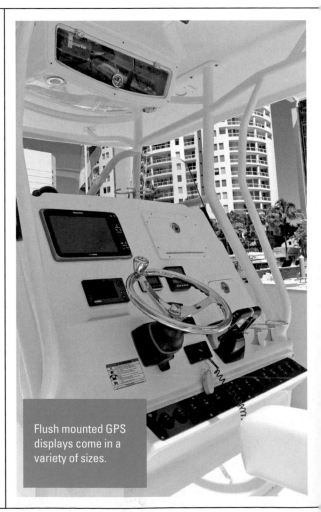

Flush mounted GPS displays come in a variety of sizes.

Fish Finder

Most GPS displays also double as a fish finder. You can choose to show the fish finder full screen or split screen with the fish finder on one side, and GPS, radar, navigation function, engine gauges or a host of other functions on the other side. Matching the unit to the boat and the style of fishing you plan on doing is important. For instance, on a smaller boat fishing in shallow water, you really only need to know water depth more than having the ability to see fish show up on the screen. If the water is less than 5 feet, you most likely won't want to position the boat over the top of the fish for fear of spooking them into the next county. On the other hand, if you plan on fishing offshore wrecks and reefs, a fish finder can help you locate the area of the bottom structure that has the largest concentration of fish. When attempting to catch live bait, a fish finder is invaluable. Bait schools are often on the move and having the ability to see them on the screen and position the boat over the top of the school will allow you to load up the baitwell faster so you can head out to your fishing spot sooner.

Bow-mounted Trolling Motor with GPS Autopilot

A bow mounted trolling motor with built-in GPS offers superior boat control and will allow you more time to fish.

For inshore saltwater and freshwater fishing boats, the addition of a bow-mounted trolling motor, if your boat will accept one, completes the package. The newest rage is bow-mounted electrics that have built-in GPS receivers. These trolling motors are capable of navigating on their own to a pre-assigned waypoint that not only gives you a silent approach, but will let you focus on your fishing. Another incredible feature is their ability to hold on a spot, so there's no need to deploy an anchor. Any function of the trolling motor can be controlled from anywhere in the boat by use of a remote control. Just short of arriving at the waypoint fishing spot, stop your gas engine and deploy your bow-mounted trolling motor. Use the GO TO feature on your remote control and let the electric motor bring you quietly into casting range. At that point you activate the anchor function on the remote and the trolling motor will hold your position.

When installing a fish finder on the boat, you will need to also install a transducer. What a transducer does is emit an acoustic signal that passes through the water and reflects off of an underwater object, bouncing the signal back to the transducer. That signal is passed on to the processor in the fish finder and is displayed in a variety of fashions depending on the type of unit you choose. Many of the smaller units come with the transducer supplied that will be matched to the fish finder's capabilities, but as the units get larger, the transducers are sold separately and you can choose the frequency. The frequency of the transducer relates to the width of the beam or cone angle that the unit emits. Think of it as the light beam illuminating from a flashlight. The wider the beam is, it will cover a broader area, but will give up some detail. This is best for shallow water operations. A narrow beam will give you more detail and is better for use in deeper water. Many fish finders have dual-frequency transducers that give you the ability to switch back and forth to pick the best resolution on your display screen.

Radar

It used to be that radar on a boat was reserved for the larger sportfishers, but now with the advancements in technology the price has come down and there is such a variety of units available that more and more boats of all sizes are installing these "extra set of eyes" on the water. Radar has many functions, and the size of the unit – really the size of the antenna – will depend on the length of your boat and its mission.

For navigating in low-visibility, radar will give you the ability to see objects like landmasses, weather systems, other boats and nav aids (buoys) to assist you in the navigation of your vessel. For

Radar mounted on T-top is the customary setup for center consoles.

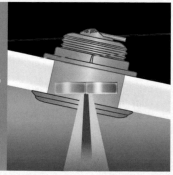

Transom-mounted transducer rides just below the water level.

Graphic of Airmar tilted-element B175 transducer, through-hull mounted.

Radar reading around boat, represented by center dot, below, shows moisture in clouds nearby.

Anglers found birds by radar and set out lines for pelagics feeding near the surface and down deeper.

Satellite Weather

Many weather systems are fast moving, and once you leave port you are at the mercy of the weather. Even with proper trip planning, like checking the local weather report and radar prior to heading out, a weather system can build between you and your port, making the trip home anything from uncomfortable to downright dangerous. Several services offer satellite weather that can be overlaid on your GPS moving map, much like having radar but with far more range. Radar has its place but its range is limited to the signal strength of its antenna. Even the most powerful units have limits of approximately 72 miles and that will be affected by weather, the antenna's height off of the water, and even the curvature of the earth. Satellite weather can be used to watch the development of weather systems and their course of travel, far before they become a factor to your boating.

So with a satellite weather link, you may ask yourself why bother with radar? The main difference is time delay. Onboard radar lets you see weather in real time, whereas weather information from satellite may be as much as ten minutes old. If you are watching a system develop in the distance and want to run for port ahead of it, the time delay is not a factor. But if you have to pick your way through a squall, searching for the areas of the least amount of falling precipitation, you will want the most up-to-date information available. A perfect scenario is having both: radar for close, up-to-date info, and satellite for distant weather you can't see beyond the horizon.

fishing, radar can help you find flocks of feeding birds that will normally lead you to feeding schools of fish as well. The biggest consideration in choosing the proper radar unit is choosing the type and size of the antenna. A higher power output level will increase the radar's signals reflecting off of objects and let you see through precipitation for better target acquisition. Open array antennas, the ones that look like spinning helicopter blades, are longer and give you a greater resolution on your display screen. The smaller closed array antennas, the ones that look like a birthday cake, may lack some of the detail of the larger antennas, but still do an amazing job. Other benefits of operating a radar include letting you quickly determine the range of targets from your boat with the use of distance rings and setting up a guard alarm that can alert you when any object enters a pre-determined range ring.

If you have to pick your way through a squall, you will want the most up-to-date weather info.

The boaters aboard the vessel had better be prepared and have a plan for getting through the incoming weather that they either ignored or did not know would soon be on them. Above, a Lowrance unit shows some serious storm weather on satellite.

Jack Plates

Jack plates have two basic functions: to allow a shallow draft boat to run in skinnier water and to increase a high-performance boat's top-end speed. Both enhancements are a product of a jack plate's ability to raise an outboard lower unit vertically on the transom while underway. The higher you lift the lower unit in the water column, the less drag you have, so your top-end speed will increase and the lower unit will stick down less so you can run in shallower water.

So you may ask yourself why not just mount the motor permanently at that height? The problem is hole shot, or the boat's ability to get on plane. If the motor is not deep enough, the propeller cannot grab enough water and will start to slip or cavitate because the thrust of the outboard is trying to overcome the weight and drag of the boat. As the boat planes off, the drag decreases and you can start to raise the motor without the fear of cavitation.

Jack plates are primarily a two piece design with a mount portion that bolts directly to the transom of the boat, and a sliding plate that the outboard motor bolts to. To control the height of the motor, typically you will have a rocker switch flush-mounted near the steering wheel, but the most popular is the flapper style switch, much like a car's blinker switch that allows a driver to keep both hands on the steering wheel.

To start off, you put the jack plate in its full down position. As you throttle up and the boat starts to plane off, you can lift the jack plate accordingly while watching the engine RPMs to know when you have to maximum height set for whichever trim configuration you are running in. One word of caution; be careful not to raise the outboard lower unit too high out of the wa-

ter and allow the water pump it to suck air into the cooling water pickups. You could overheat the powerhead and cause damage.

Jack plate on this bass boat can raise the engine to increase boat's speed and let the vessel run in shallower waters.

The higher you lift the lower unit, the less drag you have.

Poling Platform

Boats used for prowling super-shallow water, often called flats boats, will have a poling platform incorporated into their design. Much like an offshore boat uses a tuna tower to gain the advantage of height, so does a flats angler with the use of a poling platform. Standing on a platform lets you see farther ahead of the boat, making it easier to spot an unsuspecting fish, and glare is reduced allowing you to see better down into the water. The extra height also doesn't let another angler on the bow to block your view.

Perhaps the biggest advantage of a poling platform is boat control. When you use a push pole to propel the boat through the water, it is far quieter than any bow-mounted electric motor, and it also allows you to turn and stop on a dime. If you want to hold the boat in position, you simply drive the push pole into the flat at an angle and it acts like an anchor without the hassle of wet ropes and noisy anchor chains.

When you use a push pole to propel a boat, it is far quieter than any other method of propulsion.

With the height, the angler poling can see farther and better and alert caster to fish nearby.

Trim Tabs

One of the most misunderstood aspects of running a boat is proper trim angle, but it actually has the largest effect on ride quality and economy. Manufacturers design their hulls for optimum performance at a particular angle of trim, normally in a slightly bow-up attitude, but as you load your boat with gear, fuel, and people, it's hard to get it just right. Trimming your outboard motor will help rotate the bow up or down on the latitudinal axis of the hull, but will do little to help with roll or list from side to side. That's where a pair of trim tabs can allow you to dial in the perfect running angle.

Trim tabs are a set of stainless steel plates that are attached at the transom of the hull. The size of the plates depends on the hull size, and the travel of the tabs is controlled either by a hydraulic pump and cylinders, or worm gear actuators. The controls are typically a set of rocker switches located near the steering wheel on the helm, and allow you to operate the tabs together or independently. Lowering both tabs will push the bow of the boat down, which can give you a softer ride into a head sea. Running back through a rough inlet, it would be desirable to raise both tabs to allow the bow to rise so you don't stuff it into the wave in front of you. When you raise or lower one tab at a time it will allow the boat to roll on its longitudinal axis. This is especially useful where you want to balance your load from side to side or offset the effects of motor torque. A properly trimmed boat is more efficient and enhances the ride quality for your passengers.

Trim tab on transom is controlled by switch near the steering wheel at the helm, left.

Bow-mounted multiple rod holders allow these tournament crappie anglers to cover water.

butt into makes the job of winching in line from the depths less fatiguing. Many times, especially if you're deep dropping, you may just leave the rod in the holder throughout the fight.

Kite fishing is another tactic where having additional rod holders mounted at the bow is a must. As the boat drifts, it's best to face the bow down current. Many craft assume this position automatically, and holding the boat into the current stern-first makes it much easier to control. Place a trident, which is basically three rod holders joined together onto one mount, in one of the gunnel-mounted rod holders at the bow. Put your kite rod in the center holder on the trident, and the other two trident holders are used for fishing two live bait rods at one time. Once you've experienced the excitement of explosive surface strikes, you'll be hooked on this type of fishing.

Rod Holders

Most fishing boat manufacturers include at least four gunnel-mounted rod holders in their list of standard features. Normally these four holders are installed at the stern with two rod holders facing straight aft and the two forward angled out slightly. For a typical four-bait spread while trolling, this set up is fine, but there are many other fishing techniques where additional gunnel-mounted rod holders would come in handy.

In the case of deep dropping or drifting while bottom fishing, several more rod holders mounted on either side of the boat, facing straight off to the side will make handling a heavy bottom fishing rig much easier. Depending on the length of the boat, rod holders spaced out from bow to stern will allow multiple anglers to fish on the same side of the boat without getting in each other's way. While you're bottom fishing you may be holding the rod, but when it's time to bait up or tie on a new rig, having a holder close by that you can put the rod

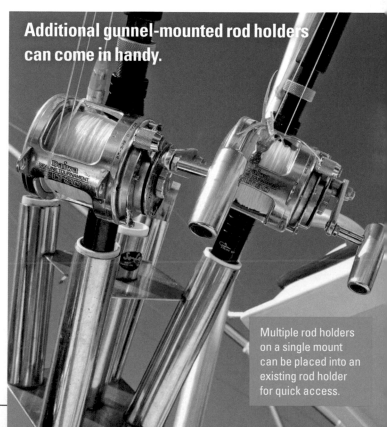

Additional gunnel-mounted rod holders can come in handy.

Multiple rod holders on a single mount can be placed into an existing rod holder for quick access.

Be sure to size the rod holders to the size of your equipment. Most stainless steel gunnel rod holders will handle the majority of rods that anglers commonly use, but if you are pursuing large offshore pelagic fish, and especially if your plan on deep-dropping with an electric reel, choose a rod holder that's up to the task. Also consider mounting the heavy duty rod holders with a backing plate under the gunnel. It will help spread the load from the strain of an epic strike and may save you from watching your prize rod and reel end up over the side.

Rod holders are a crucial convenience on fishing boats, and many think the more the better.

Downriggers

Downriggers work in a similar fashion to outriggers, they just cover a different part of the water column. Normally, a downrigger is mounted on the gunnel of the boat, just forward of the rod holder, and a weight is attached to the downrigger line, commonly called a cannon ball because it resembles one. Above the cannon ball is a release clip that your main fishing line attaches to. The base mount for the downrigger rotates so you can swing the end of the downrigger arm inward to attach your fishing line to the clip and then swing the arm out again to get it away from the boat. If you don't want to permanently install the outrigger base to your gunnel, a mount is available that slides into a gunnel-mounted rod holder. This makes the downrigger portable to be used on multiple boats.

Using your fish finder to locate what depth the fish are at, you can use the line counter that is part of the downrigger to lower your bait to the desired depth. Let your bait out several feet from the boat and attach your fishing line to the downrigger release clip. Disengage the reel and let out line at the same rate the downrigger line is deployed. Once the desired depth is reached, lock the downrigger and engage the reel.

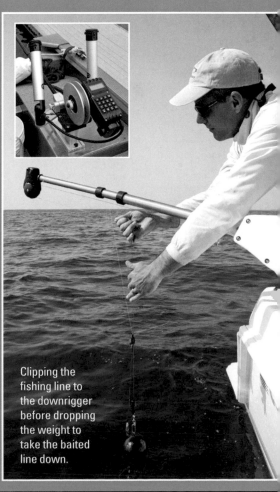

Clipping the fishing line to the downrigger before dropping the weight to take the baited line down.

Outriggers

Trolling is one of the most popular ways of fishing offshore. Whether you use lures or rigged fresh bait, this technique is very effective and can be relaxing since the boat is doing most of the work. Having a wider spread on your baits allows you to cover more water and will increase your chances of hooking that trophy catch. That's where a set of outriggers comes in.

Constructed out of fiberglass or aluminum, outriggers are basically two long poles that deploy out of either side of the boat. There are a few different ways of rigging the lines associated with them, but the result is the same. When you attach your main fishing line to a clip that is then run out to the end of the extended outrigger, it spreads your fishing lines apart. When your fishing lines are separated it accomplishes two things: It lets you cover more water and allows the boat to make sharper turns without your lines becoming tangled.

When a fish strikes, the clip that holds your main fishing lines releases so that you are free to fight the fish to the boat. The two most common type of release clips are adjustable to compensate for the size and drag of the bait you're trolling with. One is like a large version of a clothes line clip that simply holds your fishing line at whatever distance you have it deployed. The other has an open catch that allows your fishing line to slide through. That way you can adjust the distance the bait is away from the boat without having to retrieve the clip back to the boat first.

To use an outrigger, you let your fishing line out to the desired distance away from the boat. Next, grab the fishing line close to the end of the rod and attach it to the outrigger clip. As you run the clip out to the end of the outrigger pole, let enough line out from your reel at the same time so that you don't put too much tension on the clip and cause the line to pop out. Once the clip reaches the end of the pole, engage the reel and sit back and wait for the action.

When a fish strikes, the clip that holds your main line releases so that you are free to fight that fish.

With lines spread out with outriggers, these trollers cover more water. Right, closeup of fishing line clipped in.

These anglers chose the right spot to set their anchor pole down, as the hookup by front angler attests.

Shallow Water Anchor

This innovation, which is growing in popularity among shallow water anglers every year, is a game changer. A shallow water anchor allows you to stop your boat on a dime and hold it in position without disturbing the surrounding environment. In the past, if you wanted to anchor your boat, it involved opening a hatch, pulling out an anchor, chain and rope and dropping it over board. Two inherent problems with this procedure are noise, and by the time the anchor sets, your boat may be out of position.

Shallow water anchors consist of a mount and solid rod, typically made out of composite fiberglass, and either a hydraulic pump or a vertical drive to deploy them. When an angler finds an area he wants to fish, he engages the anchor mechanism with a remote control or a console-mounted switch, and the fiberglass rod is lowered into the bottom. The advantage with this system is that it's silent and fast, plus you can retrieve the anchor and re-deploy it as many times as you want without dealing with a wet rope or muddy anchor and chain. The limit of depth you can use a shallow water anchor in is approximately 12 feet.

There are some less-expensive options available of shallow water anchors that are commonly referred to as stick pins. These are manually-deployed much like a push pole is used in flats fishing, but the pins are generally smaller and lighter in weight than a push pole. Either system will allow you to hold your boat's position in shallow water without alerting the fish of you presence.

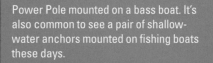

Power Pole mounted on a bass boat. It's also common to see a pair of shallow-water anchors mounted on fishing boats these days.

Baitwells

Round baitwells keep the baits from bumping into corners and damaging themselves and increase circulation.

Portable Baitwell

It's hard to imagine a fishing boat without a live baitwell, but some manufacturers may have a design that leans more toward the family, or in some cases your boat may have a built-in baitwell but it's not of sufficient size to keep the type of bait you want to use alive. Portable baitwells come in all sorts of shapes and sizes. Some are manufactured out of fiberglass but the majority of the aftermarket wells are fashioned out of a roto-molded plastic. These are the most popular, mainly because they are lighter and less expensive than ones constructed out of fiberglass and gel coat.

Many tournament anglers use portable baitwells in addition to the ones molded into their boat's deck layout because of the volume of bait they need to carry for a full day of fishing. Another nice feature of a portable well is that when you're not heading out to fish, the well can easily be removed to free up valuable cockpit space.

Some anglers may use a standalone pump as part of the boat's raw water plumbing just for a portable baitwell, but many more simply use the boat's raw water washdown system if one is already installed.

Many tournament anglers use portable baitwells in addition to the ones molded into their boat's deck layout.

Rigging Livewells and Release Wells

Plumbing water into and out of a storage compartment on a boat is commonly referred to as a baitwell, livewell or release well. Which type of well it is depends on the intended use.

Baitwells are typically used for just that, bait. Water flow is important because a large number of small, nervous fish swimming around in a confined

It's important to know how many of a species you can place into your baitwell without crowding them and decreasing their survival rate.

Plumbing and pumping water – whether it is from surrounding waters or recirculated in closed wells – can be managed a variety of ways depending on your needs for baits, livewells and release wells.

area consume a massive amount of oxygen. Supplying an adequate amount of oxygenated water to keep your bait healthy can be accomplished by one of two ways. The best way is to keep a constant flow of water coming into the baitwell from the bottom and allowing the existing water to overflow out of the baitwell near the top. This will bring in the surrounding oxygen saturated water, and at the same time remove waste generated by the bait. In some cases it may not be practical to have a fresh supply of water for your baitwell. In smaller boats, installing pumps and plumbing may not be practical. Or if the water quality where you are is poor, to introduce the outside water could kill your bait. In this scenario, a pump mounted inside of your baitwell can be rigged to a spray bar that will circulate the water, and at the same time oxygenate it. Another concern with a baitwell is the need for rounded corners. Swimming baits have a tendency to bunch up in a corner, and the added stress of this will cause your bait to die prematurely.

Livewells are the equivalent of a baitwell but most are larger in quantity of gallons, and may have squared off corners to allow for a maximum interior size. Livewells are most prevalent on boats that are used for fishing

Now that fresh baits are in hand, it's a matter of quickly and efficiently caring for them to keep them lively and healthy.

tournaments. The ability to bring your prize catch to a weigh-in, alive, can account for more points awarded. Many tournaments penalize an angler for bringing in a dead fish to be weighed. Just as water flow is important in a good quality baitwell, that holds true for a livewell too. Livewells are designed to keep larger fish alive, so you may not have the numbers of fish to deal with as in a baitwell, but larger fish do consume more oxygen than smaller fish do. The same plumbing set up for a baitwell can work just as good for a livewell. The interior design can incorporate squared off corners due to the fact that larger fish confined in a livewell tend to suspend in one place since they don't have the room to swim around. Livewells also have another benefit; they allow you to cull your catch throughout the day. If you are limited to a specific number of fish that you can legally keep or will be accepted at a tournament weigh-in, a livewell will keep the fish you land alive. In the event you happen to catch a larger fish than one of the fish you have in your livewell, you can release one of the smaller ones to stay within the limits.

Release wells are just larger versions of a livewell and are found on many saltwater bay boats where the species you fish for are larger in size than if you were angling from say, a bass boat in fresh water.

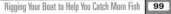

Joystick Control

As boats get larger, control becomes more of an issue, especially in close quarters like a marina or fuel dock. Current, wind and waves all have an effect on the boat, and getting the boat into a slip or up to a dock can be a challenge, even for an experienced captain.

With a twin motor setup, better control is made possible by the ability to put one motor in reverse and one in forward to spin the boat with the thrust of the motors. But on some models the outboards are mounted so close together that the benefit of the twin motors versus a single motor is minimal.

Motor manufacturers now offer an option of adding a joystick control at the helm which literally

Joystick control – a relatively new innovation – promises to make boat control easier.

allows you to move the boat in whatever position you tilt the joystick. A joystick control seamlessly integrates the steering, throttle and shift functions, as well as the outboard propulsion and direction. Whether you want to move forward or backward, sideways or diagonally, or pivot in place, just move the joystick in that direction and the boat will follow. The control system independently positions each outboard to coordinate thrust direction and amount. This thrust vectoring enacts forward and reverse shifting simultaneously, positioning each motor at different angles, or setting each outboard to a different gear or RPM.

LED Lighting

Fishing at night can be highly productive. In the summer, once the sun is high on the horizon, fish will move deeper to find cooler water and escape the sun. Nighttime brings out a host of tiny sea creatures that hide during the day but come out after dark to feed; this starts the food chain cycle. In high pressure areas, fish that are wary during daylight hours drop their guard at night, and with leaders harder for them to see, your catch ratio is sure to go up. Adding lighting both above and below the surface of the water can make nighttime angling safer and more productive.

Before we get into where to install lights on your new boat, let's talk about the benefits of LED lighting over other light sources. Over the years, vast improvements have been made in the LED industry to where now these light have the same level of output of low-wattage halogens. LEDs are extremely long-lived, are impervious to vibration and give off very little heat. Using about a tenth of the wattage of a halogen while producing similar output, they are far less of a drain on your batteries, and most are waterproof.

The most common lights installed on a boat are called spreader lights. These can be mounted on a tower facing into the cockpit or on a T-top facing forward or aft. These lights will give you great illumination when trying to rig baits at night and will light up the cockpit. One drawback is that when looking out toward the horizon at night with your spreader lights on, your night vision will be diminished. To counteract this, many anglers also rig their boats with under gunnel rope lighting. LEDs are available in a string of rope lighting that comes in a multitude of colors, with some rope lighting even having the ability to change colors by the way of a remote control. Rope lighting will illuminate

Under gunwale lights add a cool look and useful illumination for low light conditions.

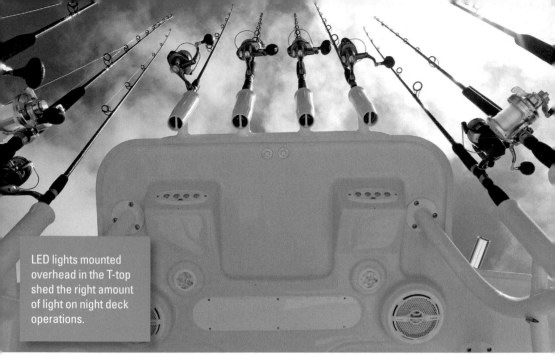

LED lights mounted overhead in the T-top shed the right amount of light on night deck operations.

the cockpit with a much softer glow that will still give you enough light to see, but not adversely affect your ability to see at night.

Some manufacturers are now using LEDs for nav lights on their vessels. Although they may cost a bit more than the typical bayonet socket bulbs you may be familiar with, LEDs will give off more light, last much longer, and are not as susceptible to corrosion.

Perhaps the best application of a LED is in the form of an underwater light. Most of the time you will find two or more lights mounted on the transom of the boat facing aft, but several

manufacturers also make LEDs that look more like a thru-hull fitting, and can be mounted just about anywhere you have access to your bilge area to shoot down from the hull. At rest at night, it doesn't take long at all for a swarm of small bait fish and shrimp to gather in the light of an underwater LED. That starts the food chain, and not far behind the bait, will be hungry predators.

So there you have it. A novice boater can outfit his or her boat with a variety of rigging options and circumvent years of trial and error to become a better fisherman plus safer boater in the process.

Underwater LED lights not only orient anglers to night spots, but they draw baitfish and action closer to the boat.

Rigging Bass Boats

Many advancements in high performance bass boats have been spurred on by professional bass fishing competition.

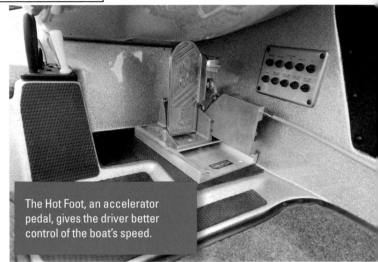

The Hot Foot, an accelerator pedal, gives the driver better control of the boat's speed.

How a boat is rigged can have a huge effect on your angling success and that is especially true of a bass boat. Many of the advancements in high performance bass boats over the years have been spurred on by the highly competitive bass fishing tournament circuits. Gaining an edge over a fellow competitor can be something as simple as a few more miles an hour in top end speed, dual livewells or above deck rod holders. But the real beneficiaries of these improvements in bass boat designs are the weekend anglers. The same features that propel a tournament pro to the top of the leader board also help the average angler catch more fish.

Starting at the bow, every bass boat needs a good quality electric trolling motor. Bass are primarily ambush feeders and having the ability to quietly position the boat to make a cast that presents your lure or live bait in the right spot is paramount. Sizing the trolling motor to the boat is important. Many bass boats today top the 21' range and if the electric trolling motor is too small to handle the hull's displacement you will find yourself constantly running on full power and depleting the batteries power supply prematurely.

Batteries are another area where it's not a good idea to cut corners. A deep cycle battery or batteries are a must for supplying power to a trolling motor. They are specifically designed to be charged and drained through multiple cycles. Try that with a typical start battery and you not only will run out of juice sooner but you'll

There's no shortage of space for tackle boxes and gear in this reach-in, in-deck storage unit.

Forward deck is carpeted for maximum traction, with ample room around chair for two anglers to work off the bow of the boat.

This trolling motor is rigged for foot control, with fish finder.

Trolling motor controlled manually or by foot.

be replacing the battery(s) more often as well. On the other hand, to crank your outboard, you need to have a start battery that carries more cold cranking amps and is designed to give you a quick shot of power then an immediate recharge from the engines electrical system.

Electronics have come a long way too over the years. A dash-mounted chartplotter will help you navigate an unfamiliar body of water and most have a built-in fish finding depth recorder to show you the structure beneath the boat. Mount an additional fish finder up on the bow and attach the unit's transducer to the foot of your trolling motor. That will let you keep track of the water depth as you work along a shoreline and see any hidden structure that will hold bass.

Bass feed in all sectors of the water column. Early in the morning and late in the evening they regularly strike topwater plugs. As the sun rises on the horizon, spinnerbaits and crank baits may be the lures of choice. Midday with the sun directly overhead, a plastic worm flipped into the shade of a dock or overhanging tree will generally draw more action. The size and color of the lures you choose will depend on water quality and cloud cover. Unless you want to spend a good part of your angling day changing lures, having an assortment of rod and reel outfits at the ready will increase your odds at landing that lunker. Deck-mounted rod holders will keep your rod combos accessible, organized and secure for running at high speeds.

Batteries are another area where it's not a good idea to cut corners.

CHAPTER 6

Safe and Smart Boating

Being out on the water and enjoying the variety of activities that are unique to boating is at times fun and exciting, and other times very calming and relaxing. For some boaters though, it can sometimes be a little bit too relaxing – especially when combined with sun exposure and the side-effects of wave and boat motions. If inexperience, inattention or recklessness comes into play, operating their boat puts them and anyone in their path at risk. Add alcohol, and they have a recipe for disaster. SB

Always remember: Safety is no accident!

Smart boaters know that boating requires a responsible attitude toward safety to avoid mishaps (right) and protect people.

Don't Be Complacent

In the majority of fatal boating accidents, life jackets are stowed onboard, but not worn.

Don't let ideal conditions lull you into a false sense of security, either on the water or at the docks.

Every year on U.S. waterways, thousands of boating accidents take hundreds of lives, cause thousands of injuries and millions of dollars in property damage. Most of these accidents are fairly easily prevented.

People tend to let their guard down when they're having a good time, especially when boating close to shore in calm waters where they feel safest. It's human nature. But these are actually the conditions in which at least half of all recreational boating fatalities occur. Too often, when boating conditions are really good, things go really bad. And unfortunately, it can be blamed mostly on one thing – a false sense of security. This is the culprit in the majority of fatal boating accidents. This com-placency shows itself in the fact that in the majority of fatal accidents, life jackets are stowed onboard, but not worn.

But accidents happen –that'll never change, right? It certainly can change if more boaters would be willing to accept the fact that powerboating is an inherently risky activity, and that they should always expect the unexpected... and be prepared for it simply by wearing their life jackets. The majority of fatal boating accident victims, who otherwise could have survived, drown because they were not wearing their life jacket – even though it was right there in the boat, just a few feet away when the unexpected happened.

The U.S. Coast Guard recommends that you wear– not just have onboard – a life jacket while boating. But don't just do it because it's recommended. Do it because you value your life, care about your passengers and their safety, and because you're a smart, responsible person.

One real-life case that truly exemplifies the importance of this vital safety rule took place nearly 3 miles off the coast of Key Biscayne, Florida. Four recreational fishermen who were thrown overboard from their boat, which had taken on water and capsized, survived after one of the men was able to swim to shore to get rescue dispatched for his three companions, who endured more than 10 hours overnight in the water. "These four men returned home safely to their families because they were smart, prepared and wore their life jackets," affirmed U.S. Coast Guard Seventh District's Public Affairs Officer, Lt. Commander Gabe Somma. "We cannot stress enough that emergencies on the water can happen at any moment, and that this incident illustrates the need to have safety equipment onboard and readily available." He added, "The conditions got pretty rough that night. If these men had not been wearing their life jackets, their ordeal would likely have had a much different outcome."

So please, know before you go: Prepare and practice so that you'll know what to do and not to do before venturing out on your boat for fun in the sun on the water.

If you bring along your furry family member, protect them too with a doggie PFD.

injuries that are serious enough to immediately incapacitate and prevent them from being able to swim at all, even if conscious. Additionally, if otherwise uninjured during a boating accident, the sudden impact of any collision can and often does knock victims unconscious.

No matter how carefully a parent watches over or holds onto their child while boating, they can't protect him or her from drowning nearly as reliably and effectively as a life jacket. So parents, even if you live in one of the few states that still have inexplicably-low age requirements for children's life jackets, please don't let that or ideal boating conditions lull you into a false sense of security. The safety and lives of your children are in your hands.

Both children and adults need to wear life jackets. Age and experience do not float. More than half of all boating fatalities are men over 30 with over 100 hours of boating experience. Having life jackets aboard does not save lives, wearing them does.

Always remember – boating safety is a shared responsibility, but the operator of a boat is ultimately the one who is morally and legally responsible for the safety and lives of all passengers aboard the boat, and also for any death, injury or damage resulting from his or her operation of the boat. Legal responsibility lies with the boat owner as well.

So play it safe and smart – don't allow yourself or anyone in your boat to become another easily-preventable, tragic statistic. Complacency kills – please wear your LIFE jackets.

The Need to Wear PFDs or Life Jackets While Underway

Most adults don't and won't wear a PFD while boating unless they're required to by law, or when it seems necessary – such as when water skiing or caught in a squall. The common, potentially-deadly misconception is the notion that, "I'm a good swimmer so I don't need a life jacket" or "I can put it on in the water" or "my kid swims like a fish – he'll be fine." This false sense of security is unfortunately a very common attitude among boaters, and comes from the old "That'll never happen to me" school of thought. What these people don't realize is that one of the primary reasons so many good swimmers drown as the result of boating accidents is because they sustain

Since recreational powerboats have no seatbelts for high-speed accident protection, life jackets are all the more critical.

Having life jackets aboard does not save lives, wearing them does.

Sobering Stats from the USCG document, "Recreational Boating Statistics 2012":

- In 2012, the U.S. Coast Guard counted 4,515 accidents that involved 651 deaths, 3,000 injuries, and $38 million in damage to property as a result of recreational boating accidents.

- 70 percent of all fatal boating accident victims drowned, and of those, 84 percent were not reported as wearing a life jacket (or a PFD: Personal Floatation Device).

- Operator inattention, improper lookout, operator inexperience, excessive speed, and machinery failure rank as the top 5 primary contributing factors in boating accidents.

- Alcohol use is the leading contributing factor in fatal boating accidents; it was listed as the leading factor in 17 percent or 111 of the deaths.

- A relatively low percentage of deaths (14 percent) occurred on boats where the operator had received boating safety instruction. Only 9 percent of deaths occurred on boats where the operator had received boating safety instruction from a NASBLA-approved course provider.

- 24 children under age 13 lost their lives while boating in 2012. Ten of these children died from drowning. Only two of these 10 children were wearing a life jacket as required by state and federal law, the other 8 were not wearing a life jacket.

- The most common types of vessels involved in reported accidents were: open motorboats (47 percent), personal watercraft (19 percent) and cabin motorboats (15 percent).

- 7 out of every 10 boaters who drowned were using vessels less than 21 feet in length.

Alcohol use is the leading contributing factor in fatal boat accidents.

Crowded conditions on the water are cause for more caution and for more patience with nearby boaters.

USCG Life Jacket Requirements for Recreational Vessels

A USCG-approved, wearable life jacket or PFD of suitable size is required for each person onboard any vessel of any size, and must be in good and serviceable condition. Children must have properly-sized life jackets designed for children. Boats 16 feet and longer must also have a Type-IV Throwable Floatation Device, which shall be immediately available within arm's reach. Life jackets or PFDs must be properly stowed – meaning readily accessible, not locked in a closed compartment, have other gear stowed on top of them, or stored in unopened packaging.

Dad has the kids geared up for safe fishing on Mirror Lake in Lake Placid, New York.

Life Jacket, PFD or Life Vest – Which Is It?

These terms are used interchangeably throughout the boating and watersports industries, as well as by the USCG and state law enforcement agencies. However, you may come across literature or website info that makes an adamant distinction between a life jacket and a PFD (Personal Floatation Device).

So is there a difference? Technically, yes. Even though it's very common to see what is technically defined as a PFD referred to as a life jacket – and vice versa. Even the USCG and life jacket/PFD manufacturers use these terms interchangeably. In fact, as of May, 2014, the USCG had the following notice posted on their website, "Note: The Coast Guard is working with the PFD community to revise the classification and labeling of PFDs. When completed, this information will be updated and hopefully be somewhat easier to understand. Meanwhile, spending a few minutes to understand the many options available to find a PFD that you're willing to wear could mean the difference between life and death for you or a loved one."

Life jackets – or life vests – are designed to turn most unconscious wearers face-up in the water, although some types are designed to do this more reliably than others. All life jackets are either Type-I or Type-II, and are brightly-colored for high visibility rescue purposes. They're bulkier and less comfortable than most PFDs, but provide life-saving buoyancy when worn properly.

PFD's – most types anyway – are not designed to a turn an unconscious or exhausted wearer face-up in the water, although a few types are (such as certain automatic inflatables). But they absolutely are capable of saving your life by keeping you afloat when the unexpected happens. PFDs are made in Types-II, III and V, and are designed for a wide variety of uses, buoyancy categories and styles.

Children's Life Jacket Requirements

Laws requiring any child under a certain age to wear – not just have onboard – a properly-fitting, USCG-approved life jacket while boating, vary from state to state. Most states have appropriate age requirements, but a few states still have unbelievably lenient laws, such as Florida, where they apply only to children under 6 years of age while in a boat underway.

In states with no children's life jacket law requirements, the USCG requires any child under 13 on a boat underway to wear a properly-fitting, USCG-approved life jacket or PFD. This USCG regulation does not change or supersede state laws. Children's age and wearing requirements for life jackets for each state are conveniently listed on the Boat U.S. Foundation website at: boatus.org/life-jacket-loaner/state-requirements

Life Jacket / PFD Types

Selecting the right type of life jacket or PFD for different types of boating activities and conditions is crucial. Be sure to choose both the appropriate type and correct size for the most effective, life-saving protection.

Type:	Best Use:	Advantages:	Disadvantages:
Type-I Offshore Life Jacket	Rough offshore or remote open waters where the possibility of rescue may be delayed. Sized child to adult. Available as: inherently buoyant life jacket.	Provides maximum buoyancy. Designed to turn most unconscious wearers face-up in water.	Bulky, not comfortable for extended wear.
Type-II Nearshore Buoyancy Vest	Calm nearshore or inland waters where there is a good chance of a relatively quick rescue. Sized infant to adult. Available as: inherently buoyant life jacket or automatic-inflatable.	Will turn some unconscious wearers face-up in water. Less bulky than a Type-I. Inflatable Type-II PFD's turn as well as a Type-I foam life jacket.	Not designed for long hours in rough water. Basic, foam Type-II's provide less buoyancy than Type-I, and may require wearer to tread water to keep head sufficiently above surface.
Type-III PFD or Floatation Aid	Calm, protected inland water where there is a good chance of fast rescue. Sized infant to adult. Available as: inherently buoyant, manually-inflatable, or automatic-inflatable PFD. Fishing vests, ski vests, floatation jackets (float coat), and general purpose PFDs are examples. Important: each PFD's intended use and speed ratings are listed on its inside label.	Lightweight and comfortable for continuous wear. The most-used PFD type, made in a wide variety of designs for many recreational purposes. Certain models are feature-rich.	Designed to keep conscious wearers afloat – but will not turn them face-up if unconscious. Not intended for extended survival in rough water or offshore.
Type-IV Throwable Floatation Device	Designed to be thrown to a conscious person needing assistance. Not wearable – it is a floatation aid to be grasped and held onto by the user temporarily until assisted. Available as: buoyant cushion, or ring or horseshoe buoy.	Intended for inland water with boat traffic where help is always present, but can be helpful anywhere.	Not for an unconscious person. Not intended for extended survival in rough water or offshore.
Type-V PFD or Special Use Device	Protected inland or calm nearshore waters where with a good chance of quick rescue. Sized youth to adult. Only to be used for the specific activities that each model is designed for, as listed on the label. Certain automatic-inflatables, float coats, and kayak vests are examples. Most must be worn at all times to meet USCG requirements. A Type-V label will also list its performance as Type-I, II or III.	Continuous wear requirement prevents being unprotected. Certain Type-V models provide hypothermia protection, such as float coats. Wearer turn-over performance varies by Type and model.	Not intended for extended survival in rough water or offshore. Can be less safe than other types if not used according to label specifications.

Type-I Offshore Life Jacket.

Type-II PFD Basic.

Type-III Ski Vest.

Inflatable PFD Type-V with Type-II Performance.

Type-III Fishing Vest.

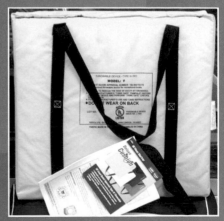

Type-IV Throwable Floatation Device.

Life Jacket / PFD Options

PFDs have become progressively more high-tech and are now much more comfortable, lightweight and even sporty-looking to wear. Barely anyone wanted to wear the few options of decades past. But with today's modern fishing and ski vests, and particularly the new automatic-inflatable PFDs, you can safely cruise and fish in both comfort and style.

Inherently Buoyant
- Every type, designed use, and size of life jacket and PFD is available in inherently buoyant models that use foam floatation. If it's not an inflatable, then it's inherently buoyant foam.
- For swimmers and non-swimmers.
- Durable, basically maintenance-free.

Inflatable: Advantages
- Inflatable air chamber inflates either automatically upon submersion into water or when manually activated – depending on the model.
- Automatic-inflatables also have manual pull-cord for backup or optional activation.
- Certain models can turn most wearers face-up faster than foam life jackets.
- Certain models will keep some unconscious users face up.
- Superior buoyancy performance.
- High visibility when inflated.
- Much more comfortable than foam life jackets.
- Coolest and most comfortable PFD to wear in warm weather.
- Compact, low profile and lightweight design allows for maximum mobility.
- Must be worn (can't be stowed) in order to meet USCG requirements for vessel PFD quantity – a great excuse to wear it!

Inflatable: Disadvantages
- Manually-activated models aren't as safe as inherently buoyant PFDs or automatic-inflatables because they will not provide any floatation if the wearer is unable to pull the cord for any reason, and aren't recommended for non-swimmers.
- Certain manually-activated models require multiple steps to deploy.
- Require regular maintenance and inspection and to work properly and remain USCG-approved.
- No insulation against hypothermia.
- Not appropriate for activities involving frequent water entry.
- Cannot be used for high-speed watersports or personal water craft (jetskis).
- Not suitable for children under 16.
- Certain automatic-inflatable models can inadvertently inflate if the inflator is exposed directly to water.

HIT Inflatable (Hydrostatic Inflator Technology)
- Automatic-inflatable PFD that won't inadvertently inflate due to rain, spray or humidity.
- Will automatically inflate when submerged in 4 or more inches of water.
- Less maintenance than standard inflatable.
- Available in Type-II and Type-V models.
- Expensive but worth it.

Proper Type and Fit Are Essential

Just the right size for her, this PFD is snug but comfortable.

Simply throwing on any PFD or life vest isn't enough. It absolutely must fit properly if it's expected to help save one's life, or even just to be comfortable to wear while in the water. It should be in good, sturdy condition, and fit snugly to the body when tightly fastened with the straps cinched up and buckled or zipped up, without being too tight to easily breathe of course.

Check the manufacturer's label on the inside of the vest to confirm that it's the right size, weight capacity and appropriate intended use for the type of boating activities you'll be doing. For any watersports that involve some speed – tubing, skiing, wakeboarding – every rider or skier must wear a PFD vest that is designed and labeled for watersports, regardless of age or state.

To confirm a proper fit, particularly for sizing children: Have them stand with their arms sticking straight up in the air (like they're signaling a touchdown), grab the life vest by the arm openings and try to pull it up and off. If it slides up fairly easily with little or no resistance, then it's too big and

A PFD that is too large for its wearer will ride up when in the water, and could accidentally slip off.

you'll need to try the next size down. Be sure to adjust the straps accordingly and check it as well. There should be no excess room above the arm openings.

A properly-fitting, tightly-fastened life jacket or PFD will make it easy to keep the head and upper shoulders above the surface of the water. If it's too loose, buoyancy will push the PFD's arm openings up into the armpits, and the top of it up to the ears, and it could accidentally slip completely off. And a PFD that's too small may not provide enough buoyancy to sufficiently keep its wearer afloat. Also – adult-sized PFD's will not work for children and should never be considered "good enough." Doing so would put the child at risk, and is illegal too. The general rule for proper sizing: If it fits you well – it will float you well.

At first glance, this ski vest seems to be a suitable size, but it doesn't pass the test for a proper fit.

The Cold Facts: PFD's and Cold Water Immersion

Another very good reason to wear a life jacket while boating in cold water, whether underway or stopped for fishing or anything else, is to help survive cold water shock and hypothermia. Cold water (generally considered to be temperatures around and below 70°F/21°C), is a game changer in terms of surviving boating accidents or even just falls overboard.

Many boaters have fallen into cold water and quickly drowned less than ten feet from their boat, caused by the immediate effects of cold water shock. Unlike hypothermia, sudden cold water immersion can lead to death in just a few minutes, and in some cases instantly, by causing cardiac arrest. Cold water shock can cause involuntary gasp reflexes that force victims to hyperventilate and faint, or inhale water and drown. The colder the water, the more severe the response.

The longer a person remains immersed in cold water, the less he's able to do what is necessary to save himself, and the more likely it is that he'll succumb to hypothermia. And he may be unable to save himself at all if not already wearing a PFD upon entering the water. Both physical and mental capacities can quickly deteriorate, making it extremely difficult to perform any functions requiring manual dexterity.

Within just a few minutes it may be impossible to tie a line, open a package of flares, or to use any communication device or other safety equipment. As disorientation sets in and voluntary motor function begins to worsen, so will the ability to swim, tread water, or hold on to anything.

But a PFD can definitely help you stay alive longer in cold water by providing energy-saving floatation, and at least some insulation to help retain a survivable core body temperature. Wearing a Type-III or Type-V floatation jacket (float coat) will provide more insulation against hypothermia than a vest-type, but Type-III's won't necessarily turn an unconscious wearer face-up in the water. Any type of PFD must fit snugly to provide these potentially life-saving protections from cold water immersion and drowning.

Cold water survival methods can vary, depending on the situation and who you ask. This has been the subject of some controversy, and still is. If your boat capsizes or sinks in cold water, do you stay with the boat or any nearby means of floatation, hoping that rescue arrives in time? Or do you swim for it, and try to race hypothermia to shore? If you can make the swim, will you be physiologically capable of pulling yourself out of the water or even walking once you get there? Obviously, making the right choice can be a matter of life or death.

But there can be no definitive, "Do it this way or you could die" answer or cardinal rule because each situation presents its own, unique set of circumstances and variables. One constant factor for which there is no doubt – wearing a PFD is crucial to the survivability of cold water immersion.

Type-III Float Coat, a potential life-saver that keeps you warm on chilly boating days.

Why You Need a Boating Safety Certificate

The more you know, the safer you and everyone around you will be.

To be a proficient boater requires a unique knowledge base and skillset, as well as a particular mindset that goes a long way toward being a good boat captain – a responsible attitude toward safety. Knowing how to safely handle navigation, boat traffic, waves, wakes, currents, wind, inclement weather, tides, anchoring, docking, trailering, fishing by boat, watersports towing, and learning the terminology, what equipment is needed and how to use it, the maintenance and storage requirements, what to do when the unexpected happens, and all of the pertinent rules and regulations, can all seem overwhelming for people new to boating. But after some time and effort put into learning and practicing the basics, along with due care for safety, they soon find out that a lot of it really just comes down to good ol' common sense, and that their efforts are being well-rewarded.

Most states now require powerboat operators to carry a boating safety certificate, verifying that they've passed an approved boating class, or at least an online course. This has a lot to do with the statistics that consistently point to boat operator inattention, inexperience and excessive speed as the cause of the majority of boating accidents. The majority of these accidents that involve fatalities occur on boats where the operator had not received boating safety instruction.

Even if you're confident in your own abilities and level of caution, there may be other boaters out on the water to be concerned about who aren't as cautious or experienced. So even if your state doesn't require you to do so, taking a safety course just might help you avoid being included in those unfortunate statistics. A boating safety certificate could also possibly qualify you for a boat insurance discount.

Whether required to or not, every boater should take a boating safety course, preferably from a NASBLA-approved (National Association of State Boating Law Administrators) course provider. Boating safety education laws vary by state. For the requirements in your state, check online at: boat-ed.com or boaterexam.com/usa where you can also take the courses.

For additional online boating safety courses, go to uscgboating.org and click on SAFETY>Boating Safety Courses.

A U.S. Coast Guard MH-65C Dolphin helicopter crew from Air Station Los Angeles conducts a flyover of the Point Vicente Lighthouse in Rancho Palos Verdes, California as part of a memorial service for fallen service brothers.

United States Coast Guard Requirements
– Including but not limited to:
(Contains info from USCG Vessel Safety Check form ANSC7012)

1. REGISTRATION NUMBERS:
Must be permanently attached to each side of the forward half of the vessel in format according to state regulations in block letters no less than 3 inches high and in a color contrasting with the background. A space or hyphen must separate the letter and number groupings and the state decal: FL 1234 AB [14] or FL-1234-AB [14].

2. REGISTRATION / DOCUMENTATION:
Registration and Documentation (if applicable) must be onboard and available. If documented, numbers must be permanently marked on a visible part of the interior structure. The documented boat's name and hailing port must be displayed on the exterior hull in letters not less than 4 inches in height and contrasting with the background.

3. LIFE JACKETS / PFD's:
A USCG-approved, wearable Life Jacket or PFD of suitable size is required for each person onboard any vessel of any size. Children must have properly-sized Life Jacket designed for children. Boats 16 feet and longer must also have a Type-IV Throwable Floatation Device which shall be immediately available within arm's reach. Life Jackets / PFDs must be readily accessible and shall not be locked in a closed compartment, have other gear stowed on top of them, or stored in unopened packaging.

4. VISUAL DISTRESS SIGNALS:
Boats 16 feet and longer used on coastal waters or the Great Lakes are required to carry a minimum of either: 1) 3 daytime and 3 nighttime pyrotechnic devices, 2) 1 daytime non-pyrotechnic device (flag) and 1 nighttime non-pyrotechnic device (SOS light), or 3) a combination of 1) and 2).

5. FIRE EXTINGUISHERS:
Every power boat is required to have onboard a minimum of 1 USCG-approved Marine Type B-I Fire Extinguisher that must be readily accessible and verified as serviceable.

Fire Extinguisher Type and Quantity Minimum Requirements by Vessel Size:

Vessels less than 26 feet: 1 Type B-I. Vessels 26 feet to less than 40: 2 Type B-I or 1 Type B-II.

All boats must carry a sound producing device (horn, whistle) capable of a 4-second blast that is audible for half a mile.

6. VENTILATION:
Inboard and I/O boats with gas engines in enclosed compartments built after Aug.1980 must have a powered ventilation system. Those built prior to that date must have natural or powered ventilation. Boats with closed fuel tank compartments built after Aug.1978 must display a certificate of compliance. Boats built before that date must have either natural or powered ventilation in the fuel tank compartment.

7. BACKFIRE FLAME ARRESTER:
All gas powered inboard or I/O (inboard/outboard) motorboats must be equipped with an approved backfire flame control device.

8. SOUND PRODUCING DEVICES:
To comply with Navigation Rules and for distress signaling purposes, ALL boats must carry a sound producing device (whistle, horn, siren, bell) capable of a 4-second blast that is audible for ½ mile. Device requirements vary by state and boat size.

9. NAVIGATION LIGHTS:
All boats must be able to display navigation lights between sunset and sunrise and in conditions of reduced visibility (fog, rain, haze). Boats 16 feet and longer must have properly installed, working navigation lights and an all-around anchor light capable of being lit independently of the running lights.

10. MARINE SANITATION DEVICES:
Any installed toilet must be a USCG-approved device. Overboard discharge outlets must be capable of being sealed. Check your state and local requirements.

11. STATE & LOCAL REQUIREMENTS:
Must be met before "Vessel Safety Check" decal is awarded.

12. OVERALL BOAT CONDITION:
Requirements include but are not limited to: 1) Vessel must be free of deck and fire hazards, in good overall condition, with bilges reasonably clean, and sound hull structure. Motor horsepower must not exceed the USCG capacity plate maximum. 2) Electrical and Fuel System: The electrical system must be protected by either fuses or manual reset circuit breakers. Switches and fuse panels must be protected from rain and spray. Wiring must be in good condition, and properly installed with no exposed conductor or deteriorated insulation. Batteries must be secured and terminals covered to prevent accidental arcing. Self-circling or kill switch mechanisms must be in proper working order.

State officers, like these Florida Fish and Wildlife Commission agents, patrol waters to enforce laws and ticket violators.

Once-over Checklist:
Boat, Safety Gear and Trailer

Before venturing out on a boating trip, you should always complete a once-over check of your boat, trailer, safety equipment and the weather. If you go boating as infrequently as most boat owners do, it's fundamentally important to ensure that everything is mechanically good-to-go, and that you're fully-equipped with all of the necessary and required safety gear, prior to heading out. Spending just 5 or 10 minutes on this can easily save you many long hours of distress out on the water.

Start in the front and systematically work your way back through the boat, checking all compartments and storage areas. Safety equipment that would require quick access in emergency situations should be kept easily accessible for a quick grab-and-go, and should never be covered up by a bunch of miscellaneous, non-essential stuff. If towing, make sure all of the trailer lights are working and that the tires aren't underinflated. If you don't – you could very possibly wind up on the side of the road, dealing with either a traffic ticket or a flat tire. Also remember to check your local weather for any fronts moving in, or any possibility of afternoon pop-up storms... just to be sure that your planned boating day is still a go.

You can also get a free Vessel Safety Check from the U.S. Coast Guard Auxiliary or U.S. Power Squadrons. Here's the website to get started: vdept.cgaux.org

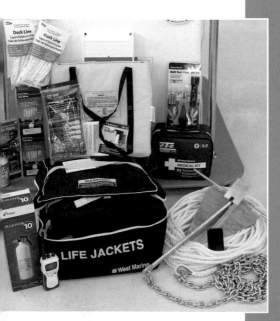

Coast Guard Kit, plus some of the more important extras that should always be kept onboard.

USCG Required + Recommended Boat & Safety Gear Checklist

√ USCG-approved Life Jackets or PFD's:
   1 for Each Person – must fit properly
√ Type-IV Throwable Floatation Device
√ USCG Marine Type B-I Fire Extinguisher(s) UL
   Rated 5-B:C or 10-B:C or 1-A 10-B:C
√ Horn or Whistle
√ Daytime & Nighttime Visual Distress
   Signals/Flares – required by some states
√ Anchor w/attached Chain and Line of appropriate length
   (even if you don't plan to use it)
√ Fully-charged SmartPhone or Cellphone(s)
√ VHF Marine Radio (fully-charged if portable)
√ Dock Lines: 2 minimum, 4 is better
√ First Aid Kit
√ Tools/Repair Kit (w/spare fuses, nav. light bulb, prop
   cotter pin, etc.)
√ Emergency Backup Bilge Pump Kit (clips directly to
   the battery)
√ Extra Propeller
√ Boat Hook
√ Binoculars
√ Compass
√ Paddle – only feasible for lighter boats under 20 feet

As these boaters will soon find out, being caught out in a storm in an open boat is no place to be.

Weather is Everything

The same foul weather conditions that the average motorist wouldn't be too concerned about driving through can quickly turn a boater's leisurely day into a nightmare of dangerous lightning, stinging, blinding rain and winds that churn the water up to barely passable. Most longtime, regular boaters have encountered at least one severe squall or harrowing experience out on the water in which they were caught off guard by sudden, violent storm conditions that put them through a perilous trial they'll never forget. For most boaters, the smart ones anyway, it only takes one life-threatening boating trip like this to permanently alter their attitude towards weather.

Up until very recently, getting hammered by unexpected, bad weather while out boating could often be blamed more on unreliable weather forecasting than a lack of foresight or experience. Thankfully, boaters today stand a much better chance of avoiding the consequences of inaccurate forecasts by taking advantage of the high-tech, wireless technology that brings us real-time weather-tracking radar or satellite imagery, accessible while boating anywhere on the planet.

You should still check the weather forecast and local weather radar for approaching inclement conditions shortly before leaving for your trip. Don't rely too much on the accuracy of forecasts from the night before your boating day, since weather can often be unpredictable. A follow-up check of current weather conditions halfway through your boating day is also a very good idea. If you have an internet-enabled smartphone (or onboard weather imagery electronics), you can keep a watchful eye on any threatening weather movement in your area. VHF marine radios also have a built-in NOAA weather channel that always broadcasts local weather information and any advisories or warnings.

For all boaters everywhere, a healthy respect for lightning, heavy rain, high winds and rough water conditions should be a no-brainer, but some people – especially those in vacation mode – just don't think enough about anything that might ruin their boating plans, regardless. Always stay a step or two ahead of dangerous, or at least miserable boating conditions.

Good Communication is Key to Safe and Smart Boating

Good and reliable two-way communication is vital to maintain safety and security. As the captain of any vessel always should, keep your passengers well-informed of the imperative safety rules and precautions that you expect them to follow.

Always have at least one other pair of eyes watching out for anything that could present a problem so that they can warn you in time to avoid obstacles such as swimmers, inattentive boaters, boat wakes, shallows, or partially-submerged objects.

Two of the most important resources that a safe and smart boater needs onboard are a smartphone and a VHF radio. Always bring along

Two of the most important resources that a safe and smart boater needs onboard are a smartphone and a VHF radio.

at least one fully-charged cellphone, or preferably an internet-enabled smartphone. Keep them dry in a resealable plastic bag or waterproof housing which you can usually talk and hear through.

Relying on a boat's battery power as a source for charging up a low or dead cellphone battery could be a regrettable decision. If you break down out on the water and the boat's battery should happen to die, or if the power outlet quits working, you'll find yourself in a classic Murphy's Law predicament.

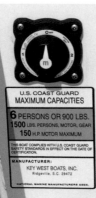

USCG Maximum Capacities Plate.

Every boat should have at least a portable/handheld VHF marine radio onboard, especially if there's any chance of boating outside of cellphone coverage range. The ability to call for assistance or to get critical information for any of the many questions or problems that can arise while boating is essential.

Getting directions or weather radar updates, calling for help with boat-related or mechanical problems, and calling 911 or Mayday for emergency assistance are all accessible from almost anywhere... but only if you remember to charge up and bring along your communication devices.

It may also be helpful to monitor VHF marine radio broadcasts for urgent marine navigational and weather information, which is broadcast over VHF Channel 22A in all coastal areas of the U.S. including the Great Lakes, major inland waterways, Puerto Rico, Alaska, Hawaii and Guam. Broadcasts are first announced over the distress, safety and calling Channel 16 before they're made on Channel 22A.

Never Overload Your Boat

Always heed the Persons Capacity limit without exceeding the combined weight limit of Persons + Motor + Gear posted on your boat's

USCG Maximum Capacities Plate.

Overloading is one of the more commonly overlooked or ignored safety violations that boaters get ticketed for. It can at best get you an expensive citation that also requires you to take a safe boating course, and at worst cause your boat to handle very poorly on the water and capsize much more easily than normal.

Also often-overlooked, but very important, is proper weight distribution. It's fairly common to see too many people in a group gravitate toward the bow seating area, seriously overloading it forward. This is unsafe because it will plow the bow into the water, causing the boat to handle very poorly, and could swamp the front

Overloading is a commonly overlooked safety violation. Never overload your boat, and always properly distribute the weight of passengers and gear.

of the boat. Too much weight aft may sink your transom low enough to let water to come over the back, especially in rough conditions or when coming off plane from high speeds.

A good captain will make sure that his passengers and heavier gear are all seated and stowed with regard to balanced weight distribution. While underway, your boat should not list (lean) to port or starboard, and should never be disproportionately overloaded forward or aft.

Know the Depth Ahead of Your Course

Keep it deep. By no means are all shallow water areas marked as such.

Basic depth finders aren't designed to be used for any navigational purposes.

On shallow waterways, only the main traveling channels and channels leading into docking or boat ramp facilities, or shallow tributaries are marked. Some channels aren't very well marked, and others aren't marked at all, or may have been partially filled in with shifting bottom material. This leaves the vast majority of shallow boating areas and unsafe or unnavigable water, unmarked. A common misconception among inexperienced boaters is that all shallow or otherwise hazardous areas of water are somehow marked, but this is definitely not the case.

For this reason, it's very important to keep a nautical chart onboard that shows the depths of your local waters, and to pro-actively navigate according to its details. If you happen to do all of your boating on a deepwater lake, or if you have a marine GPS system onboard that displays all water depths, then you probably don't need a chart for depth-tracking purposes.

Whatever you do, don't rely on a basic, electronic depth or fish finder to keep you out of areas where it can get too shallow, or less than 3 to 4 feet deep. They aren't designed to show what the depth of the water is where you're heading to, and can only give a current depth reading directly below the boat, or at best just a few feet out in front of the boat. If you're moving along at any rate above idle speed,

their depth readings won't help you to avoid shallows, so you could easily run aground onto a sandbar or shoal, which can certainly be a problem ranging from inconvenient to catastrophic.

If the waters you boat in have any shallow areas other than just the shoreline, it's very important to carefully follow your chart until you become well-familiarized with your boating area. It's the best and least expensive way to keep your boat sufficiently deep.

Never Allow Anyone to Perch on Your Boat While Underway

Never operate a boat while passengers are sitting on the edge of, or in any way hanging over the bow, gunnels, sides, stern or swim platform. This is grossly negligent and irresponsible boat operation, is hazardous to life and limb, and is illegal.

To give a clear understanding of the dangers of boat propellers: a typical three-blade prop running at 3,200 RPM can inflict 160 impacts in 1 second. A typical boat propeller can travel from head to toe on an average person in less than a second. It would be very naive for anyone to think that they could turn off the motor in time if someone perched on the edge of their boat should fall overboard. All passengers should always remain properly seated while the boat is underway, and children naturally require extra-close attention and supervision.

The larger the wake, the more caution is required to avoid squirrelly situations.

boat operators soon realize the need to slow down to avoid catching air and banging the boat's hull down onto the water, jarring everyone and everything onboard. This is a kind of "automatic" lesson that every boater quickly learns one way or another, regardless. When approaching another boat's wake, you should aim your bow at a 45 degree angle to the oncoming wake as you reduce speed. This will allow the bow to move up and over the wake with a slight roll and help to prevent pounding your boat's hull.

Not as obvious – but also imperative to know – is that while cruising or running at speed, there can be a dangerous situation for any boat passengers standing or sitting in the bow area of a boat. If an inattentive boat operator doesn't slow down in time to safely float over a boat wake, and fails to quickly give advance warning to his unsuspecting passengers not looking forward, they can easily get catapulted up into the air by the sudden ramping effect of the wake – resulting in serious injury. This is actually a fairly common, but easily-preventable peril.

Boat Wakes Dangers

Did you know that as a boat operator, you're legally responsible for your boat wake and any subsequent damage or harm that it does to anything or anyone in your wake? Novice, or just plain inconsiderate boaters aren't always aware – or sometimes don't care – that their wake could potentially wreak havoc on others; such as people trying to refuel, load, or board their vessels.

Normally there are "NO WAKE" signs posted in areas where boat wakes could seriously rock other docked or anchored boats. But signs can't be everywhere, so oftentimes boat operators simply need to be courteous and use common sense to prevent creating a wake, even in areas that aren't necessarily No Wake Zones. Speed should be limited to 5 mph when you're within a few hundred feet of a shore, marina, pier, dock, anchored boat, canoes, kayaks or people fishing.

When cruising out on the water and negotiating other boat wakes, even the most inexperienced

Boat operators are liable for harm caused by their wake.

Avoid Using Spray-on Sunscreens Onboard

Spray-on sunscreens shouldn't be sprayed onboard because they can quickly turn your boat into a slippery, potentially-hazardous place to be. They may be labeled as being "greaseless" or a "dry formula," but they don't soak into a boat's hard surfaces and vinyl like they soak right into skin. It doesn't take very much sunscreen overspray to make boat surfaces dangerously-slick, and even more so when wet.

They make boat cleanup harder than usual, too, since another "side effect" is oily dirt and footprint stains. Also, certain types of sunscreens contain dyes that can stain the surface materials of your interior, particularly white vinyl.

Fishing Safety Concerns

Other than cruising – which practically every boater does and enjoys – fishing is the most popular boating activity. When caught up in the excitement of catching a fish, it's easy to forget about safety. A fishhook to the eye accounts for more than a third of fishing-related eye injuries. A sinker or lure body striking the eye causes nearly half of these injuries. It may seem that a hook in the eye would be much worse, but a sinker or lure strike to the eye can cause the eyeball to rupture, and results in permanent blindness in about half of the cases.

Fishing in a boat can increase the risk of eye injuries for one simple reason... two or more people are sharing the same confined casting space. To help prevent traumatic eye injuries while fishing by boat, practice the following precautions:

➤ Always wear fishing sunglasses that provide side protection.

➤ Always wear a ball cap or a visor – they can intercept a hook or lure.

➤ Spread out from each other on the boat as much as possible.

➤ Check behind you before casting – and make sure anyone fishing behind you knows to do the same.

➤ For snags – cut your fishing line rather than fighting to pull it free.

➤ Remove or cover fishhooks from fishing rods before transporting. Exposed hooks should be covered with fishhook safety covers.

Gaffs can be a danger when their big, sharp point is left unprotected. A carelessly-placed gaff can impale an angler running along the gunnel while chasing a hooked fish. A protective cover should always be slipped over the point when it's not being used. And obviously, gaffs must be used with extra caution when wrestling large fish into the boat, since they can slip off or break through the fish while being pulled upward.

Fish can also present very real hazards to anglers. Several different fish species – both saltwater and

Fishing in a boat requires a few extra common-sense safety precautions to bring home nice catches like this, unscathed.

freshwater – have dangerous defense mechanisms that you need to be aware of in order to handle them safely. These can include: razor-sharp teeth, serrated back edges of gillplates, needle-sharp fin spines, and stinging, toxin-covered spines. Fish can even cause injuries just by jumping high out of the water and into your boat. Always study-up ahead of time on the fish varieties that may be caught in your fishing region, or region you're visiting. This way you won't learn the hard way just how much pain certain fish can cause.

Also, always keep your deck and gunnels well-organized and free of any clutter or loose dock and anchor lines. Someone could easily trip and fall when moving around the boat while fishing, and get seriously injured or possibly even get knocked unconscious and fall overboard, which is actually a fairly common occurrence.

Never Anchor a Boat From the Stern Alone

Not only should you never anchor a boat from the stern alone, you must never, ever attach the anchor line to any portion of the stern, in an attempt to release and retrieve a stuck anchor from the bottom (of a river, lake, ocean) using the thrust power of your motor. In certain conditions and situations, doing so could very quickly drag down the stern and swamp or capsize your boat. This is especially dangerous to do in waters with a steady current. Sadly, people have lost their lives as a result... solely due to not knowing any better.

(Note: this safety rule does not apply to the use of hydraulic, temporary anchoring devices known as shallow water anchors or power poles, which are mounted to the sterns of some fishing boats. They're designed and function very differently than traditional anchor tackle.)

There are certain instances in which it is relatively safe to use a stern anchor in combination with a bow anchor; however, it is much more common and safe to anchor a boat from only the bow.

If your anchor gets stuck to the bottom, there are a few fairly safe and sometimes-effective methods to break it free, but none of them involve attaching the anchor line to any rear portion of the boat. No anchor is worth risking the safety of you and everyone onboard your boat, just to save an easily replaceable piece of cheap metal.

Also, never anchor within or too close to any channel or busy boat traffic area. This would impede and frustrate other boaters passing through. It's usually a fineable offense as well, not to mention a good way to get seriously rocked by the wakes of larger boats or yachts.

> Anchoring a boat from the stern can cause it to swamp, capsize or sink.

Watersports: Safe Towing Requires Boat Handling Experience

To safely tow passengers behind a boat for watersports requires a fairly advanced level of boating experience, and isn't recommended for novice boat operators. This applies particularly in areas with busy boat traffic. All aspects of operating and maneuvering your boat should be second nature or at least comfortable and reasonably effortless for you – before ever towing anyone in the water. You should be able to confidently pilot your boat without looking down at the controls or gauges for more than a second. Familiarity with your boat and experience at your helm is the key.

You need to be able to maintain control while

Watersports Hand Signals

➤ Cutthroat hand motion = Stop the boat / Cut the motor
➤ Thumb down = Slow down
➤ Thumb up = Speed up
➤ OK sign = Speed OK
➤ Twirling finger pointing up = Turn boat around
➤ Hand wave or hands together and raised overhead = I'm OK (signal after every fall)

turning your head back frequently so that you can keep a watchful eye on the rider. (In certain states it is illegal to tow any type of skier without a rear view mirror and/or at least one other person onboard to be a spotter.) You also need to be able to turn off your motor instantly, just in case you accidentally get your boat too close to anyone in the

All aspects of operating and maneuvering your boat should be second nature before ever towing anyone behind your boat.

Safety Rules for Watersports Towing

water. The best way is to keep your safety lanyard (kill switch cord) attached to your PFD.

Warn riders to keep their fingers away from the rope as much as possible, especially right before being pulled up by the boat. A finger can actually get popped right off the hand if it gets caught in a slack rope that instantly gets yanked by the boat.

When ready to pull the rider, watch the tow rope just prior to accelerating to make sure it isn't catching onto any part of the boat or motor. If it gets caught in the prop, it can get tightly wound to the point of being extremely difficult to cut off and remove. If presented with this problem be sure to first pull the key out of the ignition switch as a safety precaution.

Avoid the sling shot effect. When turning your boat around, if you maintain or increase your speed centrifugal force will rapidly accelerate your rider exponentially, possibly forcing them into a high-speed wipeout. Instead, slow down as you begin the turn, but not so slow as to cause the rider to lose too much momentum and allow too much slack in the tow rope.

When turning your boat back to retrieve a fallen rider, never speed up to make long, wide-sweeping, high-speed turns. Instead, immediately slow way down and make a slower and much tighter 180-degree turn. This not only gets you back to them faster, it also burns a lot less fuel.

Always turn your boat motor OFF before allowing anyone in the water to get anywhere near the

> Keep your head on a swivel – know what's ahead of both your boat and your rider at all times.
> Never follow behind another boat that is towing a rider.
> If a boat is following closely behind yours while towing – change course or let them pass.
> Never tow anyone in shallow water: 6 feet is the minimum depth needed.
> Never tow anyone in an area that hasn't been established as a safe ski run – even in deeper water there can be hidden, submerged objects.
> The distance you keep from any docks, pilings, shorelines, etc. should well-exceed the length of your tow rope. This prevents the rider from being slung into them during a turn.
> Always be courteous – stay a safe distance from other skiers, swimmers and boats.
> Never back your boat in reverse toward any person in the water.
> Think twice before allowing two passengers to ride together on a tube. The bouncing around on the water and wakes can force their heads to collide, causing head or facial injuries.
> Always use correctly-sized, USCG-approved, Type-III watersports vests that are labeled accordingly. All skiers or riders of all ages are required to wear one in every state. Never use Type-II life jackets for watersports – they're not designed to stay on during high-speed falls.

propeller to avoid serious injury or death. Also, never restart the motor before looking to make sure that nobody is anywhere around the boat. A common but dangerous misconception is that it's safe to just put the boat in neutral, and leave the motor running while passengers get in or out of the boat. The problem with this notion – it's actually possible for a maladjusted shift cable to cause a prop to continue to turn while the shift lever is set in the neutral position. It's also not inconceivable that someone could accidentally shift the boat into gear while someone else is still in the water near the prop. Both of these scenarios do happen, and with very real consequences.

If boat traffic gets to be congested, find another open ski area or just call it quits. Not only is it too dangerous to have several boats trying to tow skiers in one area, but all of the boat wakes make the water way too bumpy for fun or safe riding.

These boaters rescued by the Coast Guard were fortunate to get back home uninjured.

Coast Guard Response boats, like this one off Jacksonville, Florida, are always at the ready in case of emergency.

Don't Drink and Boat: It's Just Not Worth the Risk

From the USCG document, "Recreational Boating Statistics 2012": Alcohol use is the leading contributing factor in fatal boating accidents. With a blood alcohol content of 0.08 or higher, it is illegal to operate a vessel on all federal waters in all U.S. states. Alcohol has many physical effects that directly threaten safety and well-being on the water. When a boater or passenger drinks, the following occur:

➢ Cognitive abilities and judgment deteriorate, making it harder to process information, assess situations, and make good choices.

➢ Physical performance is impaired – evidenced by balance problems, lack of coordination, and increased reaction time.

➢ Vision is affected, including decreased peripheral vision, reduced depth perception, decreased night vision, poor focus, and difficulty in distinguishing colors (particularly red and green).

➢ Inner ear disturbances can make it impossible for a person who falls into the water, to distinguish up from down.

➢ Alcohol creates a physical sensation of warmth – which may prevent a person in cold water from getting out before hypothermia sets in.

➢ As a result of these factors, a boat operator with a blood alcohol concentration above .10 percent is estimated to be more than 10 times more-likely to die in a boating accident than an operator with zero blood alcohol concentration. Passengers are also at greatly increased risk for injury and death – especially if they are also using alcohol.

Boating under the influence (BUI) can be a life-changing mistake.

Never, ever operate a boat while intoxicated. Although many state laws do permit open containers on boats, it is still basically ZERO tolerance for any intoxication of a boat's operator. If you do drink and boat – and get caught – you'll also face the same stiff penalties, fines and life-changing legal troubles that apply to getting a DUI on the road.

Nearly half of all boating accidents involve at least one alcohol or drug-impaired boater. Research has proven that one third the amount of alcohol that it takes to make a person legally intoxicated on land, can make a boater equally intoxicated while on the water. This phenomenon is only exacerbated by sun exposure and the motion-caused side-effects of being on a floating boat.

So even if you feel 100 percent comfortable with having a few beers or drinks while at the helm, why not just save it for later and not risk any sort of trouble at all.

Additional Boating Safety & Potentially Life-SavingTips

▷ Always prepare and file a float plan that includes: where you're departing from, your planned destination(s), expected return time, and all persons that will be onboard, before leaving for any boating trip. Leave it with a reliable family member or friend who can be depended on to notify the USCG or other rescue organization if you don't check in as scheduled. Download a free float plan form online at: floatplancentral.org

▷ Take extra water, food, and fuel – if appropriate. Use the 1/3 Rule: after 1/3 of your fuel is used, start to head back in. This leaves about 1/3 of your fuel for emergencies.

▷ Always keep your boat's safety lanyard (kill switch cord) attached to your PFD or clothing. If the unexpected happens and causes you to fall away from the helm or overboard, it will instantly shut the motor off. This is particularly important if boating alone to prevent the boat from continuing on without you, or turning around and running in what is known as the "Circle of Death" which can result in propeller strikes.

▷ Make sure that all lines are secured inside of the boat and out of walkways. A carelessly placed dock line can fall and get tangled in the propeller, or cause someone to trip and fall overboard.

▷ Stay a minimum of 100 feet away from all objects when cruising.

▷ Always be aware of what other boaters are doing; remain vigilant at all times – head on a swivel. Look and listen. Just because you can see a boat coming toward you, doesn't mean that they can or will see you. Always assume that they don't. Make sure you always allow yourself an "out" in case you need extra room to maneuver around or away from a careless boat operator. Failing to keep a sharp lookout is the most common cause of boating collisions.

▷ Do not exceed safe speeds or the speed at which you feel comfortable. Safe speed is the speed that ensures you will have ample time to avoid a collision and can stop within a safe distance. Safe speed

Before getting under way, attach your boat's safety lanyard to your PFD or clothing.

varies depending on conditions such as visibility, wind, water conditions, navigational hazards, boat traffic congestion, the maneuverability of your boat and your skill level.

▷ Don't follow too closely behind any boats traveling ahead of you – especially ones towing a skier. Stay at least 100 yards behind. You never know when they might stop suddenly or make a completely unexpected maneuver.

▷ When boating in shallow areas, pay close attention to channel markers and always refer to your chart as a navigational guide to help keep your boat in safely deep water. Straying from a marked channel can potentially spell disaster. You could run aground, damage your boat, and possibly hurl passengers out – caused by the sudden stop.

▷ Always turn the boat motor off before letting swimmers board, to avoid risk of serious injury.

▷ Pay attention to tides. Being stranded on a sandbar or mud flat can be a safety hazard.

▷ Keep your boat maintained. One of the top five causes of boating accidents is mechanical failure.

Tips For What To Do In Case Of:

(Not to be considered professional medical or emergency response advice.)

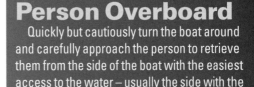

EPIRB with GPS (left), for large lake or offshore rescue. Personal locator beacon (PLB) (right), dispatches help at the push of a button.

Powerboating does present encounters with risks and hazards. The outcome of your encounters will be determined by your knowledge, skill and attitude toward safety. So why not make boating emergencies less likely to happen in the first place by taking the proper precautions? Prepare for and know what to do in any situation in case of an emergency. The following are only examples of some of the things that can be done to self-assist when one of the many things that can go wrong while boating happens.

Major Medical Emergency

Remain calm. Focusing on what needs to be done right now will help to avoid panic mode. Call 911 on your cell phone, and/or call "Mayday-Mayday-Mayday" on VHF radio channel 16. If neither are possible then flag down anyone nearby for help by any means available. It is imperative to know either where on shore you will be able to meet emergency crews, or if you're not sure or if you're immobilized, where exactly your current location is. If unsure of your current location, look for channel marker numbers or distinctive landmarks. Keep in mind that distances on water can be very difficult to judge. Nearly everyone will tend to grossly underestimate the distances between their location and distant visible points.

If your boat has been damaged beyond use and is adrift, anchor it from the bow and make sure it sets hold so that you won't lose your position. If your boat is operational then head directly ashore with due caution to a nearby location, but preferably where an ambulance will have realistic accessibility.

Administer first aid using the best-available first aid supplies, and to the best of your ability until EMT help arrives and takes over. If possible, request the guidance of a qualified 911 or USCG dispatcher for first aid suggestions until emergency crews arrive.

Person Overboard

Quickly but cautiously turn the boat around and carefully approach the person to retrieve them from the side of the boat with the easiest access to the water – usually the side with the swim ladder, if applicable.

If there's any boat traffic in the area, sound your horn or whistle continuously during the time that it takes to get your boat back to retrieve your fallen passenger. This will help to draw the attention of any inattentive boaters toward you, so that you can point emphatically at your passenger's location in the water.

Grab or have someone grab and have ready your Type-IV throwable floatation device to toss to the person if they're struggling or cannot swim.

Turn the engine OFF when you're within close enough distance to slowly coast up and stop the boat close to the person, and help them aboard. If the victim is unconscious or in need of assistance, anyone who jumps in the water to help him or her, should be wearing a PFD and have the Type-IV device at ready for added buoyancy if needed. If unconscious in the water, assume that there could be head or neck trauma and carefully bring them back onboard while someone calls 911.

Unrepairable Mechanical Breakdown or Out of Gas

If the boat is adrift, anchor it from the bow and make sure that it sets hold so that you won't drift away, unless by chance it's safe to just keep drifting along with a current or wind that happens to be pushing your boat toward where you need to get to. If it's getting later in the day immediately call friends, family, or a boat towing service that can come to help you, since it is very difficult to find a stranded boat in the dark of night. Give them your exact location with plenty of detail.

If you're not able to or aren't having any luck with calling for help by cellphone, wave down a nearby or passing boat and ask them for a tow, or help getting towed in before nightfall. If no one else is around, then you'll need to hail for assistance on VHF radio channel 16.

Night Boating Precautions

Once the sun goes down, so must the speed at which you operate your boat.

Some of the most serene times to be on the water, enjoying the outdoors, can be when you're relaxing in your boat as the sun sets and the stars come out. Once darkness settles in, though, it becomes extremely risky to operate a boat at cruising speed.

The darkness of night (combined with alcohol in most cases) has been a major factor in far too many boating fatalities and life-changing injuries. But you can greatly reduce your risk for such catastrophe by simply going easy on your throttle and strictly keeping your speed to an idle-speed crawl. That way, if you do hit something, damage and the chance of injury can at least be lessened. If that's just too slow, then think of it this way –

you shouldn't go any faster than you're willing to run into a solid object with your boat. (Keeping in mind that if that object happens to be another boat with people onboard, you'll be held responsible, regardless of how dark it is.)

Even on moonlit nights when visibility on the water is better, your eyes can play tricks on you and convince you that you're seeing things you're not. Boats – or their running lights – can appear to be much closer or much farther away than they really are. It can look as though they're traveling away from you when they're actually coming toward you. (Hence the reason for the green and red navigational light system.) This is why it also helps to maintain a straight and steady track at night.

Sudden Strong Storm

If safe harbor is within visible distance, turn on your navigation lights and head in cautiously. Safe harbor is NOT just any shore or dock. Many areas would be much too rocky or shallow to approach—or would be very treacherous to approach in high winds, such as directly exposed docks or piers. When you get to a reasonably safe spot, to prevent boat damage and/or injury, use care and common sense when tying off your boat in relation to wind and waves.

If visibility is less than 100 feet, anchor your boat from the bow with scope ratio of 10:1 or as close to 10:1 as possible to allow for a 360 degree swing surrounding your anchoring spot. Make sure that it sets hold. (See Chapter 10 for anchoring info.) Do not anchor in a channel or high traffic area because other boats could easily crash into yours due to limited visibility. Turn on the lights and anchor light, and try to wait it out. Do not attempt to continue on in low or no visibility conditions. You would be at high risk for collision.

If there is lightning in the area, do NOT go seek shelter under any tall trees! During a lightning storm, no one can be 100 percent safe anywhere outdoors, but statistically you're actually less likely to get struck by lightning in a boat (without a sailing mast) out on the water than you are sitting underneath a tall tree on land. Don't risk it though. Get indoors as soon as you possibly can if lightning or thunder is moving your way.

Boating at night, in calm conditions can be a time of peaceful serenity and productive fishing, but it always requires an extra level of caution and vigilance at the helm.

When under way, turn off or dim any bright interior lights. They will significantly reduce your night vision.

Bright interior lights in your boat will significantly reduce your night vision. So if any are on and glaring toward your eyes at all, turn them off or dim them if possible. Turn your stereo off, too, since you'll need to rely on your hearing almost as much as your vision. If you have binoculars onboard, they can be surprisingly helpful at night, but never attempt to operate a boat while simultaneously looking through them because your depth perception will be nil. Keep your speed to a crawl and proceed back in with extra caution and vigilance.

Offshore Boating is a Whole Other Ballgame

Anyone who buys a boat built for offshore fishing or cruising, needs to either already have, or be willing to invest the time, effort and cost of attaining the specialized knowledge and skills that are quite literally vital to return to port safely after every trip offshore. To captain any sea-going vessel, miles offshore – where you're often completely on your own – also requires the understanding that safety is always priority number one.

As the owner or operator of your boat, you're ultimately responsible for the safety of your passengers. But your crew also needs to be familiar with the safety precautions, location of all safety equipment onboard your boat, and at least the most basic boat operating procedures. Also teach everyone onboard how to use the communication devices, place a Mayday call, deploy the life raft, work the autopilot (if applicable), and how to anchor. The more familiar your crew is with your boat and how to handle it, the better you'll be able to fulfill your responsibilities as the captain. They'll need to know what to do and how to do it, in case something happens to you, right?

Always prepare and file a float plan that includes the vital information about your trip.

https://beaconregistration.noaa.gov/rgdb

The online beacon registration takes only minutes to complete.

Heading offshore for trophy fish like this mahi-mahi, and returning safely every time, requires a whole other knowledge base and skillset beyond what is required for inshore boating.

Everyone onboard should be familiar with safety precautions, location of safety equipment and at least the basics of boat operation.

Make it mandatory for everyone to pay attention to your boat orientation before heading out, even kids. If things go from bad to worse – they'll have to help out, and possibly have to know how save themselves. And there probably won't be enough time to explain everything to them then.

Always prepare and file a float plan that includes: where you're departing from, your planned destination(s), expected return time, and all persons that will be onboard, before leaving for any boating trip. Leave it with a reliable family member or friend who can be depended on to notify the USCG or other rescue organization if you don't check in as scheduled. Download a free float plan form online at: floatplancentral.org

Offshore boats require substantially more safety equipment and electronics than inshore boats do. Type-I or Type-II life jackets designed for offshore survival are a must. For vital communications, a DSC-VHF radio isn't USCG-required, but is

> **An EPIRB, life raft and flare gun should be onboard every size of offshore boat too.**

highly recommended, and a satellite phone is definitely recommended as well since cellphones don't work miles offshore. An EPIRB, life raft and flare gun should be onboard every size of offshore boat too. Even unsinkable boats should carry a life raft because of the possibility of capsize turtling and onboard fires. An array of electronics for navigation, depth sounding and weather tracking are all needed equipment. And extra provisions should also be brought along for every trip offshore – for more than just the time you expect to be out there, just in case.

Covering all that one needs to know to be a proficient, offshore boater, would be well beyond the scope of this particular book. But even if you read every book available on the subject, you should still team up with a seasoned, qualified, offshore boating captain who can show you the ropes hands-on. Experience is the best teacher, but it is best gained with the help of a highly-experienced pro.

CHAPTER 7

Trailering, Launching, Loading

Most first-time boat owners don't yet know the importance of having a good, dependable trailer underneath their boat. But if you've ever headed out for a fishing trip only to have it cut short by a flat tire or worn out wheel bearing, it's a lesson quickly learned. In addition to standard maintenance, there are plenty of sound practices and habits that can make the job of trailering, launching and loading easier and yes, even enjoyable. SB

Before you head out on the open road, it's always a good idea to give your trailer a thorough once-over.

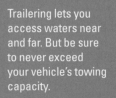

Trailering lets you access waters near and far. But be sure to never exceed your vehicle's towing capacity.

With motor up and braced in place, along with other preparations, this boater is ready to roll out.

Sizing the Trailer to the Boat

Some manufacturers don't help new boat owners learn proper trailering practices by including a trailer with their boat/motor/trailer package that is qualified as adequate, when adequate means the trailer is sized to carry the load of the boat, rigging and motor(s), but that's it.

When buying a new trailer, it costs very little to increase the gross weight of the trailer to include all of the gear you will be loading into the boat, with some leftover capacity to spare. Even though you may be within the gross weight spec on your trailer, if your entire load is close to or at the maximum gross vehicle weight (GVW), you will subject the trailer to more stress, and at the least your tires will suffer and show premature wear.

The formula is simple. Add up the weight of your hull, rigging and motor(s). Now include the weight of batteries, a full fuel tank and any other additional capacities like 2-stroke oil tanks, water tanks and added accessories. To that total add in the weight of the trailer itself. Next you need to include gear that will be carried. Tackle, tools, dive gear, coolers and personal effects all add up. Consider the weight

of things you will occasionally carry, like ice, a good day's catch, or in the case of transporting live bait, the weight of the water and the bait in the baitwell.

With all of the above weights totaled, you get a clearer picture of what you will be asking your trailer to carry. Then add an additional 10 percent to the total possible weight and round up to the closest available trailer capacity.

You don't want to size the trailer too much above the total GVW needed because the suspension will be too stiff and the ride will be rougher for your boat. If you size the trailer properly it will not only last longer but it will be easier on your tow vehicle as well.

USCG Max Capacities plate applies to the boat's weight limits, not the trailer's. Below, trailers support boats with bunks or, as seen below, rollers that ease the boat on and off.

U.S. COAST GUARD MAXIMUM CAPACITIES

6 PERSONS OR 900 LBS.

1500 LBS. PERSONS, MOTOR, GEAR

150 H.P. MOTOR MAXIMUM

THIS BOAT COMPLIES WITH U.S. COAST GUARD SAFETY STANDARDS IN EFFECT ON THE DATE OF CERTIFICATION.

MANUFACTURER:
KEY WEST BOATS, INC.
Ridgeville, S.C. 29472

NATIONAL MARINE MANUFACTURERS ASSN.

Preparing for the Road

Before you head out on the open road, it's always a good practice to give your trailer a good once-over. Few trips to the ramp don't include some preparation in getting the boat ready, so be sure to allow some time devoted to the trailer as well. Start at the hitch and work your way around the trailer back to the tongue. For the same reason pilots use a check list to insure a safe flight, a person new to boating may want to come up with their own list to make sure they don't miss anything prior to trailering their boat.

1. Compare the size of the tow vehicle's trailer ball to be sure it is the proper size for the trailer coupler.

2. When lowering the tongue jack, be sure that the lower tab on the coupler latch doesn't get trapped on top of the trailer ball.

3. Close the coupler latch and install a latch pin or trailer lock.

4. Be sure that the trailer jack is fully retracted, or in some applications rotated in the vertical position and locked.

5. Hook the trailer safety chains or cables to the tow hitch on the vehicle. (Tip: Criss-cross the chains so in the event that the trailer becomes un-latched, the chains in the crossed position will have a tendency to keep the trailer from swaying side to side.)

6. If trailer is equipped with brakes, hook break-away safety lanyard to tow vehicle's hitch.

7. Plug in the trailer light harness to the tow vehicle.

8. Turn on the tow vehicle's flashers and parking lights so that when you do the rest of the walk-around, you can check the trailer lights.

9. Check trailer tire condition and inflation.

10. If the hubs are equipped with bearing protectors that allow you to add grease, this may be a good time to insert a few squirts, depending on how long it's been since the last time it was done. Also look behind the wheel hub to see if any grease is being slung out. This could be a sign of a failing spindle seal.

11. If it's been a while since you checked your trailer wheel lug nuts, torque them down with a lug wrench to the proper foot-pounds. (Tip: New trailer wheels' lug nuts will need to be checked more frequently for the first 200 miles as they seat.)

12. Check brake and side marker lights.

13. Secure tie-down straps at both the bow eye and transom eyes.

14. Inspect trailer winch to see that the ratchet catch is engaged and there is sufficient tension on the winch strap.

15. If the trailer is equipped with brakes, make sure they are functioning by lightly testing before getting on a major roadway.

Image labels (top photo): Trailer ball sized correctly · Coupler · Breakaway safety lanyard · Hydraulic surge brake actuator · Safety cables · Light harness

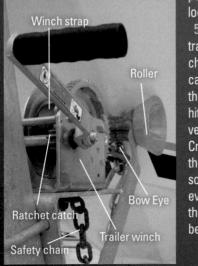

Winch strap · Roller · Ratchet catch · Bow Eye · Trailer winch · Safety chain

Backing Your Boat Trailer Tips:

While reversing, put your hand at the bottom of the steering wheel, turn your hand in the direction you want the trailer/boat to go.

When backing up, use all the room available at the ramp to maneuver your vehicle and boat into the best position to approach the ramp.

Launch Ramp Etiquette

It's been said that the best form of free entertainment is a boat ramp on a Saturday afternoon. Between the curse words, congestion and frayed nerves, it can be quite a spectacle, but it doesn't have to be. With a little preparation and common courtesy, launching and recovering a boat is really not that hard.

If you are a first-time owner of a trailerable boat, go to a big, empty parking lot early one morning or later in the afternoon, when there is not a lot of traffic, and practice backing your trailer. Time and time again, it's backing up that presents problems for someone new to boating.

When you get to the ramp, it's best to have two people to launch and retrieve a boat: one to drive the tow vehicle, and one to operate the boat. Always prepare your boat for launching or the drive home in the staging area at the ramp, not on the ramp itself. Once you have successfully launched the boat, back away from the ramp area while your driver parks the tow vehicle and trailer. You can return momentarily to pick them up. Reverse that procedure when you recover the boat. Drop off the driver, back away and return once your trailer is in the water. Remember, the staging line is formed by vehicles with trailers, not boats in the water.

Launching

As stated before, prepare your boat for launching well away from the boat ramp. Most ramps have a staging area where you can transfer equipment and gear to the boat without holding up anyone else who is ready to go. Disconnect your tie-down straps but it's best to leave the trailer winch secured, especially on a steep ramp, until the boat is in the water. Check to make sure your boat plug(s) are installed. If necessary, tie a line to the bow to help control the boat once launched.

Have the driver back the trailer into the water deep enough for the lower unit to be submerged while the boat is still on the trailer. This is so that if you experience engine trouble, you can easily retrieve the boat. Start the engine and ensure that cooling water is being picked up by the water pump with the water pressure gauge or the tell-tale water stream from the powerhead. With the engine now running, have the driver submerge the trailer

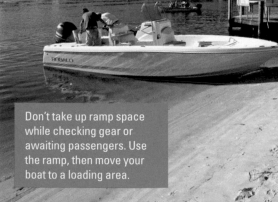

Don't take up ramp space while checking gear or awaiting passengers. Use the ramp, then move your boat to a loading area.

until the boat floats free and unhook the winch strap. Put the boat into reverse and back off of the trailer, away from the ramp area and wait for the driver to park the tow vehicle.

Typically, one person will back the trailer down as another takes the helm.

Often it's backing up that presents problems for someone new to trailering.

Launching a boat alone takes some practice but is easily accomplished. 1. Back down to prepare boat as you would with an operator at the helm. 2. Unstrap safety straps. Check that line from boat is tied to trailer.

3. Back boat down until it floats off, still tied to trailer. 4. Untie boat from trailer and take line to dock to tie it off while you park vehicle. 5. Pull out of ramp to go park vehicle/trailer. Return to boat to untie it and slowly back away from dock for your trip.

Retrieving

Return the driver to the boat ramp dock and have them back the trailer into the water with approximately two-thirds of the bunks submerged. The depth needed for any particular boat will vary depending on the hull design and the slope of the ramp, so take a mental note each time you launch your boat so you can adapt to different locations. Trailer designs vary; some boats have to be winched on, while others can be driven on. In either case, once the trailer is in the water, slowly motor the boat onto the trailer, keeping the keel in the centerline of the trailer. Once the hull nestles into the bunks, either attach the winch cable and crank the boat onto the trailer, or apply the throttle a little at a time to move the boat forward against the bow stop. A word of caution when loading under power: On shallow ramps you may hit your lower unit and damage the housing or the propeller. Power loading can also erode the sediment just beyond the edge of the ramp.

With the boat now on the trailer, be sure that the winch strap is attached to the bow eye with the winch ratchet catch engaged, and crank the winch strap tight. Also be sure to hook the trailer's safety chain or cable to the boat's bow eye. Shut off the engine and trim the motor up. Pull the boat out of the water, to the staging area, to secure for travel over the road. In the staging area, perform an abbreviated walk-around and secure the tie-down straps to the bow and transom eyes. Secure the outboard motor(s) for travel with the trailer lock bracket or transom saver.

Trailer designs vary; some boats have to be winched on, while others can be driven on.

Approach the trailer slowly, in full control of the boat. It helps to keep the motor trimmed down to give the boat the best steering and control in tight dock quarters.

Let the boat coast up onto bunks in a straight position. Once boat makes contact with bunks, apply thrust to let the engine push the boat higher up onto bunks.

Boat can be hand-cranked with the winch strap up into position so that the bow comes flush to the bow stop. Trailer and boat are now ready to be pulled out of ramp.

Trailer should be submerged deeply enough to let the boat move up on bunks easily.

Keep It Clean

Before leaving the staging area, remove any plant life that may be hanging from the trailer, remove the drain plug and drain any livewells. This will help prevent the spread of aquatic nuisance plants and animals.

A little motor thrust and a little hand cranking gets the boat into proper position on trailer.

One person can control the boat from the dock with the bow line and stern line. Alternately, one single line from bow to stern can be used to control the boat.

CHAPTER 8

Boat Operating and Handling

Now the real fun begins – learning how to run your boat to get the best performance out of it – and how to master increasingly difficult boating and navigation challenges. Beginning boaters may view their first times docking with a bit of trepidation, but all boaters should exercise caution when running rough inlets, navigating at night and operating at high speeds – all subjects covered in this chapter.
It all comes down to taking the time to learn the best way to meet those challenges and practicing them under the right conditions. SB

Even if you have years of boating experience, take the time to get used to how a new boat handles.

Pulling up to the docks to fuel up, above, and navigating shallows to catch baits, right, may take a few tries to master.

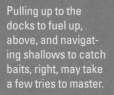

Turning at high speeds isn't a maneuver you'll want to rush into. You'll have to know how the boat handles first.

Getting to Know Your New Boat

Two similar hulls can run differently with changes in horsepower and layout.

Even if you have years of boating experience under your belt, the first time you operate a new boat you should spend some time to get used to the handling characteristics before heading out into open water, running at wide open throttle, and most importantly, maneuvering in close quarters. Different hull designs, types of propulsion and environmental conditions all have an effect on how a boat reacts.

Before leaving the dock, get familiar with the systems on the boat and walk around the deck, at rest, to see how tender the boat is. In other words, how the boat reacts to weight transfer. When you first get underway, motor to an area where you can safely see how the boat turns at low speeds. Some single engine craft are a handful when trying to maneuver around a dock, and a crowded marina is no place to find out that it will only reverse in one direction. The other end of the spectrum is running at high speeds. This is where you need to take your time

and gradually work your way up to wide open throttle, especially with high performance boats like bass boats. Even two similar hulls can run differently with changes in horsepower and layout, so take your time to get acquainted with your new boat.

Loading

As mentioned in Chapter 6, the combined weight limits posted on your boat's U.S. Coast Guard Maximum Capacities Plate should never be exceeded. It should be used as a guideline only, and does not depict how the boat should be loaded. Just because the capacity plate lists 7 persons, for example, doesn't necessarily mean that it's a good idea to load it that way.

Prior to getting underway, use common sense when loading your boat. Everyone onboard should have a safe, comfortable place to sit, but again, proper weight distribution of your passengers (and gear) is also necessary and important for safe and proper boat handling.

Proper Trim

Many things can affect the performance of your boat: hull design, power, props, etc., but the one thing that goes consistently underused is proper trim. Running at the right attitude will increase your speed, reduce your fuel consumption and greatly improve the comfort of your ride. The angle at which your bow meets the water and waves has a direct correlation as to how efficiently you operate your vessel, and in many situations, improper trim can be a safety concern as well. Getting the running surface of your hull to have the least amount of wetted surface drag will increase your efficiency, and should be your goal most of the time. But in some cases it's actually better to have more of the hull in the water to allow your bow to knife through the waves. It's dialing in the "sweet spot" that is so important, and understanding that it's a moving target as conditions change.

When you're running into a head sea, it's best to let the bow come down and give the entry of the V a chance to slice into each wave. In a following sea is where you will want your bow high, out of the water. Either riding the back of the swell or overtaking them, you don't want to allow your bow to stuff into the backside of the wave in front of you.

Adjusting the attitude of your hull means adjusting the trim angle of either your engine/out-

The top boat is trimmed to keep the bow down. The boat below is running with the bow high for the least drag on the hull.

It's dialing in the sweet spot that is so important when it comes to trim.

Trim tabs help to provide maximum attitude control, and can offset the effects of a boat's unbalanced weight at high speed.

drive, or by use of trim tabs or a combination of both. What you'll soon find is that small adjustments can have a big effect, and something as simple as a passenger moving from one side to another or up to the bow, may require you to counter that change in weight distribution. On some boats, it may be best to run

Proper use of your trim tabs will help to get your boat running efficiently at high speeds.

Trim tabs, which are installed on many boats, can help you to fine tune your running attitude by creating lift at the stern, allowing the boat to run higher and reduce its foot print. The two independently-adjustable metal plates at the transom are controlled by a switch panel at the helm, and can also compensate for a hull running with a list due to propeller torque effect or unequal weight distribution.

a full down trim to get the hull to plane off, then immediately trim up as the speed increases. So now that you want to adjust your boat's trim attitude, what are some of the indicators to guide you, and how do you do it?

So if you're looking to improve your boat's efficiency and ride, all you may have to do is adjust your attitude… running attitude.

To start off, look at the spray as it exits to either side of the hull. If it's too far forward that tells you the bow is plowing through the water which can cause the boat to bow steer and have poor fuel economy. If the spray is too far back towards the transom, unless you are running a bass boat, your bow is too high and a percentage of your thrust is being wasted along with exposing the bottom of the hull to impact waves for a rougher ride. Once you have established what you feel is a good trim attitude, you can fine-tune it or "dial it in" by using your RPM gauge, plus GPS and fuel flow gauge. These three pieces of electronics used to be considered luxuries, but now are installed as standard equipment on even entry-level craft. Once you have reached your desired speed, whether it's cruise or wide open throttle, and feel you have the proper attitude, adjust your trim angle while watching your RPMs, speed and fuel consumption to get the best performance.

Trim adjustment for either your outdrive or outboard is normally controlled by a rocker switch(s) built into the throttle control handle. Trim the engine/outdrive up and the bow rises, too much and the hull can porpoise and the prop aerates or cavitates. Down trim can lower the V entry of the hull into waves to soften the ride – too much and you will plow through the water. Proper drive trim keeps the thrust generated from the propeller as parallel to the water's surface as possible.

Reading Current and Wind

Once you leave the dock, your boat is at the mercy of the wind and currents. Even though you may have reverse, it's not the same as brakes on a car. Propellers are not nearly as efficient when turning backwards as they are going forward. For those reasons it's best to always keep an eye on what the wind and current are doing and how they will affect your boat.

The higher the profile your boat has, the more it will be affected by the wind. Much like a sailboat, the wind will have a tendency push the boat, usually in the direction where the bow will be facing downwind. Lighter boats will be pushed faster, and the less weight you have on the bow, the quicker it will want to weathervane away from the wind.

Current, on the other hand, has about the same effect on all vessels. Since you're resting on top of the water, your boat will want to travel down current at close to the speed of the current itself. At operational speed, out in open water, those two forces trying to take control of your boat will be of less concern, but when you get in tight quarters and you don't have the momentum of speed to help counteract the effects, you really need to pay attention to your boat control. There are three main

Running in rough seas, you'll want to trim your bow down to let the v-hull help to cut through the waves so you have a better ride.

Once you have established a good trim attitude, you can fine-tune it or "dial it in" by using your RPM gauge, GPS and fuel flow gauge.

areas where you will want to stay the most alert: inlets, channels and marinas.

On any given day, the conditions offshore may be fine, although a little bumpy, nothing that you would feel unsafe navigating. Going through an inlet with the wind and current in the same direction, conditions are rarely more severe than they are offshore, but if you encounter an inlet where the wind is against the current, that 3- to 5-foot sea can build to 6 to 8 feet before you know it. The best practice is to stop short of the inlet and see what direction the current is flowing, and then check the wind. Plan your passage through the inlet based on the size of your boat and your ability as a captain.

Weedlines like this one offshore get pushed together by moving currents.

Channels are another area where a boater can get into trouble unless they stay vigilant. The biggest potential for a problem is where the current is flowing 90-degrees to the channel. You may be holding a constant heading, but your boat may actually be traveling as much sideways as forward. If you find yourself in this situation you will have to drive the boat in a crab, where you will be traveling in a straight line down the channel but your bow will actually be pointed several degrees into the current.

Close quarter operations, mainly docking, is where current and wind can really foul you up. Here, patience and planning can keep you from an embarrassing moment, or worse yet, an insurance claim. The best practice is once you get close to the dock, but are still in open waters, stop and let the boat come to rest. Watch what the wind and current do to the boat and get a feel for the direction they want to push you. With that in mind you may want to pick a different dock or area of the marina to tie up, one where the drift created by the forces can either be counteracted or may actually even help you. It's easier to power into a current or wind than it is to attempt to pull away from them when they are acting to push you into a seawall or piling.

Wind and waves have more of an effect on the way a boat handles the faster you go.

Boaters, while running at high speed, are properly paying attention to their course ahead to maintain safety.

High-speed Operations

With today's larger outboards, computer-aided hull designs and composite construction, the average top-end speeds of many boats have steadily increased over the last decade. While the new designs have led to a more stable ride at high speed, operating a boat at over 50 miles per hour, things happen very fast. Floating debris, another inattentive boater, and unexpected rough water can all turn a fun day on the water into a tragedy. Safe boating requires control and staying alert at the helm, but as the speed of

Wind and waves have more of an effect on the way a boat handles the faster you go. Even if your boat is capable of running 70 mph, is it safe to do so where you are boating? Another factor is location; many waterways have strict speed limits and with today's ultra-accurate GPS receivers, it's hard to convince a water-borne authority that you didn't

Crossing wakes at high speed can be bumpy, so the driver must alert passengers beforehand and maintain control as the wakes come and go.

It's hard to convince a water-borne authority that you didn't know how fast you were going.

your boat increases so does the level of proficiency an operator needs to have.

Operating a boat at high speeds – and for the sake of this chapter we'll consider anything over 50 miles per hour to be high speed – can be done in a safe manner. The first things to look at are the conditions.

know how fast you were going. Most important is your ability and your boat. How is it equipped and are you comfortable driving at these speeds?

Many aftermarket accessories can be added to your boat to make it safer to operate in the fast lane. A Hot Foot, mainly used in the bass boat market, is basically an accelerator much like you have in your car. It allows you to control the throttle function of your outboard while keeping both hands on the steering wheel. A jack plate, as discussed earlier, will let you raise the lower unit higher out of the water, reducing the drag and increasing the speed. A kill switch is a lanyard that attaches to you

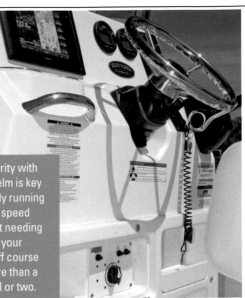

Familiarity with your helm is key to safely running at high speed without needing to take your eyes off course for more than a second or two.

Common Courtesy

When it comes to helping out other boaters, navigation rules require operators of a vessel to stop and render assistance to another vessel in distress, as long as doing so will not endanger your own vessel or the passengers onboard. This assistance can be in many forms, from a simple call to a towing operation, or to the U.S. Coast Guard if lives are at stake. Use your own judgment in your ability as a captain. Depending on the situation, if you plan on towing another vessel with your boat, be sure you are comfortable doing so. It may be better to call for assistance and stand by until help arrives.

If you plan on towing another vessel, be sure you are comfortable doing so.

and a switch that will kill the ignition in the event you are thrown from your boat. Perhaps the most important accessory is a good-quality life jacket, one that fits snugly around your upper body and has a collar for neck support.

Tournament fishermen are always looking for ways to squeeze a little more performance out of their boat, in hopes of gaining an advantage over their competition, but they didn't get to the point

of being able to operate their boat safely at high speed overnight. It takes practice. Start off slowly from a speed where you know you are capable of running your boat safely. Increase the speed in small increments to see not only how the hull reacts but how you feel at the controls. Make your trim adjustments in small increments as well, until you work your way up to running at the speed you wanted to achieve and feel comfortable.

Jumping On Plane

These boaters, in shallow waters, are jumping up on plane by turning hard right and accelerating to thrust the hull up to run.

Advanced Flats and Bass Boat Operation

Tournament fishermen didn't get to the point of being able to operate their boat safely at high speed overnight. Start off safely.

Jumping on plane in shallow water is mostly undesirable: You don't want to hit bottom and risk damaging your boat and/or fish habitat. But if you must move out quickly, and you have enough water for a straight "hole shot," put your trim tabs in the full down position. This provides transom lift, helping to offset the tendency for the bow to rise and the stern to squat when you throttle up. Similarly, if you have a power jack plate, trim the engine all the way in/down, and raise the jack plate to keep the lower unit clear of the bottom (just don't raise it so high or for so long that you impede cooling water).

What if there's only a small patch of deeper water and no other option?

There is a maneuver that can plane the boat off

quickly with the least amount of impact. It's a full 180-degree turn that will slide the boat on plane, but it needs to be practiced in deeper water until you get comfortable with it. First, attach your kill switch lanyard to your lifejacket. Not wearing either one? Don't try the maneuver! Find the deepest part of the flat, preferably with a bare area, and rest the boat there. Turn the steering wheel hard right until it stops. (A standard rotation motor gets on plane faster in a right turn.) Next, put your starboard trim tab in the full down position (left rocker switch forward, on most installations) and the port trim tab in the full up position. When you're set, go full throttle while holding the hard right turn, and as soon as the boat planes off, straighten out the turn and put your port trim tab in the full down position.

Running Shallow Water

If you fish the flats, backcountry or bays, you will from time to time be running in very shallow water. It may be that you got there by being caught by an outgoing tide or because the best fishing was on the other side of a skinny flat, but knowing how to set the boat up properly to run in shallow water is important for your safety and to minimize your impact on sea grasses.

The first things you have to consider are the limitations of your boat. What is the hull design? Do you have a jack plate and low water pickup? Secondly and most important, how well do you know the surrounding area? It doesn't matter how shallow your boat will run, if you run out of water, not only will you run aground, but running at speed can put you so far up onto a flat that waiting for high tide could be your only solution to getting off of it. To further add insult to injury, many places carry a hefty fine for running aground. The best course of action if you are not familiar with the area is to stay in the marked channels, and if you do have to get into a shallow area, go slow with your engine trimmed up.

In the case where you want to run shallow and you know the area well enough, there are some boats specifically designed for shallow water operation and ways to set the boat up that will enable you to run across water less than a foot deep with no issue. Starting with hull design, know that wide flat bottoms with a pocket at the transom, or better yet a tunnel, will let you run the engine higher on the transom. Add on some aftermarket accessories like a jack plate, trim tabs and low water pick up on the outboard's lower unit, and now you can run the motor even farther out of the water.

Knowing how to set the boat up properly to run in shallow water is important for your safety.

An aerial view of an island chain shows the extreme shallows that can catch unwary boaters by surprise and see them grounded. Below, flats boat on the move to skinnier water to fish.

Navigating Inlets

Boaters running an inlet need to stay focused, due to strong currents, wave action and traffic.

Outgoing tide, incoming waves: The basics

Every inlet has its own set of conditions, due to its construction, depth, tidal action and nearby currents. But there are a few basic principles of inlet navigation that can help boaters stay safe, as illustrated at right. If possible, speak to a dock master at a nearby marina for advice before navigating that inlet.

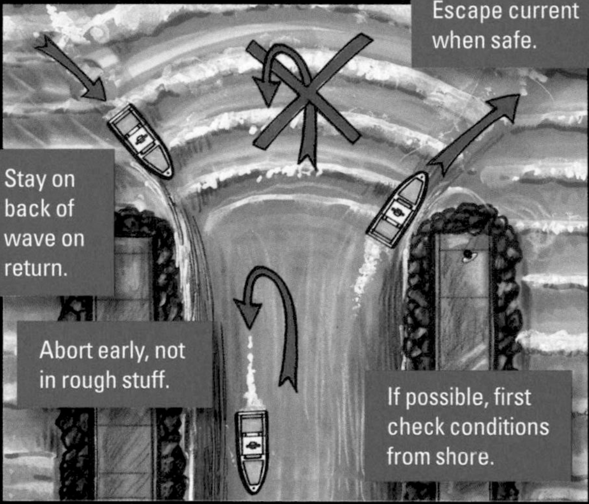

Escape current when safe.

Stay on back of wave on return.

Abort early, not in rough stuff.

If possible, first check conditions from shore.

Illustration: Joe Suroviec

Inlets, like Jupiter Inlet in Florida, are often the scene of intersecting boat traffic patterns, where boat handling and proper navigation are critical to safety.

Atlantic Ocean

Jupiter Inlet

Indian River Lagoon

Loxahatchee River

Every inlet has its own set of conditions, due to its construction, depth, tidal action and nearby currents.

Running in Rough Seas

The short answer is, don't. Images which accompany promotional materials for boats and fishing tournaments sometimes give new boaters a false sense of invincibility.

A veteran captain at the helm of a 30-foot, deep-vee center console may have the skill and equipment to "bridge" a steep headsea at 40 knots, but one might ask his passengers about the experience later.

Safety and comfort, for everyone on board, should always come before speed.

That said, there are a few things you can do to improve the ride when the seas kick up.

➤ In a quartering forward or headsea, trimming the engine in will help keep the bow down, minimizing pounding and possibly improving your envelope for comfortable speed. Trim tabs, if you have them, will achieve a similar effect – and you can lift one side of the boat or the other slightly to reduce spray, if desired. Use very minor adjustments.

➤ Assuming the waves aren't cresting or breaking, most trailerable outboard boats run best "in the trough" – beam-to the waves, though not necessarily parallel to them. Rather than heading straight into the waves, you might tack somewhat on your course, to improve comfort.

➤ When running downsea, trim the engine and/or tabs up somewhat. Importantly, be careful not to launch over a wave and bury the bow into the next wave. The relative comfort of running downsea may convey a false sense of security, causing the skipper to go too fast. If the waves are very large and steep, and you run over the back of one wave and stuff the bow

into the back of the next one, the boat may broach and capsize, or even pitch-pole – end over end.

➤ In a true storm situation, keep your bow into the seas; keep your passengers safe (PFDs on; signaling devices, too); and keep your wits about you. Ensure that all hatches are sealed and that there's nothing on deck which may slide around and obstruct a scupper or drainage port. Periodically confirm that sea water is not accumulating in your bilge or other compartments.

➤ Ocean inlets can be especially dangerous, particularly during periods of outgoing tides and incoming winds. Large "standing men" or break-

While navigating in rough seas, it's best to keep your bow pointed direcrly into the waves – use enough power to get through but not launch your boat into the air.

ing waves may form at the mouth of the inlet. At times these conditions extend well offshore, mixed with all kinds of unpredictable hydraulic effects. Best to avoid these conditions by planning your trip around calmer periods, or by plotting a course for an alternate inlet. The deeper the inlet, usually, the better the conditions. If you're committed to running a tricky inlet on a regular basis, seek local advice.

CHAPTER 9

Navigation and Waterway Rules

Good seamanship describes a large number of things that come into play for operating a boat in a safe manner: the preparation prior to the trip, keeping an eye on the horizon, navigation, weather and the general overall handling of the boat. All of these factors together have an impact on the outcome of a successful trip. SB

There are specific rules that you must follow when encountering other vessels. Know these and practice them, and your time on the water will be safer.

An angler fishing by one of the biggest navigational aids – a lighthouse marking a reef. Right, a channel marker.

Stay Alert

A prudent captain stays focused and uses every asset at their disposal to ensure that each time they leave port, the trip has a safe outcome. Plan your course with the use of a chart and follow your progress by way of channel markers or landmarks. Monitor your VHF radio, if your boat is so equipped, for weather updates, periodic broadcasts from the Coast Guard and other vessels operating in the same vicinity. Ask other passengers on board to assist in keeping a proper lookout. Electronics are great but there is no substitute for using your sight and hearing at all times, keeping your head on a swivel to be aware of your surroundings.

Avoiding a Collision

It is the responsibility of every boat operator to take action to avoid a collision. Weather, sea conditions, wind, current and other vessels all need to be taken into account when you are navigating the waterways.

Don't assume the other boat will see you or have time to avoid you.

As captain, it's your job to know what's ahead of you, AND behind you.

Maintaining a Safe Speed

Maintaining a safe speed will depend on where you are operating your boat, other traffic in the area and the water conditions. Just because you can run fast in a certain area doesn't mean it's a good idea to. The first thing to consider is the waterway. Can you safely navigate that area at your present speed? If you are running a river or channel with blind corners, be sure you have enough time to react in the event of an oncoming vessel in your way. Don't assume the other boat will see you or have time to avoid you.

Water conditions also have to do with the speed you should be traveling at. Many boats don't ride well in rough water and may be harder to control. Also take into account the comfort of your passengers. Nighttime brings with it a whole new aspect to maintaining a safe speed. As discussed earlier, reduced visibility in the dark should prompt you to use extreme caution.

Darker colored water is typically deeper and safe to navigate. But adjacent, lighter colored water, as seen here by the mangroves, often indicates much shallower areas where boats could run aground.

These boaters are running their boat in calm conditions with good visibility — conditions which let them run their small boat at higher speeds safely.

The boater who wants to pass is the give-way vessel and signals his intent to the stand-on vessel, who acknowledges the notice with a signal-answer.

Stand-on Vessel

Toot! Toot!
**Stand-on vessel:
signals agreement**

Toot! Toot!
**Give-way vessel:
signals intent**

Encountering Other Vessels

There are specific rules that you must follow when encountering other vessels. Factors are both boats' direction of travel and what type of propulsion each boat is using. Two power-driven vessels approaching each other have different rules as opposed to one being power driven and one being a sailing vessel. For the sake of this book we will deal with power-versus-power and power-versus-sail scenarios. Sail-versus-sail scenarios have a different set of rules. Also, consider how are the two vessels approaching one another? Whether they are meeting head-on, crossing paths, or one boat is overtaking another, all are factors in the proper procedure outlined for a safe outcome. To help with the explanation of the rules, we will give the definition of two terms: Give-way and Stand-on.

Give-way Vessel

The vessel that is required to take action to give right of way to the other vessel by stopping, slowing down or changing course. Any action by this vessel should be early enough or large enough to be readily apparent to the other vessel. If you are operating a power-driven vessel, you must give way to:
> Any vessel that is disabled or anchored.
> Any vessel that is restricted in its ability to maneuver, such as in tow or inhibited by its draft.
> A vessel engaged in commercial fishing.
> A sailing vessel, unless it is overtaking you.

Stand-on Vessel

The stand-on vessel is the one that should maintain its present speed and course, unless doing so would put its path in conflict with another vessel that is not giving way.

Passing Another Vessel – Power vs. Power

Meeting head-on: When two power boats are approaching each other head-on, they both should give way. Each boat should turn to starboard (the right) and give an audible signal with ONE blast from their horn.

Paths that cross: When two power boats are going to cross paths, the one to the starboard (right) is the stand-on vessel and has the right of way. The boat to port (left) should give ONE blast of the horn to signal they are giving way.

Overtaking: When a power boat is overtaking another power boat, the boat that is being overtaken is the stand-on vessel. The boat that is passing, giving way, should signal its intent in the following manner: by ONE blast of the horn to mean, "I intend to leave you on my port side," or TWO blasts to mean, "I intend to leave you on my starboard side."

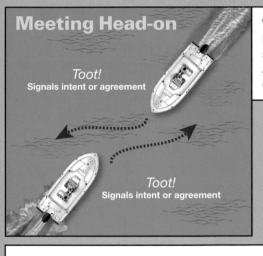

Meeting Head-on

Toot!
Signals intent or agreement

Toot!
Signals intent or agreement

When boaters approach each other head on, they both have the obligation to signal and to turn to their starboard side to avoid running the risk of a collision. As with a car on a street in the U.S., you will pass the oncoming vessel with it on your port side.

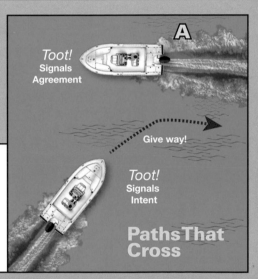

Toot!
Signals Agreement

A

Give way!

Toot!
Signals Intent

Paths That Cross

When vessels are on paths that cross, both operators must maneuver to avoid collision, but by the rules, if the other vessel is at your port side in its approach, you are the stand-on vessel. If vessel A is in a marked channel he has right of way. If in open water, demonstrate your intensions. Using your horn to indicate intent may be helpful.

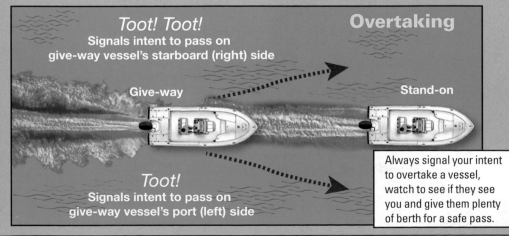

Toot! Toot!
Signals intent to pass on give-way vessel's starboard (right) side

Overtaking

Give-way

Stand-on

Toot!
Signals intent to pass on give-way vessel's port (left) side

Always signal your intent to overtake a vessel, watch to see if they see you and give them plenty of berth for a safe pass.

Passing Another Vessel – Power vs. Sail

Meeting head-on: When a power boat is approaching a sail boat head-on, the power boat must give way. The power boat should turn to starboard (right) and give an audible signal with ONE blast from their horn.

Paths that cross: When a power boat is going to cross paths with a sail boat, the sailing vessel is the stand-on vessel and has the right of way. The power boat should give ONE blast of the horn to signal they are giving way.

Overtaking: When a power boat is overtaking a sail boat, the sail boat that is being overtaken is the stand-on vessel. The power boat that is passing, giving way, should signal its intent in the following manner: by ONE blast of the horn to mean, "I intend to leave you on my port side," or TWO blasts to mean, "I intend to leave you on my starboard side."

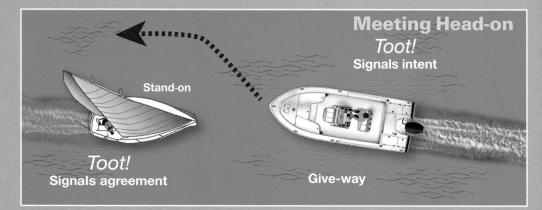

Sailboats always have the right of way when they cross paths with powerboats, because powerboats can maneuver faster. When a power boat meets a sailboat head-on, it signals its intent to give-way and moves out of the course of the sailboat, leaving the sailboat on its port side, just as in traffic on U.S. roads.

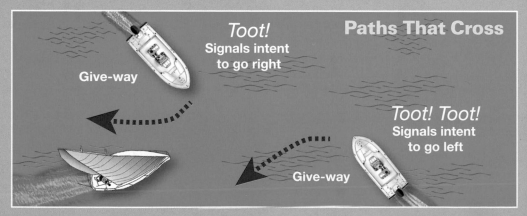

When a powerboat approaches a sailing vessel and will cross paths, the power boat always gives way and signals that intent with one signal if it will pass and leave the stand-on vessel to its own port side, and it will give a two-part signal if it will leave the stand-on to its starboard.

One of many inlets to the Intracoastal Waterway. Photo credit: John Massung www.indianriverbyair.com

In addition to the challenges that inlet waters sometimes pose for boaters, traffic in and around inlets demands strict attention.

Overtaking

Toot! Toot!
Signals intent to pass on give-way vessel's starboard (right) side

Give-way

Stand-on

Toot!
Signals intent to pass on give-way vessel's port (left) side

Rules for overtaking a sailboat are the same as for overtaking a power boat. Signal first, one or two times depending on direction of the pass, and give the sailboat plenty of room for a safe pass around it.

Never assume another boater knows your intention for a planned turn.

Nighttime Operations

As discussed earlier, at night, running at a speed reduced from daytime operations will give you more time to evaluate lights that you might see and have time to react if necessary. Always be sure your navigation lights are in working order and they are illuminated from sunset to sunrise or at other times of low visibility like fog. Lights displayed on vessels help you determine what type of craft it is and its direction of travel. After you determine if you are the give-way or stand-on vessel, use the same rules that apply during the daylight hours. If you are underway, your port and starboard sidelights should be illuminated as well as your stern light. At anchor, use only your all-round white light.

In remote areas, total darkness makes it hard to navigate when the only things that you can see are what are illuminated in the beam of your search light. Many channel markers are not lit and some don't have reflective paint. Be sure to consult local charts and navigate from marker to marker or landmark to landmark

Powerboats less than 66 feet: Use your all-round white light when you are at anchor.

Low-vis and night navigation lights include all-round white light and combination lights at the bow. Red marks port and green, starboard.

Operating in Low Visibility

All boaters should navigate in low visibility conditions, like fog, with extreme caution. Proceed at a slow enough speed that allows you the ability to maneuver immediately if another vessel suddenly comes into view. Be prepared to reduce speed to idle or stop.

what they are. City lights, dock lights, lighted buoys and other watercrafts' nav lights all tend to blend together. It's a good practice in these conditions to periodically stop the boat at rest and watch for movement in other lights that you are seeing. Before coming to a complete stop, be sure you are not going to be blocking a channel. Move to the right side of the channel center line as far as you safely can without risk of running aground and double check your bearings. At rest you will be able to see which lights are moving and which may be other vessels.

At night, GPS and radar can be invaluable in assisting you in navigating, but don't rely solely on them. There's no substitution for your own senses of sight and hearing. Also, reduce the back-screen lighting on all electronic displays enough so that you can still see them but they won't interfere with your night vision. Another tip is to avoid looking into any white light source at least 30 minutes prior to going out onto the water at night. This will greatly improve your night vision.

Lights displayed on vessels help you determine what type of craft it is and its direction of travel.

to be sure you keep your intended heading.

On the other end of the spectrum is boating at night in highly populated areas. Nighttime operations here will dictate that you distinguish between a whole series of lights, and determine

Charts

Nautical charts have several functions. Noting locations of channels and sandbars, along with water depths, are just the basics . Charts can also help you find fishing and diving spots, depending on the chart you choose. When it comes to planning a trip, a chart is an invaluable tool that will allow you to plan for distance traveled, fuel quantity needed and what navigational challenges may lie ahead. If you are new to an area, having an up-to-date chart on board is a must. It will keep you out of trouble and save you time and fuel learning an unfamiliar area. Even if you are boating in a location you know well, it's nice to be able to get a birds-eye view of the area you are

in. Charts are relatively inexpensive and can be laid out on the dining room table prior to a trip for planning – something that you can't do with the GPS mounted in the dash of your boat.

Below: Specialty charts may include GPS numbers for fishing hotspots, markers and other points.
Right: Degrees, minutes and tenths is a common format for latitude and longitude.

Artificial Reefs and Wrecks

Fishing Club Reef			
12 Concrete Rubble	27 26.800	80 10.400	55'
13 Two Bridges Reef	27 26.650	80 10.300	42'
14 Ft. Pierce Fish Haven	27 26.537	80 09.637	51'
15 Barge	27 26.20	80 09.90	54'
Donaldson Reef			
16 Upside Down Barge	27 13.954	80 06.717	58'
17 Pipe Barge	27 13.385	80 06.958	57'
18 Toilet Bowl	27 12.956	80 06.798	54'
19 Guardian Reef	27 12.913	80 06.750	60'
20 170' Barge-North End	27 12.911	80 06.809	60'
21 Wreck/Rubble	27 12.639	80 06.568	54'
22 11 Loads-Culverts	27 12.370	80 06.620	
	North to 27 12.920	80 06.950	
3409.5 62012.0 North to 43409.5 62013.1			
Capt. Al Sirotkin Reef			
23 Roosevelt Bridge	27 12.88	80 02.07	100'
24 FP&L Reef	27 12.862	80 02.063	91'
25 Tetrahedron Reef	27 12.808	80 02.342	92'
26 FP&L Reef	27 12.731	80 01.433	100'
27 Mercedes "Drega"	27 12.261	80 02.896	75'
28 David T.	27 12.225	80 02.856	76'
29 USS Rankin	27 11.326	80 01.439	130'
30 Titan Tug	27 11.305	80 01.450	80'
Ernst Reef			
31 Buses	27 09.390	80 03.220	57'
32 Corner Barge	27 09.38	80 03.29	70'
33 North Barge	27 09.35	80 03.34	70'
34 Ernst Reef Bridge Rubble	27 09.348	80 03.333	70'
35 South Barge	27 09.31	80 03.24	70'
36 Tire Piles	27 08.724	80 02.710	55'

FLORIDA SPORTSMAN

FISHING CHART

FT. PIERCE/ STUART
Very breath
to Hobe Sound

WHERE THE EXPERTS FISH

INSHORE OFFSHORE

NEW UPDATED CHARTS WRECKS AND REEFS

www.floridasportsman.com

Chart No. 06

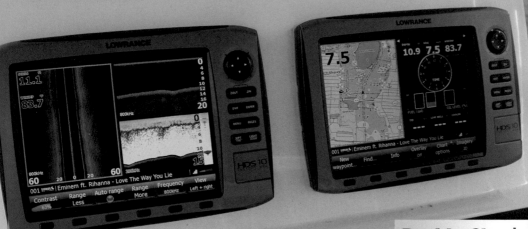

Dual multi-screen displays allow for simultaneous viewing of numerous sonar readings, left, and charts and gauges, right.

GPS – Moving Maps

As mentioned previously, technology has advanced in nautical navigation where most boats today have some form of a Global Positioning System (GPS) moving map. From the large LCD displays that are flush-mounted in the dash of a center console, to the small gimbal-mounted units that you find on bass and flats boats, a GPS could be the single most useful piece of electronic equipment you can add to your boat. With that said, they should not be considered a replacement for paper charts. Electronics can and do go out, and a mistake many boaters make is to become so reliant on technology that they lack the basic dead reckoning skills to get back to port in the event they lose power to their electronics. Think of your GPS as a complement to your paper charts, and your paper charts as a back-up to your electronics, but neither one will replace simple situational awareness.

When onboard, throughout the day, especially if you are out of the sight of land, note your position. Find your compass heading and distance back to port and make a mental note. Even go a step further by shutting down your GPS and try to navigate back home with just your compass. If you ever find yourself in the position of having to navigate solely by your compass, this practice will boost your self-confidence.

NOAA's New Chart Product: Booklet Charts

One resource boaters should not miss is the array of downloadable charts and maps available from NOAA. Now, NOAA's entire national suite of 1000-plus charts is available for free download in a handy, page-sized .pdf format in the BookletChart product line. These charts can be printed out in page size panels.

"Many people who previously did not carry charts find these very convenient to use in lieu of the full size charts," says Nick Perugini, at NOAA. "They'll print these charts at home, sometimes laminate them, paste them together and make notations on them. Obviously the page size chart is much easier to use in an open boat."

For people who do carry the full size chart of their region onboard, which is highly recommended, BookletCharts can be an auxiliary chart that can be marked up. The BookletChart download site is:

http://www.nauticalcharts.noaa.gov/staff/BookletChart.html

Compasses and Compass Rose

A compass, which is used in navigation, is an instrument that shows magnetic north. If a magnetic compass is in use, to navigate you must be able to convert back and forth between true and magnetic headings. You accomplish this by either adding or subtracting the magnetic variation – which is the angle between magnetic and geographic meridians. Most nautical charts include a compass rose that shows two graduated scales. One is referenced to true north, while the other is referenced to magnetic north. A compass rose is a circle graduated in degrees, clockwise from 0 degrees at the reference direction to 360 degrees and sometimes also in compass points. Compass roses are placed at convenient locations on a chart to facilitate measurement of direction. The compass rose can be used to help lay out a course with a protractor or parallel ruler. In the center of the rose, magnetic variation is given in degrees and minutes, with an easterly or westerly component. Also included is the annual deviation, as magnetic north changes over time. If converting from magnetic headings to true headings, a west variation is subtracted from the magnetic to obtain true. An easterly variation would be added.

When mounting a compass on a boat, keep it away from irons, speaker magnets and electrical wiring or equipment. Practice with your compass in good weather and get confident in its use. If you ever have to use it solely to return to port, it is the one instrument in your boat that will be the most reliable.

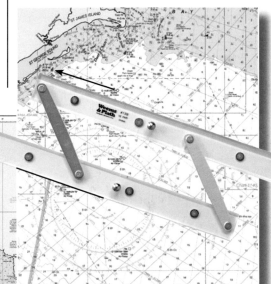

Compass roses are placed at convenient locations on a chart to facilitate measurement of direction.

Understanding how to use a compass, left, and special features on a chart will build your confidence. Top: Parallel ruler is used to plot course from artificial reef to bell buoy and home. Outer ring of the compass rose shows True course while inner ring shows Magnetic (compass) course.

Navigational Aids

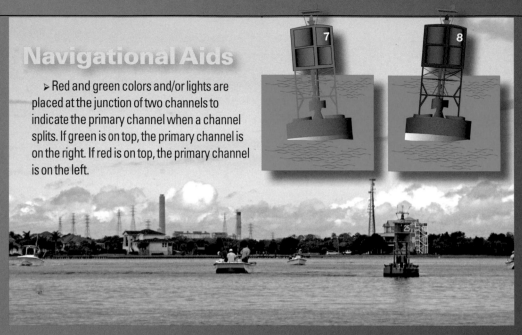

➤ Red and green colors and/or lights are placed at the junction of two channels to indicate the primary channel when a channel splits. If green is on top, the primary channel is on the right. If red is on top, the primary channel is on the left.

➤ Daymarks are permanently placed signs, attached to structures like posts in the water. Common daymarks are red triangles (equivalent to nuns) and green squares (equivalent to cans). They may also be lighted.

Red Right Return

➤ Red colors, red lights and even numbers mark the edge of a channel and should be passed on your starboard (right) side as you enter from the open sea or head upstream. Numbers usually increase consecutively as you return from the open sea. The old saying "**Red Right Return**" in most circumstances lets you know you are returning from open waters or heading into a local marked channel.

➤ Green colors, green lights and odd numbers mark the edge of a channel and should be passed on your port (left) side as you enter from the open sea or heading into a local marked channel. Numbers usually increase consecutively as you return from the open sea.

Common daymarks are red triangles (equivalent to nuns) and green squares (equivalent to cans).

➢ Can buoys are cylindrical-shaped and are green with odd numbers. They mark the edge of a channel on your port (left) side as you enter from the open sea or head upstream.

Intracoastal Waterway (ICW)

The Intracoastal Waterway (ICW) is a chain of local channels linked together to provide an inland route along the Atlantic and Gulf of Mexico coasts. Channels that are part of the ICW are identified by yellow symbols on the channel markers and buoys that are also used for navigational aids. When following the ICW from New Jersey through Texas, any marker that has a yellow triangle should be passed by keeping it on the starboard (right) side of the boat. Any marker that has a yellow square should be passed by keeping it on the port (left) side of the boat. It doesn't matter which shape or color the marker or buoy is when you are using the yellow symbols to follow the ICW, but these yellow symbols should be used only as guides and you should refer to the navigational aid color and shape to keep you in navigable waters.

➢ Nun buoys are cone-shaped and are red with even numbers. They mark the edge of a channel on your starboard (right) side as you enter from the open sea or head upstream.

Red Right Return in the ICW

If on the Intracoastal or ocean, a good rule of thumb to follow is if you're heading in the direction of Texas, keep the red markers on your right. When heading away from Texas, keep the green markets on your right.

Texas = "Return"

Navigational Aids

Channel markers and buoys guide boat operators safely through the waterways. They also identify dangerous or controlled areas and give direction and information. Knowing the different types of markers and their meaning will aid in your navigation. Basically there are two types of markers, lateral and non-lateral. Lateral markers mark edges of safe waters for navigation like channels. These markers use a combination of colors and numbers which may appear on either buoys or permanently placed markers. Non-lateral markers give information other than edges of safe navigation, like closed areas, danger zones, idle zones, swimming areas, etc. Typically these markers are buoys with orange markings and black lettering.

Here is a descrition of markers and buoys:

Non-navigational markers are buoys that give warnings, directions and boundary information.

Digital Navigation

With the advancements in GPS units both in range of sizes and affordability, few boats don't have some form of moving map that includes marine charts with topography, nav aids and details of channels plus structure. Many GPS units even have high resolution satellite imagery with aerial photography of ports, harbors and marinas. I'm still a big advocate of having paper charts on board as a backup to the electronic software but with a current GPS moving map, navigating is as simple as following your track on a screen. You can even go so far as adding an auto pilot coupled to the GPS for hands free operation of your vessel.

Most GPS units come pre-loaded with some type of mapping software. These maps are just

Channel markers and other navigational aids will appear on mapping software in GPS units.

that, they are electronic versions of a paper chart and most GPS units come with a built-in broad version that covers the US and a lot of the islands. If you want more detailed data, additional memory chips are available for many units that have premium mapping and more information about points of interest. For instance, when you toggle the unit's cursor over a particular marina, a pop-up screen will list all of the services offered at this location, along with contact info. Now move the cursor over to a buoy and a pop-up screen describes the nav aid. Adding one of these detailed mapping chips lets you get the maximum use out of the unit's capabilities. Other memory chips are also available to load into your unit a list of waypoints that show fishing hot spots, even what type of fish you would most likely encounter when fishing there.

A GPS with a moving map will not only allow you to find fish more easily but will add an extra margin of safety for you and your crew. Many of the new GPS displays are very intui-

Important tracks and way-points gathered while on the water, as in photo below, may be stored in chartplotter and used trip after trip.

tive and along with helping you navigate, they can also be used for a variety of other tasks like depth finding, radar, engine gauges, weather, and even as an audio system.

A word of caution, these new GPS units have so much information at your fingertips you may have a tendency to spend too much time with your head looking down at the display screen instead of what's ahead of the boat. Use the GPS as a reference to your our navigational skills and make sure your head stays on a swivel to get the big picture of the area and other traffic that's around your boat at all times.

There's no substitution for a paper chart and a good quality compass. Learn to read charts and be able to navigate without relying solely on your electronics.

In the best-case scenario, digital navigation goes hand-in-hand with old-time paper chart navigation and boating know-how. Always have paper charts as backups and keep a running log – whether jotted down or mentally – of your position at all times. When scouting for fish, make notes of conditions and in shallow, of tides. And always corroborate your position on your GPS chartplotter to document safe passage in shallows, into and out of channels and into new waterways.

CHAPTER 10

Anchoring

Although it's not a USCG requirement, anchors are mandatory in many states because they're considered very important safety gear. Enforced or not, keeping an anchor with an attached chain and line onboard is strongly recommended. Even those who have no use for one for fishing or any other recreational purpose still need an anchor for unexpected and emergency applications.

You may not need an anchor very often, but when you need it – you really need it. For example, if your boat breaks down and you're out a good distance with no anchor, your boat will drift with the wind and/or current, which could leave you drifting helplessly into a predicament. It's almost always far better to stay put in one spot because locating a boat in need of assistance is a lot easier when it's not on the move. If you break down and just happen to be drifting directly toward a safe shoreline, then you may not have to anchor, but you certainly can't count on that sort of luck all the time. SB

Anchors are mandatory in many states because they're considered very important safety gear.

Boat anchored near bridge to drift back baits to where fish hold near structure. Yellowtail, right, often caught on anchor.

With plenty riding on your anchor's reliability, your choice of ground tackle is important.

Anchoring

Ground Tackle: the anchor, chain, shackles and line.

There are times when having an anchor is an absolute must in order to protect your boat and passengers from imminent danger. When caught by a pop-up storm or squall – it'll happen sooner or later – the conditions can suddenly become unnavigable due to nil or extremely limited visibility and dangerous, gale force winds. To drive your boat in such conditions would be blindly putting yourself at great risk for collision with another boat or solid obstacle. Without an anchor to secure your boat in one safe spot, you could very possibly drift into a hazardous situation.

Anchoring a boat is actually an easy task if you have the right gear and always keep it ready. But there's a little more to doing it correctly and effectively than just letting the anchor plop into the water. So let's cover the basics and take a look at some numbers. You'll have it wired in no time.

Choosing the Right Anchor

With plenty riding on your anchor's reliability, your choice of ground tackle is important. Ground tackle is the anchor, chain, line and shackles combined. Having the right set-up will make consistently-reliable anchoring a lot easier and

safer than using gear that's inadequate for your boat or incompatible with your boating area.

First and foremost – the actual anchor. There are several different types, each designed for effective holding in various kinds and densities of bottom materials or beds. The type of anchor you need is determined by your boat's weight, size and type, and even more so by which kind(s) of riverbed, lakebed or seabed you'll anchor in: sand, mud, clay, gravel, rocks, coral, etc, and whether or not it's covered with aquatic grasses or weeds.

Areas with aquatic vegetation growing on the bottom can be especially tricky to set and hold

Anchored at a favorite, secret fishing spot.

anchor in, especially if densely covered. These beds usually require a heavier anchor that is designed to penetrate through and into to the bottom... where they might not stay set for long. Grassy-bottomed areas are notorious for weak or "false" settings because the anchor will frequently catch on roots or protrusions that easily break loose from the bottom. This releases the boat, setting it adrift with the anchor sliding across the bottom and not re-setting due to being fouled with the big clump of grass that it broke off.

So your anchor choice starts on the bottom. If not yet familiar with exactly what lies beneath the waters of your boating areas, be sure to check with local boaters and people in the boating business to find out which kinds of bottom materials or combinations there are.

Two is Better than One

There really is no universal, all-purpose anchor. However there are some designs that work well in most applications. The popular fluke or Danforth types, and the state-of-the-art scoop or plow designs are examples. Having at least one of these types will suit many boat owners adequately.

But there are many regions or local areas with significant variations in bed materials where you really need to carry two different types of anchors onboard, and keep them both readily-available. For instance, there can be a hard-pack sand bottom within a few hundred yards of a mushy-soft mud bottom, both with or without aquatic grasses. Anyone carrying only a fluke anchor would soon realize that they tend to drag across hard, flat bottoms with no soft surface material to dig into. There is another advantage of keeping two anchor types onboard: You won't be left anchorless if one gets stuck and can't be retrieved, which is a possibility anywhere.

Holding Power

The heavier and larger a boat is, and the more water it displaces, and the more windage (wind resistance of a vessel's profile) it presents – the more holding power its anchor must provide. Holding power is the rating of an anchor's average-tested, horizontal load capacity to stay set before breaking loose – measured in pounds of pull force. Holding power requirement increases exponentially as wind speed increases. As the wind speed doubles, the holding requirement quadruples. In other words, for safety's sake, if you keep just one anchor onboard, be sure it's rated as a storm anchor so that you'll have sufficient holding power for all conditions.

The weight of an anchor is no doubt a factor in its ability to penetrate into bottom material and catch hold. But it's actually the anchor's holding power, which is determined by its design and size, that has the most bearing on its adequacy and reliability.

Anchor Holding Power Requirements: Horizontal Loads					
	BOAT LENGTH				
WIND SPEED	15 ft.	20 ft.	25 ft.	30 ft.	35 ft.
17 mph / 15 knots Lunch Hook	60 lbs.	90 lbs.	125 lbs.	175 lbs.	225 lbs.
34 mph / 30 knots Working Anchor	250 lbs.	360 lbs.	490 lbs.	700 lbs.	900 lbs.
48 mph / 42 knots Storm Anchor	500 lbs.	720 lbs.	980 lbs.	1400 lbs.	1800 lbs.

If your boat is above average weight, windage or beam, be sure to select for the next boat length up.

Anchor Types

Just as for any purchase involving an important piece of safety equipment, it's wise to do a little homework online to help you compare all of the different options. Most of the anchor makers' websites advertise the reasons why their brand and designs are the best, so it's also a good idea to read a few impartial anchor test comparisons online.

The following anchor types are recommended for the types of boats outlined in this book, and represent some of the more popular, reliably-effective anchor designs available.

Pivoting Fluke / Fluke / Danforth / Lightweight Anchor

Advantages

➤ Holds very well in soft sand and mud
➤ The most commonly-used anchor for trailerable-sized boats
➤ Excellent holding power-to-weight ratio
➤ Available from very inexpensive to relatively expensive
➤ Fortress anchors have an adjustable shank/fluke angle to adjust for sand or mud bottoms

Disadvantages

➤ Not compatible with most types of rock, coral, clay or kelp bottoms
➤ Larger ones can be somewhat awkward to handle
➤ Prone to getting stuck on bottom objects, becoming difficult to retrieve or unretrievable
➤ Tends to drag across hard, flat bottoms and slide across dense weed beds without digging in
➤ The flukes and stock (crossbar) are prone to fouling by vegetation, mud clumps, and the rode (anchor line), preventing the anchor from resetting

Claw / Bruce Anchor

Advantages

➤ Holds well in most types of bottoms, good option for gravel
➤ Allows for a 360-degree turn without releasing from the bottom
➤ Stays set dependably though wind and tide changes
➤ Resets well and easily retrieved

Disadvantages

➤ Performs less well in sand and mud
➤ Can be cumbersome to stow.
➤ Comparably heavy weight

Claw anchors are best suited for use in gravel bottoms.

Delta / CQR / Plow Anchor

Advantages
➤ Holds in a variety of bottom materials: sand, gravel, rocks, coral, kelp, and particularly mud
➤ Their designs and weight can dig right in and hold well
➤ Good resistance to wind and tide movements
➤ Less likely to foul in the anchor rode than fluke types
➤ Best suited and very popular for larger, heavier powerboats 30 feet plus.

Disadvantages
➤ Must be very heavy to work as designed – can require considerable upsizing
➤ Can have difficulty holding in hard sand or other hard bottoms
➤ Not practical for most boats under 30 feet.

Photo: Courtesy of Rocna Anchors

Scoop / New Generation Anchor

Advantages
➤ Certain designs have the highest all-around holding ability in varying bottom conditions
➤ Hold more effectively than most anchor types in mud, sand and grass
➤ Resistant to fouling
➤ Set quickly and reset themselves easily if wind or current changes direction
➤ Certain designs incorporate a round roll bar that self-rights the anchor on the bottom
➤ The Rocna has excellent surface area-to-weight ratio, giving it the highest holding power of new generation anchors

Disadvantages
➤ Expensive
➤ On some boats, the anchor types with an attached roll bar can clash with the boat's anchor bracket/roller, bow pulpit or bow platform

Richter Anchor

Advantages
➤ Popular for small/mid-sized fishing boats in areas where grapnel-type anchors are effective
➤ Versatile for a variety of bottom conditions (except for soft materials)
➤ Easy to retrieve, rarely gets stuck

Disadvantages
➤ Performs less well in soft sand and mud
➤ Not rated for storm wind conditions – best suited for smaller boats in protected, inland areas

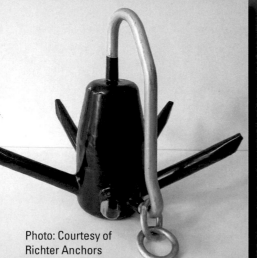

Photo: Courtesy of Richter Anchors

The Rode to Anchoring Success

To complete your ground tackle set-up, you also need the appropriate type and length of both anchor line and anchor chain, which together make up the anchor rode. It's best to use removable anchor shackles to connect the anchor to the chain, and the chain to the line. Shackles not only prevent rope chaffing, they also make quick work of replacing any part of your ground tackle trio. For brackish and saltwater use, stainless steel shackles last longer and are much easier to remove the screw pin from than galvanized ones – which will eventually lock up. (It is a good idea, though, to secure the pin with a plastic ziptie or "seizing" wire to prevent it from working its way out at the wrong moment.)

Don't be tempted to omit the chain from your ground tackle and just attach the anchor directly to the line, as some boat owners naively do. The anchor chain is a key component, and without it you can't expect for your anchor to set and stick reliably. The chain's weight helps to keep the anchor shank horizontal, which is essential to both setting ability and holding power. Its weight also forms a curve in the rode that helps to absorb shock loads from wakes and rough conditions. And it won't chafe from rocks or sharp objects on the bottom.

Every boat's anchor should have a galvanized or stainless-steel chain of the appropriate length and diameter attached to it. Anchor chain lengths typically run between 4 and 30 feet, depending on the weight, size and type of boat. A 14' flat-bottomed, aluminum john boat would do fine with 4 feet of chain, whereas a 32' walkaround boat would need a 30-footer. A few extra feet can only help too, since even a 15 mph wind can lift short lengths of chain off the bottom.

For your anchor line, use three-strand, nylon anchor rope. (Not to be confused with polypropylene rope, which is no good at all for anchor lines because it floats... not OK when other boats are motoring by.) Nylon rope is strong, light, easy to handle, and elastic – which is what you want. Three-strand offers the advantages of both elasticity and lower cost.

To determine how much anchor line you'll need in order to make a sufficient length of anchor rode, simply multiply the deepest depth of water you'll be boating in by 10, and add on an extra 10 or 20 feet. This is important. Not having a long enough rode can make it difficult or impossible to set your

Complete ground tackle sets are available in ready-to-go packages.

West Marine

TRADITIONAL Anchor & Rode Package
Ensemble d'ancre avec chaîne/câble
For Boats up-to 31 ft.(9.4m)

ESSENTIAL GEAR 13
Anchor | Chain | Shackles | Line

- **ALL HOT-DIPPED GALVANIZED STEEL**
  13.45 lb Fluke Anchor (6.10kgs)

- **PREMIUM ANCHOR RODE**
  200 ft.- 7/16 in. with Five Tuck Eye Splice (61.3m - 11.1mm)

  15 ft.- 1/4 in. Proof Coil Chain (4.6m - 6.4mm)

  2 - 3/8 in. Bow Shackles (9.6mm)

Don't be tempted to omit the chain from your ground tackle; it's a crucial component that is key to reliable anchoring.

anchor. More about this is just ahead.

As for rope diameter, figure 1/8 inch of diameter for every 9 feet of boat length. For a 27' boat, you'd need a 3/8" nylon anchor line. But even for considerably shorter boats, 3/8" is the minimum recommended diameter because ¼ inch and smaller sizes are difficult to grip and more prone to tangling.

When stowing your new ground tackle in your boat, if it has an anchor locker be sure to securely tie the end of the line to the hardware mounted inside so that you won't accidently lose everything. Did you know that the end of a rode is actually called the bitter end?

Ground tackle should always be organized and ready to run freely at a moment's notice. You never know when a sudden and urgent matter could pop up that would necessitate a real quick anchor drop. If your motor stalls and won't restart as you're drifting toward trouble, you don't want to be digging your anchor out from underneath piles of stowed gear and supplies. And you really don't want to pull out a rat's nest of tangled ropes and dock lines. Always keep your anchor readily accessible, with the rode neatly coiled – wherever you stow it. You'll be glad you did.

Anchor Size

Anchor size recommendations vary by manufacturer and model. Once you've decided which type of anchor(s) you'll need and which brand and model you want, you'll find the appropriate size of anchor for your boat size listed on the manufacturer's anchor selection chart. These reference charts or selection guides are typically found on your marine supply retailer's display rack, conveniently placed right there with the anchors. They're also posted on each anchor manufacturer's website.

It's important to note that the anchor manufacturers' recommendations are basic guidelines based on boat length. Since boats of the same length can be vastly different in weight and windage, and because anchor loads are more dependent on those two factors than boat length, use these guidelines only as a starting point. Be sure to factor in any above-average weight, windage (wind resistance), or beam if applicable to your boat, and up-size accordingly.

Ground tackle should always be organized and ready to run freely at a moment's notice.

It might take a few attemps to get your anchor to grab and set for the position you want your boat to hold at a spot to fish.

Quick Tip:

Mark your rode every 10 feet with a permanent marker – measured from the anchor, back. This will take the guesswork out of paying out (feeding out) the correct length of rode to set your anchoring scope.

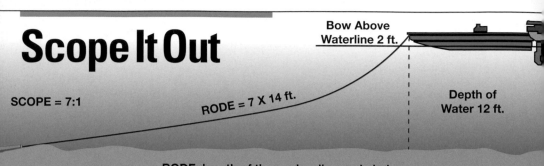

Scope It Out

Bow Above Waterline 2 ft.

SCOPE = 7:1

RODE = 7 X 14 ft.

Depth of Water 12 ft.

RODE: length of the anchor line and chain
SCOPE: ratio of length of anchor rode in use to the vertical distance from the bow of the vessel to the bottom of the water

Scope is the ratio of length of deployed anchor rode, to the vertical distance from the bow cleat of the boat to the bottom of the water. Since anchors hold best when the rode is as near to horizontal as possible, rather than just guessing how much rode is needed, calculating scope helps to ensure a sufficiently horizontal rode angle for the conditions you're anchoring in. Here's how to easily calculate your scope:

1. Choose the necessary scope ratio based on the wind, water conditions and any current. Use the chart below as a general guideline. Example: there's a light breeze and the water is fairly smooth, but there's a steady current, so a 7:1 scope would be needed.

2. Add the depth of the water to the vertical distance between the water surface and your bow cleat. Example: it's 8 feet deep, plus you've got about 2 feet from surface to bow cleat = 10 feet.

3. For 7:1 scope: 7 x 10 (ft.) = 70 feet of rode (from anchor to bow cleat or tie-off point).

AnchoringTips

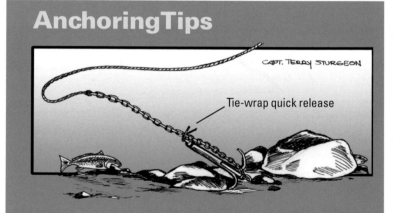

CAPT. TERRY STURGEON

Tie-wrap quick release

Special trip rig for temporary fishing anchorage in rocky areas. Chain is shackled to ring at bottom of grapnel anchor (above) or hole drilled through crown of Danforth anchor (below). Plastic wire tie(s) or heavy twine secure chain to anchor shank. If anchor is stuck, moderate pressure in opposing direction should break wire ties and allow anchor to be pulled out backwards.

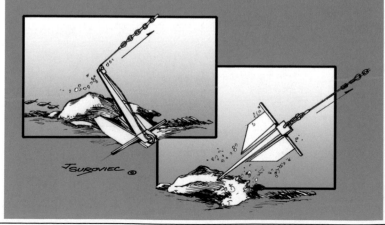

J SUROVIEC ©

Recommended Anchoring Scope

Wind-generated Water Conditions	Scope	Max. Potential Holding Power
-------------	2:1 (not advised)	35%
Calm/Glassy to Light Breeze/Ripples	3:1	53%
Gentle Breeze/Wavelets	4:1	67%
Breeze/Light Chop	5:1	77%
Moderate Breeze/Choppy	6:1	85%
Fresh Breeze/Very Choppy	7:1	91%
Strong Breeze/Rough, White Caps	10:1	100%
Near Gale/Very Rough	10:1	100%

Data listed is an aggregate average of generally-accepted parameters for anchoring scope.
Figures are approximate and assume a flat seabed.
Strong currents will necessitate increased scope.

Scope Adjustment

➢ Scope of less than 3:1 significantly reduces holding power.
➢ Scope beyond 10:1 does not significantly increase holding power.
➢ If your anchor won't stay set, you may need to increase your scope.
➢ If you do any boating in deep lakes, keep a long enough rode onboard for up to a 10:1 scope in case you break down out in deep water on a windy day.

Picking a Good Anchoring Spot

➢ Before dropping anchor – especially in unfamiliar areas – take precautions to avoid any problems.
➢ Check the depths around your intended anchor site.
➢ If in a tidal area, be sure that you'll have enough depth at low tide.
➢ Check your chart for any known, underwater obstructions that you may not be able to see.
➢ When anchoring near other boats or obstacles, allow for a 360 degree radius of open space from your anchor to your stern for the possibility of switching wind direction. Don't assume that all of the anchored boats around you will swing the same direction at the same time.
➢ Anchoring in a channel is prohibited unless you're in distress.
➢ Anchoring in the vicinity of underwater utility cables in prohibited; look for any posted signs and also check your nautical chart.
➢ Avoid anchoring within mooring areas; it's almost asking for trouble.
➢ If multiple boats are all anchored in one relatively tight area, there's probably a good reason; be sure to find out why.
➢ Obviously, on windy days – the more protected from wind, the better the anchoring spot... as long as it's not too close to anything that could be problematic.

Dropping Anchor

Grapnels are good for jetties because their tines will bend free under pressure if caught in rocks upon retrieval and can be bent back in shape for use again.

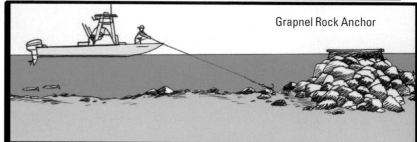

Grapnel Rock Anchor

Vital Safety Warning: boats should not be anchored from the stern, especially in a current. If you haven't already, be certain to read in Chapter 6: "Never Anchor a Boat From the Stern Alone."

1. Check the depth, determine the appropriate scope, and calculate your needed rode length.

2. Prepare your ground gear – rode untangled and readied.

3. Point your bow into the wind or current – whichever is stronger, and shift into neutral.

4. When forward momentum has stopped, lower the anchor into the water and down to the bottom. Don't throw it in (or let it plop in and scare away the fish you were about to catch).

5. Pay (feed) out the rode as the boat drifts astern (back) with the wind or current.

6. If there isn't enough wind or current to push you astern, shift into reverse and give it just enough to get the boat moving slowly backwards with enough reverse momentum to coast.

7. Once the rode has been fed out to your pre-determined length, cleat it off to the bow cleat. (This is when having your rode marked at 10-foot intervals comes in handy.) Always tie the rode off to a bow cleat using a cleat hitch so that it will hold securely and also untie quick-n-easy.

8. After the rode is secured to the bow cleat, shift into reverse and slowly back down to pull on the rode with steady tension for three or four seconds. This should ensure that the an-chor has dug into the bottom and has been set.

9. Take a sight bearing on a stationary object or two so that you'll know if your anchor is dragging.

10. If anyone will be swimming around the motor, pull out the key – just to be extra safe.

GPS Anchoring

The advent of GPS-linked electric trolling motors has changed anchoring practice for many small boat anglers. GPS trolling units allow anglers on bay boats, bass boats and other low-freeboard vessels to hold position without dropping anchor. This convenience saves anglers fishing over wrecks the risk of losing their anchor and allows anchor-free positions over sensitive vegatation or reef areas.

Anglers are reviving a sailfish before release while their GPS anchor holds their position steady and current flows to the fish.

Anchor Ball Assist

Left, dropping the anchor ball clasped to the anchor line. Quarter away from the descending ball toward deeper water until the ball ring around the line passes over the anchor shackle, suspending the anchor for you to easily lift into boat.

Retrieving the Anchor

1. To break out (release) your anchor, you'll need to position your bow directly over the anchor so that it can be lifted as vertically as possible.

2. If it's light enough to, pull your boat by hand (with the rode) up to the anchor. (This can actually be kinda fun... makes you feel like you have superhero strength! But don't strain yourself.)

3. If your boat is too heavy, or the conditions are too rough for that, slowly power up to the anchor using your motor (not your windlass), taking in the rode as you approach it.

4. Once you're over the anchor you should be able to hoist it right up, usually.

5. If it's not cooperating, and if you have a small to medium-sized boat with passengers onboard, try this: move everyone to the bow, cleat the rode tightly to the bow cleat with no slack, then move everyone aft. This may leverage the anchor loose.

6. If it doesn't, or your boat is too heavy for this to work: slacken the rode just slightly and re-secure it to the bow cleat, shift into reverse, and from the opposite direction that it was set, slowly and carefully try to pull the anchor loose.

7. When lifting your anchor out of the water, if it has any mud or weeds stuck to it, be sure to dip it into the water a few times to rinse it off. You don't want that stuff in your boat because it could eventually flow down into your bilge and accumulate enough to clog up your bilge pump. For pontoon boats (they don't have or need a bilge pump), this is of course optional.

8. Unless you're pulling in your anchor just to slowly relocate to another nearby anchoring spot, always stow it away securely. Not only is it a trip hazard lying on the deck, it's not something you want flying around if involved in a collision of any kind.

Be Eco-Friendly

Whenever you have the choice, try not to anchor in any area with seagrasses or dense weed beds on the bottom. Not only are these areas difficult for most anchors to set into and remain set, in many regions they're also very environmentally sensitive.

In saltwater regions with endangered coral reefs, any reef damage done by anchoring or accidental vessel grounding is a fineable penalty. One way to avoid anchoring to a coral reef in such areas is to use mooring buoys, where provided. Another alternative is to anchor in the sand located beyond the edge of the reef.

Boat anchors and chains can damage and harm the aquatic vegetation in lakes, rivers and estuaries. Naturally, most species are very important to the health of their ecosystems. So if you must anchor in such an area, please do so with care.

➤ Don't drop anchor until your boat has stopped coasting. This will prevent dragging it through the vegetation unnecessarily.

➤ When moving your boat to another spot – even a short distance – lift the anchor off the bottom rather than letting it drag. Dragging an anchor while under power is actually illegal in some areas.

➤ It's particularly important to clean any vegetation and soil off of your anchor before leaving the area so that you won't inadvertently transport invasive species from one area to another.

CHAPTER 11

Docking

This may sound a bit crazy at first, but docking a boat is in many ways a lot like golfing – or more precisely, like putting. Fortunately though – for all of us the huge difference is that just about anyone can learn to consistently dock at a pro level. For two things that seem so completely different, there are a lot of similarities. To do well, they both require confidence, forethought, con-centration, aiming for a target, accounting for wind, reading the current or the green, proper technique, finesse, patience, etiquette, and most of all... practice and experience.

For either skill, reading and watching instructional material and videos will certainly help to get you started on the right track, but experience is for-sure the best teacher. Just as for any skill that requires practice and experience in varying settings and conditions, you really have to get out there and get the feel for it before you can gain the confidence needed to perfect your technique. SB

For docking, practice and experience are for-sure the best teachers.

Center consoles backed into boat slips for a lunch break (above). Unloading rewards of a good day's fishing (right).

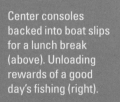

Ins and Outs of Docking

Familiarity with the slow-speed handling characteristics of your boat is key to honing your docking skills.

For docking – and for any close-quarter boat maneuvering – getting the feel for it is all about familiarity with how a boat handles and maneuvers at minimal speed. And maneuvering a boat into just the right position is all about confidently controlling both momentum and rotation – while simultaneously either using the wind or current to your advantage, or compensating for their adverse affects as much as possible. Since there can be night and day differences in how different boats handle, familiarity with the slow-speed handling characteristics of your particular boat is key.

With so many things to have to try to think about, control and adjust for all at the same time, it's no wonder that docking a boat can be somewhat of an intimidating task for most novices. Thankfully, practice and experience make it easier and easier to do, and eventually – for most boaters anyway – the confidence and control become practically second nature.

Boat docking and golf share other notable parallels as well. First, having too many bystanders telling you what they think you should do while you're trying to do it, is usually very counterproductive. Second, even the best will sometimes miss their mark and have to circle around to try it again. And third, the greater the degree of dif-

Busy marinas, like Roland Martin's Marina and Resort on Lake Okeechobee, can be intimidating for novice boaters, but patience in docking at them always pays off.

Boat Docking General Guidelines

- Forget everything you know about parking a car.
- 5 mph is 4 mph too fast for safe docking.
- 95 percent of docking occurs while coasting in neutral, unless it's windy.
- Coast, don't power toward the dock.
- The slower you go, the easier docking is, and the more time you'll have to make adjustments or corrections to your approach. You want to control your boat's momentum and using reverse can help.
- But reverse is not a boat's equivalent of brakes. Dropping into reverse and flooring it should almost never be necessary, unless as a last-ditch effort to avoid imminent collision.
- Using frequent, abrupt throttle bursts of high-revving power while docking is a common bad habit among unskilled boaters. This actually makes maintaining control of an intended docking maneuver more difficult because it usually only produces extra momentum that has to be countered and adjusted for.
- Unless dealing with an unusually strong wind or current, intermittent, light throttle bumps in and out of gear will do the trick. A throttle bump is a subtle, 2-second, very-low RPM thrust of forward or reverse throttle. Easy does it.
- If you have no docking experience or it's been years, start with practicing slow, precise maneuvers in an open area of water exposed to a breeze or current. This helps to get the feel for your boat's handling characteristics; how well it steers and responds to subtle throttle bumps and adjustments. Pick a spot in the water and practice approaching an imaginary dock from different angles, positioning your boat parallel to it. "Calibrate your brain" to gauge the distances needed to compensate for wind and current upon approach. The more confidence you gain in your ability to control your boat in close quarters with adverse conditions, the better you'll be able to handle various docking challenges.

ficulty, the more likely you are to get a round of applause in appreciation of your impressive skills.

Docking a boat at a busy marina or in challenging conditions can be pretty stressful. But, with the help of the guidelines and steps outlined in this chapter, and with plenty of practice at your local waterfront pit stops, you'll soon be docking your boat with precision and making it look easy… like a pro.

High winds and current can make docking a more delicate operation, so look for the best place to dock given the layout of the marina.

Preparing to Dock

Step by Step

▷ Prior to approaching any dock, have your boat and passengers prepared. The stronger the wind and current, the less optional this is.

▷ At least 2 dock lines (1 bow line and 1 stern line) should be connected to the boat cleats, untangled and readied. Dock lines should be on all cleats if unsure of docking arrangement.

▷ Any necessary dock fenders should be placed at dock level on the docking side of the boat.

▷ A boat hook can also be handy to have out and ready.

▷ When preparing to dock in windy conditions, if your boat has a collapsible Bimini top, it can definitely help to fold and lay it down flat, or at least fold it prior to approaching the dock. On many boats this will significantly reduce windage and docking difficulty.

▷ When approaching any dock located within a No Wake zone, your speed should already be down to idle speed, of course. For any other dock – and in general – use the following guidelines:

1. By the time your boat is within 100 yards, your speed should be reduced to below 10 mph.

2. By the time your boat is within 50 yards, your speed should be slowed to 5 mph or less.

3. Within 3 boat lengths of the dock, you should be just barely drifting in toward it. This will reduce chances of damage or injury.

Approaching the Dock

1. Be confident – you're prepared, you know how your boat handles, and you're well aware that slowly coasting in neutral makes it easy to control and adjust your approach.

2. Anticipate – scan the entire area ahead of you to look for any boats that are on the move or about to cast off. Yield to other boats where appropriate, and also be aware of any trailing close behind – in case you need to back up. Think out your planned line of approach to the dock ahead of time, accounting for wind or current and how they'll either help or hinder you.

3. Concentrate – aim for your targeted docking spot, keeping your hand on the shift lever, ready to adjust your momentum at any second.

4. Use proper technique and finesse – remember, if you gauge your speed to slowly coast in neutral upon approach, you'll only need intermittent, subtle throttle bumps to control your momentum – regardless of whether forward or reverse gear is needed.

5. If wind or current will slowly push your boat toward the dock, set up your final approach to sidle parallel to it, using just enough reverse thrust to counter your momentum.

6. If docking into a wind, try to approach at a narrow angle of less than 45 degrees, turning just short of the dock so as to slide alongside parallel. A steady wind can make this easier said than done.

Whenever possible, have a passenger ready to toss a dock line to a dock attendant once you're close enough.

If docking into a wind, try to approach at a narrow angle of less than 45 degrees, turning just short of the dock to slide alongside it.

Nice-n-slow, wake-free final approach.

Gradual turn to position boat parallel to dock.

Using correct methods, no help needed on dock.

Tie off boat fairly snug to dock for safety.

So if necessary, there's a simple method to counteract the wind: The bow line can be wrapped around a piling or dock cleat, and then with the motor turned toward the dock, use slow but steady reverse power to pull the boat parallel to the dock.

7. Any time you feel uncomfortable with how your approach is going, just start over (if possible). Docking skills require just the right balance of patience and urgency; too much or not enough of either has been the root cause of many a boat docking mishap. But even the most experienced boaters accidentally bump into a dock or other boat once in a while, especially in windy conditions. Bottom line: The more you control momentum, the less likely any damage will result.

8. When in a docking situation involving a lot of backing up in reverse, such as when fighting a strong current or wind that keeps pushing you off

target, some boaters find that it's helpful to stand at the helm with a sideways stance. This makes it easier to turn your head astern and forward, rather than constantly wrenching your neck to look back over your shoulder.

9. When pulling up parallel to a dock, if forward momentum continues to carry your boat forward – as is usually the case – the stern line will be needed first so that it can be pulled on from the dock or wrapped a half-turn around a piling to bring the boat to a complete stop. The bow line won't do much good (yet) for this docking method, since you can't exactly push on a rope, and pulling on it from the dock will allow the rear of the boat to swing out and away from the dock. Sound like a no-brainer? You'd be surprised how often people pulling forward alongside a dock, mistakenly toss their bow line over first to a dock attendant.

Docking Scenarios

Each docking scenario you approach may be slightly different – the first time you see it. But with practice you'll gain confidence and control with your boat's maneuvering and your own handling skills. Caution is the best rule to let guide your approaches. Illustrated below is a common tight-quarters maneuvering scenario, where the boater must pull into a slip directly between pilings.

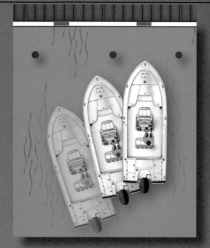

Following the below instructions will swing the bow to the right, which will allow you to move straight into the slip.

In single outboard vessel, when approaching at an angle, shifting into gentle reverse power while simultaneously turning the wheel away from the direction of the turn, will slow forward momentum and at the same time pull the bow around for a straight, bow-forward entrance into the slip.

In a vessel with two engines, the same straightening of the boat can be controlled by powering with the throttles. Gently forward on the port engine and reverse on the starboard will pull the bow to the right.

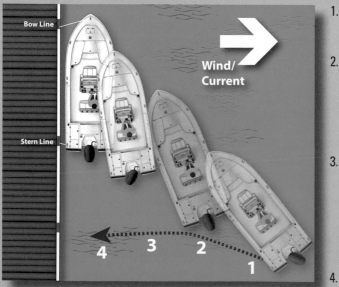

1. Final approach should be at about a 45-degree angle to dock. Bow and stern lines ready.
2. Coasting in neutral, turn wheel to position the boat parallel with dock. If wind/current is strong enough to push boat away, it may be necessary to initially attach only bow line to the dock.
3. If wind has pushed boat's stern from dock, shift into reverse with rear of motor turned to dock. Easy does it. Not too much reverse power is needed to swing stern. Promptly secure both bow and stern lines to dock cleats.
4. Tie boat to dock with lines.

1. On final approach, coast in neutral and let wind/current take your boat to dock. You shouldn't need to use any forward thrust. You will, however, usually need to use reverse power to slow and control your momentum.
2. With practice, you'll learn how to time your final, hard turn of the wheel in order to rotate your boat to the side that you want to dock on and "land" flush, softly.
3. The goal is to time your turn to have the boat positioned parallel to the dock by the time you've reached it.

Wind/Current

Bow Line

Stern Line

3

2

1

Each docking scenario you approach may be slightly different – the first time you see it. But with practice you'll gain confidence and control with your boat's maneuvering and your own handling skills.

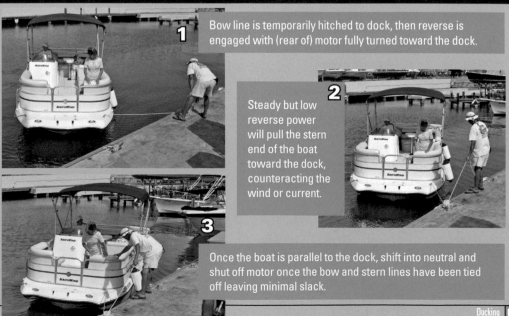

1 Bow line is temporarily hitched to dock, then reverse is engaged with (rear of) motor fully turned toward the dock.

2 Steady but low reverse power will pull the stern end of the boat toward the dock, counteracting the wind or current.

3 Once the boat is parallel to the dock, shift into neutral and shut off motor once the bow and stern lines have been tied off leaving minimal slack.

A 180 or U-turn in close quarters must be done at a slow speed and low RPM throughout the entire maneuver.

The One-Eighty

A skill often needed for slow-maneuvering in a marina and docking in close quarters is the ability to rotate a boat 180 degrees on its axis, or to turn the boat around in a very sharp, 180-degree U-turn. Sometimes this can be done in one hard turn of the steering wheel, and other times it requires a very compact 3-point turn. Which one, depends on the amount of open maneuvering space, the skill level of the boat operator, and the handling characteristics of the boat.

For some boats that have a twin motor setup, better control is made possible by the ability to put one motor in reverse and one in forward to spin the boat with the thrust of the motors. But on certain models, the outboards are mounted so close together that the benefit of the twin motors versus a single motor, is minimal.

Your steering wheel must be fully turned all the way. Being half-way turned just won't cut it.

A 180 can sometimes be done with one hard turn of the steering wheel.

Stay near the middle or your turning area. Don't swing out wide before starting your turn.

Allow any rotational momentum enough time to actually assist in the rotation of the boat.

Over-acceleration during a 180 will not only over-widen the turn, it will also roll out an unintended wake.

Unless it's windy, turning a tight 180 in a confined area shouldn't be difficult, but it sure can give some inexperienced boaters fits.

Unless it's windy, turning a tight one-eighty in a confined area shouldn't be difficult, but it sure can give some inexperienced boaters fits. Usually they struggle with it only because they haven't been taught the right techniques, which are actually easy and very effective once you learn them. Like docking, it is a skill that requires practice and familiarity with your particular boat. And adopting the same guidelines and principles that apply to docking – along with the following tips – can help you learn to easily turn your boat right around in any marina.

1. Take it slow and low... slow speed and low RPM throughout the entire maneuver.

2. Stay near the middle of your turning area – don't swing out wide before starting your turn and get too close to surrounding boats or obstacles, which is a common mistake. It's a boat, not an eighteen-wheeler.

3. Your steering wheel must be fully turned all the way. Being half-way turned or even most-of-the-way turned just won't cut it. This applies whether attempting a 180 degree on-axis rotation, a sharp U-turn, or a compact 3-point turn. For 3-point turns, every time you reverse direction and counter-steer, the wheel must be fully turned or else you'll wind up making it a 6-point turn.

4. Very few boats will turn sharply if you over-accelerate during your maneuver(s). Any more than low-RPM, light power will usually lunge the boat off axis or force it into more of a straight direction than a rotation or sharp turn.

5. If you accidentally give it too much gas, try not to overcorrect by dropping into the opposite gear and high-revving it back to your initial spot. This can set off a flurry of back-and-forth over-corrections. The more power you apply in one direction, the more you'll want to counter with in the opposite direction.

6. Be patient. Keep the wheel turned hard (left or right) and allow any rotational momentum enough time to actually assist in the rotation of the boat. Depending on your boat's handling characteristics, you may find that once your turn transitions into a spin or at least very sharp turn, you can just shift into neutral and let momentum complete the maneuver.

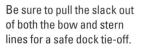

Be sure to pull the slack out of both the bow and stern lines for a safe dock tie-off.

Safe and Proper Dock Tie-off

When tying up against a dock, be careful not to leave more than a few inches of slack in between the boat and the dock. A common and potentially dangerous oversight, slack dock lines make it way too easy for someone to inadvertently push the boat away from the dock while boarding or stepping off, or loading or unloading. If this happens unexpectedly, someone could step into the gap that wasn't there just a second ago and take a nasty fall.

To prevent this, be sure to pull the slack out of both the bow line and stern line. If your bow and stern cleats don't happen to line up perpendicular to the dock cleats or tie-off points (they often won't), it may be necessary to pull and tie off roughly equal lengths of dock line. This is so that neither line will be too long and have too much of an angle in it to keep the boat firmly against the dock.

Someone could accidentally step into the gap that wasn't there just a second ago.

The safety requirement for a slack-free tie-off naturally applies to docking situations where people need access onto or off of a boat. However, for certain longer term dock tie-offs when no one will be boarding, there are necessary tie-off methods that actually require slack in the dock lines to allow for wind and wave or tidal action. We'll discuss these in Chapter 14.

When tying off your boat to a dock, to protect it (and any adjacent boats) from scratches, dings and damage caused by wind and water movements, take the time to carefully set your dock lines. Tie them off at the appropriate angles and lengths necessary to prevent contact with anything other than the dock that your boat is tied up to. If necessary, tie off an opposing spring line or two for additional constraint. Make sure that your dock fenders are securely set so that they won't shift out of a protective position.

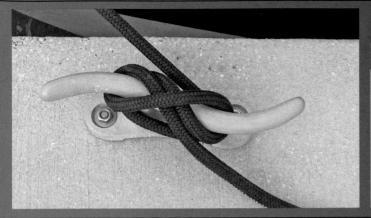

Cleat Hitch

A cleat hitch is quick and simple to tie, holds very well, and is also quickly and easily released.

Doubled Cleat Hitch

For long-term tie-offs or for an extra-strong hold, simply double up your cleat hitch.

What *Knot* To Do

What *NOT* to do; cleat tie-off overkill – looping up a mound of figure 8's, or weaving a macrame like this is completely unnecessary because it doesn't hold any better than a double cleat-hitch, and is needlessly tedious to untie.

Cleat Hitch Coiled

Coil up the excess dock line to reduce trip hazards on the dock.

No dock cleats? Rather than tying to the pilings...

... just bring each dock line one half turn around the piling and back to your boat's cleat.

The Amazing Cleat Hitch

When docking or tying off to a piling or another boat, always tie off using a cleat hitch – the one hitch that every boater should learn to do. It's super-quick and simple to tie, holds very well (if done right), and is also quickly and easily released. This is important because there will be times when a boat must be quickly untied, and you don't want to be struggling with an unnecessarily over-done hitch or knot.

What's so amazing about a cleat hitch? It's a prime example of "Less is more." Like many hitches – as long as it's tied correctly – the greater the pulling force on the line, the tighter a cleat hitch will grip and hold onto the cleat. This "holds" true despite the fact that it's so extraordinarily simple in its design, and is so quickly and easily secured.

If docking where there are no dock cleats to tie off to, utilize the dock's pilings. But rather than wrapping your dock lines several turns around the pilings and tying directly to them – an unnecessary and often ineffective chore – just bring each dock line one half turn around the piling and back to your boat's cleat, and secure it with a cleat hitch. This also facilitates dock line adjustments from onboard the boat.

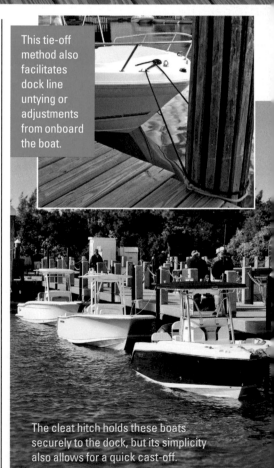

This tie-off method also facilitates dock line untying or adjustments from onboard the boat.

The cleat hitch holds these boats securely to the dock, but its simplicity also allows for a quick cast-off.

Guidelines for Tying Off Your Boat

These are a few basic scenarios for tying off your boat and leaving it at the dock for a few hours, days or even longer. In saltwater, precautions must be taken for rising and falling tides, which present dangers to boats tied at docks. If in doubt, always consult the dockmaster for best tying off practices.

In a marina slip, stern-to seems to be the common way to tie-off. It gives crew and passengers a safe, convenient point for boarding. Bow lines (1 and 2) should be put in place first as you back in the slip, cleated or hitched to pilings. These lines maintain lateral stability in the slip, while providing for vertical rise and fall resulting from tides and waves. Secondly and most importantly, include at least one midship spring line forward (3) for latitudinal control, to ensure the stern remains safely off the dock. Additional spring lines may be called for, in some cases. Finally tie the stern lines (4 and 5) crossing above or behind the engine and hitched to opposing cleats.

Similar procedure is used to tie off bow-to, if desired.

In general, always seek guidance from dockmasters and/or local boaters on the impacts of tides and currents, particularly in the case of a fixed (non-floating) dock. When in doubt, make careful observation at regular intervals, particularly during the first days and nights, and adjust your lines accordingly.

Note: Where safe to do so, an anchor of appropriate configuration may be used in place of an offshore piling, if one is unavailable.

Tip: If you'll be keeping your boat in the water for several days, once you have your lines secured at the ideal length, leave them tied to the pilings on cleats when you leave, making your next return trip a snap.

For tying off briefly beam-to, as at a boat ramp or floating dock, stern and bow lines (1 and 2) are commonly hitched to the nearest cleat.

For longer periods, to account for the rise and fall of tides (for non-floating docks), you must lengthen the bow and stern lines by cleating off to points father forward or astern. In order to keep the boat in place, add midship spring lines fore and aft (4 and 5). Specially made boating fenders should be used to protect the hull.

Disclaimer: Any time you're tying dock lines to a boat that you'll leave in the water through a change of tides or longer, your lines must accommodate for the changing water levels or the boat will be at risk.

Casting Off

1 Before casting off, let your motor warm up for a few minutes and make sure it's running smoothly. Outboards will sometimes begin to idle roughly before eventually breaking down, so it's best to check the issue at the dock – rather than heading out and just hoping it'll be OK.

without too much boat traffic coming and going.

4. Account for wind direction when you're about to untie your boat. If there's a breeze or wind blowing from the general direction of either the bow or stern, always untie the dock line that is downwind first, so that the boat will remain in place until you can untie the windward dock line.

5. Check to be sure all lines are secured inside the boat. Carelessly placed dock lines can be an accident waiting to happen. They could fall in and

Before casting off for even the best boating conditions, as seen here, be sure to go through last-minute checks.

If there's a breeze or wind blowing from the general direction of either the bow or stern, always tie the dock line that is downwind first.

2. Do you have everything needed? Plenty of gas and water, PFDs for everyone, your cellphones, sunglasses, sunscreen, a clear local weather radar, the kids used the facilities, and the captain is sober?

3. Look to see that you have clear path out,

get tangled in the propeller, or cause someone to trip and fall overboard. Use velcro straps to keep your lines secured and well-organized.

6. If everyone is completely onboard and properly seated, you're all set to go.

Casting Off Scenarios

1. If the wind/current is light or average - with a good, strong shove-off - it's usually feasible to push away from the dock, bow first. But if higher winds and/or stiff currents are keeping your boat pinned against the dock and making this too difficult, it will be necessary to back away from the dock using the following method.
2. With only the bow line still attached to the dock, turn the rear of the motor(s) away from the dock, and use reverse thrust power to slowly pull the boat's stern out and away from the dock.
3. Once the boat's stern is backed out and the boat is more perpendicular to the dock, you can then release the bow line and continue to back away from the dock.

Casting off with wind and/or current blowing/moving toward the dock

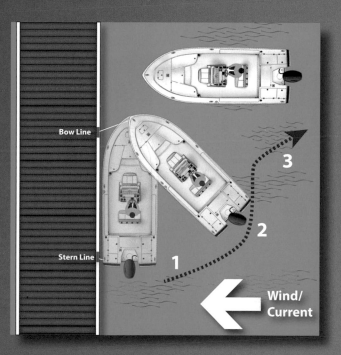

Casting off with wind and/or current coming from the direction of the dock

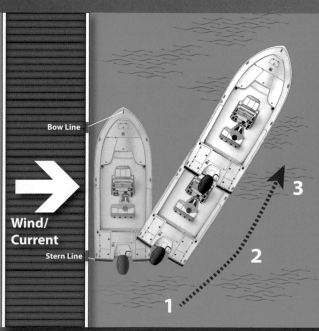

1. Release the bow line first so that your bow will lead out away from the dock.
2. Release the stern line last.
3. Simply let the wind or current push your boat off the dock and head out on your boating adventure.

CHAPTER 12

Getting to Where the Fish Are

Now more than ever before there are tools literally at the angler's fingertips that can help him find his way to the fish – inshore and offshore. Onboard electronics, including multiscreen displays with sonar readings, sea surface temperature charts and maps with waypoints, as well as radar and other tools all lend assistance to anglers targeting specific species. Once you have the tools, it's only a matter of practice with them to gain proficiency in their use. SB

Waypoints are the most valuable asset a fisherman can have for a successful day of angling and are highly coveted.

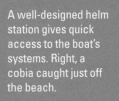

A well-designed helm station gives quick access to the boat's systems. Right, a cobia caught just off the beach.

GPSmap 740s

Home | Mark | XM | Menu

GPS Speed
0.0 kt

GPS Heading
006 M

Depth
177.3 ft

GPS Position
N 27°27.659'
W080°19.199'

GARMIN

Charts

Charts come in two versions, paper and electronic. The paper charts that most boaters are familiar with are the least expensive and have a variety of fish finding help, including topo lines, reefs and wrecks. Two advantages of paper are that you can make notes right on the chart, plus you can plan your next fishing trip in the comfort of your own home. The electronic charts that come in most GPS units have a built-in broad version that covers the U.S. and a lot of the islands. If you want more detailed data, additional memory chips are available for many units that have premium mapping and more information about points of interest. For instance, when you toggle the unit's cursor over the top of a particular marina, a pop-up screen will list all of the services offered at this location, along with contact info. Now move the cursor over to a buoy and a pop-up screen describes the nav aid. Adding one of these detailed mapping chips lets you get the maximum use out of the unit's capabilities.

The GPS unit above comes with navigational charts, which contain information that pops up on command. Additional charts for other areas or with premium mapping information, below, can be uploaded to the unit.

Adding one of these detailed mapping chips lets you get the maximum use out of the unit's capabilities.

Waypoints

The series of Florida Sportsman Fish Chips contain valuable GPS locations of fishing hotspots that can be uploaded to your GPS unit.

Now that your boat has the ability to navigate safely out to a fishing spot, how do you know where to go to find the fish? Waypoints! They are the most valuable asset a fisherman can have for a successful day of angling and are highly coveted. If you don't have a circle of fishing buddies willing to relinquish their secret spots, a viable alternative is an electronic waypoint list – like the Florida Sportsman Fish Chip – which includes hundreds of fishing hot spots, along with giving locations of underwater ledges, wrecks, reefs and structure. Furthermore, the FS Fish Chip even lists the species of fish you're most likely to catch there. You upload the additional Fish Chip waypoint list to your GPS

unit and it can help you pinpoint where to go, based on the fish you would like to target by overlaying icons on top of your electronic charts, showing their locations. Getting to the spot you choose is now just a matter of sliding the unit's cursor over the top of a particular fishing spot and activating the unit's GO TO feature to give you heading and track information to the waypoint.

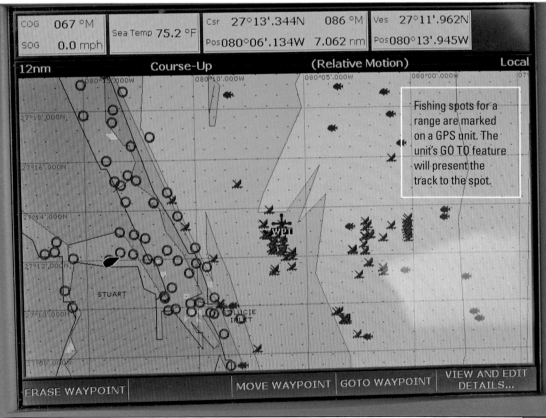

Fishing spots for a range are marked on a GPS unit. The unit's GO TO feature will present the track to the spot.

Fish Finders

After you have located what you think is the perfect fishing spot, how do know if there are fish there to be caught? The best way is by using a sonar fish finder to see what's below the boat. There are many units available for every size of boat manufactured, and picking the right unit depends on the type of fishing you will be doing and the depth of thve water you will be fishing in.

For the shallow water fisherman, a fish finder is really more of a depth finder. If you are fishing in water less than 3-feet deep, running the boat over the top of an area you plan to fish will pretty much clear the flat. In this instance you shouldn't need a large display or a unit that has a lot of features. What you mainly will need to know is how deep the water is to help you navigate to a fishing spot. Catching fish in skinny water is normally associated with casting away from the boat and not fishing straight down.

As you venture out farther into deeper water, this is where you will see the benefits of having a good quality fish finder. Fish are drawn to underwater structures. Whether it's a reef, ledge or wreck, find the structure and you'll find the fish. Having the ability to pinpoint structure or bottom contours will help you locate fish faster. Depending on current, bait and water temperature, fish will move from place to place. In some cases, even on the same reef, you will find more fish on the upcurrent side or concentrated in a certain area of the reef. That's where a fish finder is invaluable. It will give you the advantage of being able to fish where the larger concentrations of fish are. Whether you are bottom fishing or trolling, knowing there are fish down there will save you time

Onboard sonar fish finder displays the bottom, other structure and any fish marking around that structure and additional info like GPS and temperature readings, among others.

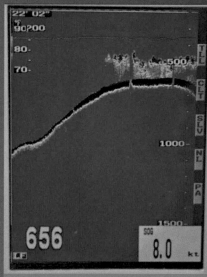

A display of fish holding above bottom in approximately 650 feet of water before a dropoff plunges deeper. Tuning and reading a display takes practice.

and fuel, plus increase your catch ratio.

Learning to understand what you are seeing on a fish finder's display screen will take some time. Reading through the owner's manual may help you learn how to turn on and adjust the unit, but there is no substitute for time on the water. Start off by using your chart to find an area that has a defined relief, or better yet some type of underwater structure. Slowly run the boat back and forth across the structure and you will begin to see a picture emerge. Along with the bottom and the structure, part of what you will see on the screen will be baitfish, larger predatory fish or even a thermocline in the water. Learning to distinguish one target from another will take some practice. For example, bait fish normally show up as a concentrated mass, larger fish will look like an inverted V and a thermocline might look like a faint bottom suspended in the water column. Once you start to understand what is being displayed on the screen, it will make a huge difference in your confidence and your catch.

Reading Water Conditions

Using sonar units effectively will reveal much about water conditions. Below, sea surface temperature charts can help direct anglers to the best spots on any given day.

An angler tuned into the environment will always be looking at the water for signs of fish and changes in depth. Changes in water color, ripples on the surface and slicks are all indicators that you should be looking for to help you locate your quarry and navigate.

Offshore rips are currents and upwellings where debris and floating grasses will form a line. These lines quite often form along a drop-off. Small baitfish will use this flotsam as cover, and their presence will attract larger predatory fish, and so starts the food chain. Find an offshore rip, which many times will have a defined change in water color, and you've found your place to start fishing.

Slicks are shiny areas on the surface of the water that are formed by oils being released from baitfish that are being fed on by larger predatory fish. Sometimes you can actually smell these slicks as they give off a strong, pungent order. A slick is a sure sign that actively feeding fish are nearby. Baitfish are structure oriented, so there's a good bet that there's structure below.

In the shallows, many fish are quite at home in just enough water to cover their backs. As they feed and move across the flats, they will actually form V-shaped wakes that give away their direction of travel. A long cast with a soft entry, well ahead of the fish, will often bring a strike. As wind and current move across a flat, any place that has a series of ripples is a sure sign that portion is very shallow also.

In this sea-surface chart made by ROFFS, colors indicate temps and hot spots are marked.

Find an offshore rip, which many times will have a defined change in water color, and you've found your place to start fishing.

Amberjack often congregate above wrecks and mark on sonar finders.

A Stealthy Approach

In deeper water, say 50 feet or more, a stealthy approach is not as necessary. Wind conditions and water clarity will come into play, but the fish are less bothered by your presence the deeper they are in the water column. Motoring over the top of a wreck in deep water is fine so you can get a look at the structure and fish that will show up on your bottom machine. Continuing to motor upwind and current to drop your anchor and let the boat drift back to the waypoint is an acceptable practice.

The reverse of that is true in shallower water on the patch reefs, rivers, bays and flats. Here you will need to actually stop short of the waypoint you intend to fish so that you don't alert the fish to your arrival. That's where the addition of a bow-mounted trolling motor, as mentioned earlier, will allow you to sneak up within range of your fishing spot.

Anglers fancast around mangrove banks and deeper waters as their boat's trolling motor pulls them along to cover more water.

Here you will need to actually stop short of the waypoint you intend to fish so that you don't alert the fish to your arrival.

To fish super shallow water, like the flats in the Keys, a poling platform is a great advantage. These small platforms that are mounted on legs above the outboard allow you to control the boat and fish from an elevated position. Being higher lets you see farther out onto the flat and deeper into the water, but the biggest advantage of a poling platform is using a push pole from the platform to quietly propel the boat across the flat without making a sound. When you see a fish you want to present an offering to, it's easy to maneuver the boat with a push pole by sliding the stern end around, and when in range, you can drive the push pole into the bottom to hold your position.

Propulsion by push pole is the time-honored method to fish very shallow water, like flats.

For boats that fish slightly deeper water but where noise is still a concern, a shallow water anchor will allow you to hold the boat's position in water up to 12 feet deep without having to deploy a noisy anchor and chain. Shallow-water anchors mount to the transom of the boat and when activated, drive a fiberglass spike into the bottom with a hydraulic ram or worm gear drive. This would let you ease the boat into casting range of a fishing area with your trolling motor, and with a remote control, lower the shallow water anchor without making a sound.

At times when fishing offshore, stealth will come into play as well. As fish get more pressure, they tend to become boat shy and when they are feeding near the surface, a boat passing overhead will drive them deeper. If you happen upon a school of fish, like tuna, busting bait on the surface, don't run in on them. Rarely will such an approach not disrupt the action. It's far better to deploy your baits well away from the school and troll parallel past the school of feeding fish. Once the boat is beyond the fish, make a hard turn half way around the school and then straighten out your course. This will drag your baits through the school without the boat disturbing them.

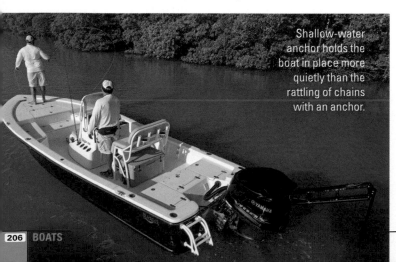

Shallow-water anchor holds the boat in place more quietly than the rattling of chains with an anchor.

Chirp Sonar

One of the latest innovations in sonar units is called CHIRP. The technology uses the same system as always, the transducer and the unit to display the information gathered.

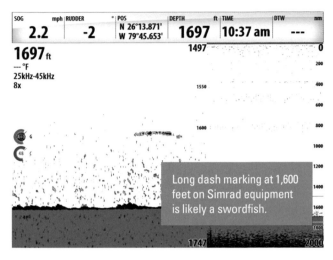

SOG	mph	RUDDER	°	POS	DEPTH	ft	TIME	DTW	nm
2.2		-2		N 26°13.871' W 79°45.653'	1697		10:37 am	---	

1697 ft
--- °F
25kHz-45kHz
8x

Long dash marking at 1,600 feet on Simrad equipment is likely a swordfish.

The transducer, of course, is the working part of a sonar fishfinder. It converts electrical pulses into sound, transmits and receives the sound (the echo in "echosounding"), then converts the return into an electrical pulse that the processor renders on the screen. You might think of a transducer as a bat's voice box; processor as the bat's brain. As the pulses strike fish, the bottom and other objects below, the duration of the returns varies, represented by the changing lines on the screen.

For years, anglers have used sonar equipment with fixed-frequency or dual-frequency pulses, typically 50 or 200 kilohertz. These systems performed – and continue to perform – very well, depending of course on a variety of factors.

Thing is, some targets and details are missed, depending on how fast the boat is moving, how close the target might be to another object, beamwidth of the pulse, output power and other factors. Maybe not a big deal, if you're mainly hunting for very large things such as wrecks or ledges. But if you're trying to "see" the sonar profile of a predatory fish within a mass of sardines 200 or even 2,000 feet beneath the boat, you're basically a bat winging through the woods in pursuit of a mosquito.

So why not do what bats do?

That's where CHIRP comes in. That translates to Compressed High Intensity Radar Pulse, and it's basically bat-speak: Like the winged mammals, CHIRP transducers deliver bursts of sound that sweep across a spectrum of frequencies. Not just one tone, but many. The "L" part of the Airmar B265LH transducer, for instance, indicates Low range: From 42 to 65 kHz, specifically. This also equates to a cone angle, 25- to 16-degree bandwidth. The Low range is ideal for marking big fish, down deep, as it produces a wider cone angle than the High range.

For complex reasons, multi-spectrum CHIRP transducer/processor combos like the B265LH and BSM-2 also deliver this high target-discrimination at far greater depths than one would expect with traditional sonar systems, at least those falling within the realm and budget of sportfishermen.

With the help of sonar, daytime swordfishing is now in reach of more recreational anglers.

CHAPTER 13

Boat Maintenance

One aspect of boat ownership that has proven to be both important and beneficial is a diligent routine of preventative maintenance and care. Getting into a regular habit of doing simple maintenance procedures and sticking to manufacturers' recommended service schedules will go a long way toward keeping your boat operating at peak performance as well as extending the life of your motor.

The boat owners who manage to "maintain" long-term happiness with their boat purchase tend to be the more conscientious ones who view routine maintenance as much more of necessity than an option or inconvenience. SB

The best way to prevent any kind of mechanical failure is to proactively maintain and check all of the systems on your boat, motor and trailer.

Routine maintenance will go a long way toward keeping your boat operating at peak performance – as well as extending the life of your motor.

An exceptionally well-maintained, renovated 1986 Boston Whaler.

Keep It Running Like New

What could fail mechanically to cause boating accidents? Anything at all that could cause a motor to stall. Fuel system problems and corroded electrical component issues are two of the most common root causes. If your motor stalls at the wrong moment and won't restart, you could literally be left powerless to prevent or avoid a collision. If your steering system fails, then obviously you could suddenly be in serious trouble. Both cable and hydraulic steering systems can fail if not maintained and checked regularly. If a shift or throttle cable snaps, you'll instantly be unable to fully-control your boat.

The best way to prevent any sort of mechanical failure – or at least to greatly-reduce the likelihood – is to proactively maintain and check all of the mechanical and electrical systems throughout your boat, motor, and trailer on a regular, scheduled basis.

5 Excellent Reasons to Maintain Your Boat, Motor and Trailer

1. Maintenance costs are typically a fraction of repair costs.
2. A well-maintained boat will retain a higher value.
3. Your boat will always be ready to go when you are.
4. Peace of mind out on the water, and on the road – knowing that all of your equipment will provide safe and reliable performance every time you go boating.
5. Boat maintenance is a real safety concern. USCG statistics rank mechanical failure as one of the top 5 primary contributing factors in boating accidents.

If your motor stalls at the wrong moment, you could literally be left powerless to avoid a collision.

Don't Forget to Flush

Motor flushing procedures vary by outboard brand, so check your manual for proper instructions.

If your boat is used in saltwater, brackish water, or dirty/polluted water, the easiest and most important maintenance procedure you can do to prevent interior corrosion in your outboard motor is simply a freshwater flush after each use. This will dislodge and flush out sand, mud, silt, salt or contaminants that have been drawn into the motor's cooling system by the water pump. If neglected, deposits can accumulate and clog or corrode the cooling passages, sensors and thermostats. Restricted water flow not only causes a motor to run hot, it also promotes exhaust system corrosion due to increased exhaust temperatures.

Motor flushing procedures vary by outboard brand, so check your owner's manual for the proper instructions. Thankfully, most late-model outboards have easy-to-use, hose attachment hardware, or a flush port built right onto the motor to conveniently attach a garden hose to. However, this method of flushing must never be done while the motor is running, and for best results, should be done right after shutting the motor off and tilting it all the way up.

The most thorough flushing is the traditional method that requires the motor to be tilted down and running in neutral, with its lower-unit raw water intakes attached to a running hose by a motor flusher (ear muffs).

Also necessary every time any boat has been used in brackish or saltwater is a thorough freshwater rinse-down of the boat, motor and trailer – top to bottom, front to back. Saltwater left to dry on any boat surface – not just metals – will leave a salt residue that facilitates and hastens rust, corrosion, deterioration or fading of virtually any material on your boat except glass, especially when combined with constant sun exposure. So after flushing your motor, hose off everything, including all canvas, upholstery, metal framework and railings, the motor and the trailer.

Outboard motor flush attachment connected to a garden hose.

Thorough outboard flushing is best done with a traditional motor flusher while the motor is running (below).

Depending on the severity, corroded battery terminals or cables can cause a host of problems ranging from unreliable starting, to an electrical fire.

How to Spot Early Signs of Potential Problems

Even if your boat is performing like new in every way, when your motor manufacturer's required or recommended periodic maintenance services become due, they should still be taken care of, especially if you're under warranty. Routinely replacing the spark plugs, filters, oil and fluid, water pump impeller and other components as recommended by the manufacturer will keep your motor running reliably, and for many years to come.

In between the scheduled maintenances, keep a close eye on anything and everything that could be a precursor to an inevitable repair or replacement. Truth is, there almost always seems to be one or two upkeep-related chores or minor fixes that could use a bit of special attention on a boat. Whether you enjoy taking care of mechanical matters yourself, or prefer to have someone else handle them, proactiveness is the key to keeping your boat and trailer in top-notch condition. Here are the more common issues every boat owner should watch for and address sooner rather than later:

➤ Loose hardware or fittings, and fraying straps or lines.

There almost always seems to be one or two minor fixes that could use some special attention.

➤ Corrosion forming on battery terminals, terminal blocks, fuses, fuse panels and holders, and inside of wiring harness connectors. Clean even slightly-corroded electrical fittings with a wire brush, reconnect them, and then protect with a marine heavy-duty corrosion inhibitor spray. Wiring harness connectors with corroded contacts should be replaced A.S.A.P.

➤ If your battery is exposed to constant moisture, it should be installed in a marine battery box.

➤ Outboard water flow indicator (aka: tell-tale, pee-stream/hole, pisser): When the motor is running, water must be streaming from the nipple hole or outflow tube to confirm good water flow and cooling system circulation. If it isn't, or indicates weak flow, this usually means debris is clogged just inside the hole. TIP: Always keep onboard a short strip of plastic such as the thin, red tube that comes with spray cans, or a thin piece of weedeater line. Use it to clear out the debris buildup while the motor is idling in neutral. If there is no clog, then the water pump is probably bad. Never continue to run a motor that isn't circulating cooling water. This would cause severe overheating and could result in a blown motor.

> Shift lever: If it has to be muscled into or out of gear, or it becomes difficult to accelerate the throttle, this usually means that one or more of the cables is worn out and needs to be replaced before it snaps.

> Cable-controlled steering system: If the wheel becomes difficult to turn, the motor end of the cable needs to be greased. If that doesn't loosen up the steering, then it usually indicates a worn out steering cable that needs to be replaced before it breaks.

> Hydraulic steering system: if there is any loose play in the steering wheel in relation to its turning of the motor, or if there is a delayed response, then either air is trapped in the system or there is a hydraulic fluid leak. If these or any other malfunctions are affecting the steering system, it would be extremely unsafe to operate the boat. It should be repaired by a qualified marine tech.

> Check fuel lines and the primer bulb for cracks, cuts or abrasions.

> Check that fuel-line clamps and fittings are rust-free, seat properly and don't leak.

> Check the bilge pump for good water flow. If it's weak it could be partially clogged with bilge debris, or the pump motor is on its last leg and needs to be replaced.

> Check behind the prop for fishing line that can get wound into the prop shaft and damage the lower unit seal, allowing water to get in and gearcase oil to leak out.

> Starting difficulties, rough idle, hesitation or sputtering, and lack of top-end power are all obvious signs that something is wrong and needs to be diagnosed and repaired before the issue(s) gets worse, causes additional problems, or completely shuts the motor down.

Preventative Maintenance Anyone Can Do

> Every 6 months spray marine heavy-duty corrosion inhibitor onto exposed metal surfaces on the powerhead (under the cowling). Also spray the battery terminals, wire terminal blocks, motor cowling latches, door and hatch latches and hinges, and seat swivel/adjustment hardware.
(But don't spray it on the timing belt, oxygen sensor or anodes.)

> Every 6 months apply marine-grade grease to all lubrication points as shown in your owner's manual to keep moving parts functioning smoothly, and to help prevent saltwater intrusion and corrosion.

> Regularly check 4-cycle oil for both correct level and cleanliness. If it feels gritty between your fingertips or is super-black, it's time for an oil and filter change.

> Replace the fuel water separator every 50 hours of use with a new 10-micron filter.

> Always make sure that the battery switch is turned off, or disconnect the battery whenever the boat will sit unused for more than a few weeks. For non-maintenance-free batteries, check for low water levels and use only distilled water to refill (wear eye protection).

> Try not to allow long periods of non-use. They'll take a toll on your motor.

Replace your fuel water separator every 50 hours of operation with a new, 10-micron filter sized for your motor.

Never crank your motor for more than 5 or 6 consecutive seconds.

If your motor will turn over but won't fire, try disconnecting and then reconnecting the kill switch.

The 5-Second Rule for Starting Your Motor (a Safety Tip)

Never crank your boat motor for more than 5 or 6 consecutive seconds, ever. What does this have to do with safety? A lot... your motor's ability to restart reliably once you're out on the water is vital to quickly getting back to shore should an incident or urgent matter arise. Continuous cranking without a successful start can and often will lead to problems beyond what is already causing the start issue, such as a dead battery or fried starter motor.

Many boaters don't realize that if a motor doesn't fire up and start running within the first 5 or 6 seconds of an initial attempt, it's not likely to start up and keep running on that attempt. The fact that our boats sit unused the majority of the time isn't a good thing for their mechanical health, and too many boat owners tend to neglect the regular maintenance required to keep their boats running reliably.

If your motor doesn't start within 6 seconds, stop and wait several seconds before trying again. If it still hasn't started and stayed running after 4 or 5 attempts, then something is obviously preventing a successful start, and it needs to be addressed. If

you simply keep cranking away multiple times – hoping against hope that it'll just somehow work out whatever is causing the problem – you're probably only going to make matters worse, not to mention the draining of your battery and the costly damage to your starting system's electrical components.

There are numerous mechanical issues that can prevent your motor from restarting after very recently cooperating just fine, but any attempt to describe all of the possible causes would be well beyond the scope of this book. The following not-too-technical suggestions apply to some of the most common, easily-resolved issues, and will sometimes do the trick:

First – if you turn the key but nothing happens at all, make sure that your shift lever is in the neutral position. Sometimes it can appear to be, but isn't quite there, so just "feel" it into the neutral position and try again. If that doesn't help, make sure that the battery cable terminals are tightly bolted. Also – if the boat has a battery switch, turn it off and on a few times to ensure that it's making full contact.

Next – disconnect and then reconnect the safety lanyard switch (kill switch). This sometimes works to "reset" or open the switching circuit, allowing motor ignition.

Then – if your boat's fuel system has one, re-prime the primer bulb several times or until it firms up. It's possible for some outboard motors to need a fuel line prime-up prior to every cold start.

If your boat or motor has a choke (applicable only to 2-stroke motors), be sure to activate the choke switch while starting if – and only if – the motor is cold or has had time to cool down... more than 30 minutes or so. Forgetting to choke a cold, choke-equipped motor could possibly flood the fuel system, which requires letting it sit for a good while before restarting. Also remember to deactivate the choke after the motor has started.

If these methods – combined with a bit of patience – don't get your motor to start, and assuming that you haven't already compounded the problem by draining your battery power, chances are you have a mechanical problem or fuel issue requiring repair.

Avoid Using Ethanol E10 Fuel If at all Possible

E10 is the controversial, very common fuel containing 10 percent ethanol blended with 90 percent gasoline. Since around 2006, and subsequently becoming much more widespread, E10 has been the only fuel option sold at the majority of gas stations and many marinas in the USA. Many gas pumps do not display "E10" anywhere

Many gas pumps don't display "E10" anywhere on them, but typically do display a label or sign indicating that the fuel being sold contains ethanol.

on or around them, but typically do display a label or sign indicating that the fuel being sold "Contains 10 percent or less ethanol" or "Contains up to 10 percent ethanol." If there is no indication at all, be sure to ask the gas station or marina manager whether or not their fuel contains ethanol, and if so what the percentage of it is. Many modern boat motors are able to be run on E10, but extra precautions must be taken to prevent contamination problems and subsequent damage. Any fuel containing more than 10 percent ethanol (E15 or E85 flex-fuel) will almost certainly damage a boat's fuel system.

Ethanol Properties that Cause Fuel System Problems

➢ Ethanol is a strong solvent. Gasoline containing ethanol or methanol can cause a formation of acid during storage and can damage the fuel system. It will clean and dissolve some parts of, and deposits within fuel systems, including fiberglass fuel tanks. These dissolved materials can clog filters or pass through and leave very harmful deposits in fuel injectors, carburetor jets, fuel pumps, valves, etc.

➢ Ethanol is hygroscopic, meaning it attracts and retains water. The lower the E10 fuel level in your tank, and the longer it sits there, the more likely water contamination is, resulting in a layer of alcohol and water forming at the bottom of your fuel tank. This is called phase separation, and can lead to damage within your fuel system and motor.

➢ Ethanol fuels have a relatively short life span. With so many different variables and factors

possible, there is no way to specify exactly how long any fuel can be expected to remain completely safe to use. However, given the right set of conditions, ethanol fuels can begin to deteriorate in as little as 15 days.

➢ Ethanol also reduces fuel efficiency compared to ethanol-free gas because ethanol contains about one-third less energy per gallon than gasoline does.

➢ Warranties don't cover fuel-related issues, so prevention is the only way to protect your boat – as well as your bank balance – from ethanol fuel-related issues. An internet search for "find ethanol free gas" will result in a few websites dedicated to providing updated lists of gas stations that sell ethanol-free gasoline, which does cost more, but is well worth the difference for boaters.

Dissected fuel line shows deterioration of inner layer, caused by E10 fuel.

Backing off of full throttle just a bit saves a significant amount of gas.

Does your local marina sell ethanol-free fuel? Check with the dockmaster if unsure.

No Access to Ethanol-free Gas? What To Do

If E10 fuel is your only available option, to help prevent the water contamination problems caused by ethanol, take the following precautions:

➤ Keep your fuel tank full with fresh gas and out of direct sunlight.

➤ Install a 10-micron fuel water separator in your boat between the gas tank and the motor. Frequently check it for excess water, and replace the filter every 50 hours of motor use.

➤ Purchase from a steadily-busy, newer gas station that sells a high-quality brand of fuel.

➤ Use a high-quality fuel stabilizer along with fresh fuel while your boat is stored. Keep in mind that fuel stabilizers do not help aged or contaminated fuel at all, and are most effective when immediately added to fuel that is fresh from the gas station or marina pump.

➤ Refer to your owner's manual for recommended proper storage procedures and also for fuel-type compatibility.

➤ Keep up with the specific fuel laws of your state; laws and fuel composition tend to change.

➤ Don't even think about putting fuel containing more than 10 percent ethanol in your boat's gas tank, such as E15 or E85 flex-fuel!

Fuel Saving Tips

1. Use only ethanol-free gasoline for the best possible fuel economy.
2. Don't cruise at full throttle. Backing off of full throttle just a bit will only reduce your speed by a few mph, but will save a significant amount of gas overall. Making a habit of this also helps to reduce the wear and tear on your motor, extending its life.
3. When turning your boat around to go back to retrieve a fallen skier or rider, never speed up to make long, wide-sweeping, high-speed turns as many boaters do. Instead, immediately slow down to make a much slower and sharper U-turn. This not only gets you back to them quicker, it also burns a lot less fuel over the course of a day.

Why Boats Are More Susceptible to Ethanol Fuel Contamination than Cars

Automobiles can have similar issues too, but are much more tolerant because of regular usage patterns and major differences in their fuel systems – specifically:

> Modern automotive fuel systems (the fuel filler, tank, fuel lines and motor components) are closed or non-vented. Once fuel is pumped into the tank, there is very little circulation of outside air (containing moisture) into the fuel system.
> Boats have vented fuel systems that allow moist air to circulate into the fuel tank as the

fuel is drawn out of the tank and as the fuel expands and contracts during heating and cooling cycles of the ambient air.

> Boats are operated and often stored in a very wet environment, increasing the risk of water directly entering the fuel system.
> Most automotive fuel tanks are smaller, and are refilled and refreshed much more frequently than boat fuel tanks, which often sit unused for many months.

If your motor gives you any warning indicator at all, don't let inconvenience be a reason to temporarily disregard it.

Warranty-Related Maintenance & Care Requirements for Outboard Motors

All new outboard motor warranties require certain periodic maintenance services to be done at the factory-recommended intervals, as detailed in the owner's manual. Skipping or taking care of them too late can void the warranty. For any maintenance you do yourself, such as 4-cycle motor oil and filter changes, always save the receipts in case you need to prove your service dates in the event of a major repair warranty claim that could be scrutinized.

Also remember that modern outboards electronically save data that can later be accessed by a technician's computer, revealing a surprising amount of diagnostic information about the history of how the motor has been run.

For example, if someone were to run their motor at excessively-high RPMs for an hour because they had accidentally driven their boat over a sandbar – result-

This sunken outboard won't be covered by warranty, which covers only normal use.

ing in a partially-spun hub (loose propeller) – and then decided to motor back to shore despite the screaming motor barely being able to move the boat along, the motor would be subjected to overheating and the possibility of internal damage. The over-revving and high temperatures from this event would be recorded in the motor's saved data, most-likely voiding any subsequent warranty coverage.

The moral of the story is to not ignore the obvious warning signs. If your motor sounds noticeably-different than it normally does, if you hear an audible system alarm beeping or sounding, or if you see a flashing warning indicator on your gauges or instruments, don't let inconvenience be a reason to temporarily disregard them. Warranty covers only normal use... continuing to run a motor that is alerting or indicating a problem could be considered abuse.

Trailer Maintenance

Keep a spare tire conveniently mounted to your boat trailer.

Warning: Towing a trailer with a bad wheel bearing can cause the wheel to completely detach from the axle, cutting it loose into surrounding traffic. Obviously this can not only lead to serious boat damage, but more importantly can be a dangerous road hazard that leads to a catastrophic accident. This scary scenario is actually not too uncommon, and is mostly due to neglected, regular trailer maintenance and checks. To help prevent this sort of boat-towing fiasco – as well as tire blow-outs and other common boat trailer troubles:

➤ Monitor your trailer tires for: low pressure, cracked sidewalls and worn tread. Trailers tires are more susceptible to blow-outs than automotive tires. Always keep them fully-inflated to the proper PSI, and use tire covers or protectant to prevent sidewall dry-rot.

➤ Frequently check your trailer wheel bearings:

A bad bearing can cause the wheel to detach from the axle.

Towing a boat on a trailer with tires that have low PSI or dry rot cracks is just asking for a blow-out.

to test for worn or damaged bearings, the trailer must be jacked up to check each wheel individually. Spin it by hand, listening closely for any grinding sound. Then grab the tire from opposite sides to check for excessive play by trying to rock the wheel back and forth. Each wheel should spin quietly and smoothly, and have no more than just the slightest hint of play. One way to tell if bearings are going bad or need to be repacked with grease is to tow your boat for 5 or 10 minutes, then park and check if the wheel hubs feel abnormally hot. If so, they should be inspected prior to further towing.

➤ Prior to every towing trip, check your trailer's lights, brake lights, and turn signals. Also check for any nicks or exposed wire in your wiring harness and tape or splice accordingly.

➤ Routinely spray heavy-duty, marine-grade rust inhibitor/lube into and between the moving parts of your trailer coupler and winch gear, as well as all of the trailer hardware and parts that are notorious for

rusting: the U-bolts and nuts, lug nuts, and leaf springs.

➤ Always keep a spare tire mounted to your trailer (with a lock on it), plus keep a jack and lug wrench in your tow vehicle that are compatible with your trailer. It's also wise to carry a flat tire kit that includes: road flares or reflectors, wheels chocks, a flashlight, a can of tire repair/sealant, extra trailer lights bulbs and fuses, and a 1-foot x 1-foot x ½-inch piece of plywood to support the jack.

➤ Trailers with a brake system should be inspected once per year.

Repack or Replace

If you use your trailer regularly in saltwater, it's best to inspect and repack the bearings annually. Since bearings are relatively cheap, go ahead and replace bearings and races while you're at it. A set of two bearings, cones and a grease seal is around $20 for 1-inch axles.

A viable alternative is to carry a spare hub and bearing assembly, run your rig until the bearing starts making noise, heating up or leaking grease, and then replace the whole works. The work time is shorter because pulling the whole hub is easier than taking out the bearings, races and seals and installing new. A hub kit is about $40 to $65 for larger axles – cheap considering the problems of not having a spare handy.

Replacing a trailer hub is an important job for trailer safety.

Check fuses for corrosion. If you find anything with a hint of corrosion, clean or replace.

Wonder Why the Lights Aren't Working?

Wonder why the lights aren't working? Fixtures do corrode over time and need replacement, but there may be other gremlins. For example: Cheap, automotive-grade butt connectors will admit moisture and subsequent corrosion into the wires. A more durable installation would include special marine-grade butt connectors with heat-shrink tubing to seal out moisture.

Replacing these components is an easy job, and would save a lot of headaches on the water. While you're at it, also:

➤ Consult a wire size chart to ensure you have the correct wire for the power demands of the device and the roundtrip distance to the power source.

➤ Double-check to see that you have the proper overcurrent protection (fuse or breaker) for each circuit.

➤ Make sure the wiring is properly supported, and not sliding on a sharp edge or abrasive surface, or immersed in bilge water.

➤ For most below-decks installations, it's best to use special marine-grade tinned copper wire that's AWG-sized, UL-listed, and ABYC and USCG approved for the application.

➤ Resist the urge to "buy cheap:" Better in the long run to forge a relationship with qualified staff at a marine supply shop, where you can buy good components and find advice.

Wire terminal blocks should be kept corrosion free with corrosion inhibitor spray.

A VHF antenna connection is corroded and needs to be taken apart and cleaned, if not completely replaced.

Batteries

Difficulties starting the engine, quirky marine electronics, trolling motors that struggle: Many of the problems new boat-owners face may be attributed to the improper maintenance or selection of batteries and battery cables.

Dual starting batteries and dual house batteries with combiner and isolator switch.

Many problems new boat owners face may be attributed to improper maintenance of batteries.

The vast majority of electrical power needs on trailerable outboard boats are served by a 12-volt DC battery, or an array of them. That includes the starting circuits for engines, as well as the navigation lights, bilge pumps, trim tabs, livewells and many other accessories. But of course not all 12-volt batteries are the same. If you're replacing a starting battery, consult the engine manufacturer or owners' manual to ensure that you select a battery rated to supply the specified minimum cold cranking amps.

On most fishing boats, it's generally best to have at least two batteries: A starting, or cranking battery for each engine, and a "house battery" which supplies current for lights, pumps and other circuits. Battery switches may be installed which can isolate the starting battery from other demands, ensuring that you have plenty of juice to fire up the engine after a few hours of fishing at anchor, for instance. With a simple "1-2-All-Off" switch, for example, you might select battery 2—the deep-cycle—only while anchored (to power lights, electronics, pumps, etc.), and then 1 when you need to start the engine. If you have difficulty starting the engine, you could select All, and thereby combine the amps of the two batteries. Note that this would produce a parallel effect: You would increase the current, which is necessary for big loads such as starting motors, but still end up with 12 volts.

For the rare higher voltage needs, such as powering high-thrust electric trolling motors, 12-volt DC batteries may be connected in series: Two for 24 volts, three for 36 volts. Note that batteries used for trolling motors should be of the deep-cycle variety, specially designed for repeated, slow discharging. While most outboard engine alternators will supply sufficient charging current to replenish the starting battery(s), it's up to you to recharge the deep-cycle ones. You should always recharge them after a day of fishing, not only to ensure you have enough current for the next trip, but to provide for maximum longevity.

A marine-grade, multi-bank battery charger, which you simply plug into a 120-volt AC extension cord at home or at the dock is a very good addition to any boat. "Smart" models are available which determine and deliver the optimal charging current to charge each battery, depending on its condition, and then automatically switch off or go into maintenance mode. Some will even tell you vital information as to the state of the battery. Make sure to carefully follow the manufacturers' installation and use guidelines for these devices, as the confined buildup of gases during charging can lead to explosive trouble.

If your batteries are of the lead-acid "maintenance" variety, remember to check the level of electrolyte periodically. Add distilled water as needed to ensure the tops of the metallic plates, visible beneath the vent caps, are submerged by about ¼ to ½ inch.

How to Check 4-Stroke Outboard Motor Oil Level

Although 4-stroke outboard motors don't use the gas/oil mixture that 2-stroke motors do, it's perfectly normal for even brand new 4-stroke outboards to consume small, to very-small amounts of 4-stroke oil during normal operation. This is due to the mechanical differences between 4-stroke automobile engines and outboards. It is because of this that 4-stroke outboards should be routinely checked for proper oil level.

Checking the oil level in a 4-stroke outboard motor is very similar to checking it in an automobile, only with the additional steps of tilting the motor up and then down, which is also necessary due to mechanical differences between 4-stroke auto engines and outboards. With the motor shut off:

1. Tilt the motor all the way up and let it sit for about 5 minutes. This is required to get a true measurement.

2. Tilt the motor down until it is level.

3. Pull out the oil dipstick and wipe any oil off of it with a clean, lint-free rag.

4. Reinsert it completely, and then pull it back out again to see if the film of oil on the dipstick is in between the low and full oil level indicator marks on the end of the dipstick.

5. If the oil level is below, at or near the low mark, slowly add oil into to the motor's oil fill, pouring in small-quantity increments until the level is at or near the full mark. Using a funnel is recommended to prevent spills.

6. If the oil level is above the full mark, it is very important to drain or pump out enough oil to get the level back down to the full mark. Running a 4-stroke outboard with too much oil in it can actually cause severe motor damage, which is not covered by warranty.

7. Always refer to your motor manufacturer owner's manual for the specific type of oil required for your motor.

Keeping Your Boat Looking Like New

If unable to keep your boat under covered storage, an investment in a boat cover and keeping it on in-between uses will definitely pay for itself over time in the form of retained boat value. Constant, direct exposure to the sun's damaging UV rays and heat, along with accumulating rain water, dirt, leaves, and bird droppings, can fade and begin to deteriorate most of a boat's surface materials in less than two years.

If shopping for a boat cover, be sure to choose a good-quality one that is well-vented. Poorly or non-vented covers that don't breathe will trap moisture and welcome mildew that can permanently stain vinyl upholstery and carpet.

Keeping your boat clean, inside and out – and protected from the elements – will ensure that it stays looking as new as possible for as long as possible. For fiberglass boats, to preserve the shine of the gelcoat, it must be kept clean and also protected

A boat cover is well-worth the extra cost, paying for itself many times over by protecting your boat and helping to preserve its long-term value.

with a high-quality gelcoat wax. Cheap waxes just don't work as well, or last nearly as long.

TIP: With just a bucket and some plain water, magic erasers or easy erasing pads work exceptionally-well for a quick, overall spot-cleaning of a boat (especially handy when you don't have access to a hose). These non-toxic, little wonders of science can cut boat cleaning time in half, and will even remove most stains and gelcoat marks with relative ease. The heavy-duty ones cost slightly more but last longer.

CHAPTER 14

Boat Storage and Winterizing

Deciding where and how to keep or store your boat, is a fairly big decision in terms of convenience, cost, security, and maintaining its overall condition. The majority of trailerable boats are kept and stored on their trailers and at the homes of their owners. Most boat owners who have this option, benefit from being able to keep a close eye on their boat, always having it readily-accessible to hitch right-up to and tow to the water, work on or clean it at any time, and not having to pay for these conveniences. But there are millions of other boat owners who don't have that option due to HOA rules or simply a lack of parking space where they live. If you either have to or choose to keep your boat elsewhere, throughout the following chapter are some key points to consider. SB

Deciding where and how to keep or store your boat is a fairly big decision.

FL 0504 MY

FL0247MB

M3 0525 M3

FL 8623 MM

B
19-34

Marinas offer a
variety of boat
storage options
and services.

Boat/RV Self-Storage Yards (Basic/Open)

Basic boat storage yards are expensive, but most provide minimal security or amenities.

Boat/RV Facilities with Open & Covered Storage Options

Boat and RV facility with both open and covered storage options.

Advantages
- Option of open storage, or paying more for covered storage.
- Most have facilities for you to service your boat: power, water, restrooms.
- Some offer shrink-wrapping service for winter/long-term boat storage.
- Fair to very good security.
- Most allow 24-7 access.

Disadvantages
- More expensive than basic yards (but typically less than marinas).
- Some may require a long-term contract.

Boat and RV storage yard.

Advantages
➢ Typically the least-expensive option.
➢ Most allow 24-7 access.
➢ Many have plenty of room to maneuver your trailer.

Disadvantages
➢ Some offer minimal or no security from theft or vandalism.
➢ Some have no power or water access for you to service your boat.
➢ Exposed to the elements, boat cover needed.

Indoor Boat/RV Storage Facilities

Advantages
➢ Max protection from the elements (and birds), no need for a boat cover.
➢ Facilities for you to service your boat: power, water, restrooms, etc.
➢ Excellent security.
➢ Some are climate controlled.
➢ Option to work on your boat during winter months.

Disadvantages
➢ Expensive.
➢ Some may require a long-term lease.
➢ Some don't allow 24-7 access.

Marinas – Dry Rack Storage – Outside & Enclosed Options

Outside dry rack storage.

Dry rack storage offers the convenience of simply calling ahead to splash your boat.

Partially-enclosed dry rack storage.

Advantages
> Convenience of not having to trailer your boat – just call ahead to have it dropped in the water.
> Most with dry storage are full-service marinas: fuel, oil, parts, repairs, detailing, concierge, etc.
> Option of an outside storage rack, or paying more for an enclosed storage rack.
> Good to excellent security.
> Most offer month-to-month terms.
> Some include splash and haul-out forklift services with the monthly fees.

Disadvantages
> Some can be expensive.
> A boat cover will be needed regardless of outside or enclosed storage.
> If the boat stacked above yours is leaking any oil or fluid, it'll drip onto your boat.
> Birds like to use boats stacked on dry racks as their condos, and highway rest stop facilities.
> You'll need to find a place to store your trailer, another possible expense.

Enclosed dry rack storage.

Marinas – Wet Slip Storage

Covered wet slip storage.

Open wet slip storage.

For wet slip storage, remember to keep your outboard(s) tilted up.

Advantages

- ➢ Your boat is always in the water and ready-to-go.
- ➢ Convenience of not having to trailer your boat, or wait for it to be put in.
- ➢ Direct access to power and water for you to service your boat in its slip.
- ➢ Some offer slips with a boat lift as an upgrade option, eliminating the need for bottom paint.

Disadvantages

- ➢ Your boat is always in the water; any boat moored long-term needs to be bottom-painted, which also requires additional routine maintenance and costs.
- ➢ Necessitates frequent check-ins on your boat for bilge pump operation and optimal mooring.
- ➢ Fully-exposed to the elements, water conditions and bird bombs – boat cover needed.
- ➢ More vulnerable to storm damage, boats in hurricane zones need to be hauled out and secured whenever threatened by hurricane warnings.
- ➢ Some are only available as a purchase or long-term lease.

Wet Slip Storage Tips

➤ Wherever possible cross-tie your dock lines across your boat slip, and use opposing spring lines wherever necessary. These are simplest and most effective ways to properly and safely moor a boat in a slip.

➤ Always remember to tilt your outboard motor(s) completely up and out of the water after every boat use, even in freshwater.

➤ A boat's initial bottom paint job must be done properly with very thorough prep work, and the appropriate type of antifouling paint for your boat hull material and the kind of water it will be moored in. Otherwise the paint won't stick uniformly, will peel off in patches, and quickly collect bottom growth. If not having the work done professionally, be sure to consult with a marine supply expert before buying your prep or paint supplies. Also, paint at least 4 inches above the waterline to prevent having to constantly clean off a scum line.

All storage arrangement options present at least one minor drawback, including the one most boaters agree to be the ultimate amenity and convenience. Boat owners who are fortunate enough to live on waterfront property with a private dock and boat lift, enjoy the luxury of anytime, immediate access to boating. But they still need occasional access to a trailer for certain service work, or if a long-distance road trip calls for it.

Use cross-ties and spring lines for a secure wet slip tie-off.

While deciding which option is best for you, keep in mind that if you live in or near a coastal hurricane zone – depending on your storage situation – you may need to have a contingency plan prepared for the 5 or 6 months of the year that your boat could possibly need to be temporarily relocated or thoroughly battened down.

A backyard boat lift is the ultimate convenience for regular boaters.

Winterizing – It's Not Just for Northern States

Winterizing is a necessary annual routine crucial to protecting your investment from freezing temperatures and periods of non-use. It's another aspect of boat maintenance that is well worth the time, effort and cost – especially when boating season arrives and your boat is as ready to fire up and get back out on the water as you are.

Winterization and long-term (2 months or more) storage procedures for outboard motors can vary significantly by type and manufacturer, so it's important to check your owner's manual for the recommended procedures for your specific motor(s) if you intend to do it yourself.

Anywhere and everywhere that temperatures can dip below the freezing point – even for very short times – outboard motors can be vulnerable to severe damage caused by any water left within the engine block or lower unit when it freezes. Expanding ice can actually crack the block or lower unit gearcase... very expensive damage that is not covered by warranty.

Fortunately this kind of freeze damage is quite easy to avoid in outboard motors since they're designed to self-drain, but it's critical to remember that the motor must be left in the fully down, vertical position for all of the water to drain out, and stay out. The motor shouldn't be tilted up even slightly because rain or melted snow can collect in parts of the lower unit gearcase, and then freeze. Another plus to keeping the motor tilted all the way down – it protects the power tilt rams.

If for any reason it's not possible to store your outboard positioned completely down, wrap a heavy-duty plastic bag around the prop and gearcase opening, and secure it tightly with bungee cords.

Some outboard owners

Winterizing for any outdoor storage should include the use of a quality boat cover.

choose to take the extra winterizing precaution of flushing non-toxic, marine antifreeze into their motors using a winterizing kit made for sterndrives and outboards. (Automotive antifreeze should never be used.) This ensures that any water trapped anywhere in the motor will not freeze. Although not really necessary if you can keep the motor fully down, it certainly can't hurt.

Anywhere temperatures can freeze, outboards can be vulnerable to damage.

Wire brushing battery posts after removing terminals for the winter.

Boat Storage Security

Boat trailers are highly targeted by thieves. Whether or not your boat is on it, always keep your trailer protected with a high-quality, heavy-duty coupler lock – the type that locks into the coupler cavity and guards it. Cheaply-made, inexpensive coupler locks and padlocks are easily sawed or hammered right off. Also use a wheel lock for a second layer of security.

Outboards are another commonly-stolen valuable in high demand. Every outboard motor should be secured with a motor lock. If you store your boat on your trailer, whenever possible park it in a position that would make it difficult for thieves to access and remove your motor(s).

If your boat is kept in a wet slip or on a boat lift, secure it to the dock with a high-strength steel cable lock. Also consider some of the new, boat-theft deterrent items on the market, such as a Dock-N-Lock, an alarm system, and a GPS boat-tracking system. And never leave the ignition keys anywhere on or in your boat.

The more measures you take to deter theft, and the more difficult and time-consuming stealing your boat, motor or trailer would be for the average criminal, the more likely it is that they'll leave your stuff alone and move on to look for an easier opportunity.

Larger marinas with extra acreage usually offer outdoor trailer storage.

Outboard Motor Winterizing and Storage DIY Steps

The following steps do not all apply to all outboard motors. Refer to your owner's manual for specific requirements applicable to your brand and type of motor. You'll need: fuel stabilizer for outboards – enough for your fuel tank's capacity, an aerosol can of Fogging Oil, and your tools.

1. Fill the fuel tank but don't top it off all the way up to the fill cap because there needs to be a bit of room left for gas expansion. A full tank will reduce water condensation, and will also help to prevent phase separation if the gas contains any ethanol.

2. Add the fuel stabilizer to help preserve the gas, and to protect the fuel system and motor from gum and varnish buildup, and corrosion. Follow the instructions on the product bottle.

Fuel stabilizer is well-worth its relatively low cost for boat storage purposes, and for helping to prevent ethanol-blended fuel contamination.

3. With the motor tilted down and running in neutral, flush the cooling system using a motor flusher connected to a hose for at least 10 minutes so that the motor runs at normal operating temperature and opens up the thermostat(s). This is important because the flushing water needs to circulate throughout all cooling passages in the engine block, and if you want to run antifreeze into the system, it definitely needs to be able to get in there too. Running the motor during this step also allows for the fuel stabilizer to circulate through the fuel lines and injectors or carburetor, which is necessary for it to protect them.

4. With the motor still running and being flushed, spray the fogging oil directly into the motor's fuel system per the appropriate instructions. Different motors call for different methods and spray locations. Some involve spraying it into the carburetor, air intakes, or fogging ports during the final seconds of the flushing process. Others don't recommend spraying it into the fuel system at all.

5. With the motor turned OFF – AND the kill

A full tank will reduce water condensation, and will also help to prevent phase separation if the gas contains any ethanol.

switch disconnected (or switched to the off position) to prevent starting, remove all spark plugs and spray fogging oil into each cylinder while simultaneously turning the motor over for 3 or 4 seconds. This evenly distributes the oil throughout the cylinders, helping to prevent internal corrosion and rust. It often requires a helper to spray while you turn the key. Another option for some (but not all) motors is to manually rotate the flywheel several times. When completed,

Disconnecting the motor's fuel filter to drain the gas and check the filter element.

Most winterizing checklists suggest that you also perform all standard maintenance tasks.

torque spark plugs to specs.

6. If your motor will be stored and not run for more than 6 months, it's also a good idea to drain the VST (vapor separator tank) or carburetor float bowls, if it has either. Simply disconnecting the fuel supply line from the motor and letting it run out the remaining fuel, won't get rid of the residual gas. But if you do your own winterizing, you're enough of a gearhead to easily follow your manual's instructions for this. On fuel injected motors just locate and remove the drain screw (if it has one, some do not), at the bottom of the VST to drain it. On most carbs, there's a small drain screw at the base of each bowl, and some models also have a drain hose. Be sure to hold a cup under each drain screw as you back it out.

7. Most winterizing checklists recommend that you also perform all of the standard, annual maintenance procedures, such as replacing the oil and filter, lower unit gear oil, fuel water separator, spark plugs, etc. And doing so is surely a great idea if you prefer to be as prepared as possible for the next boating season. However, you may want to hold off on replacing some of these things until springtime, after your first run out on the water. For example, if you install brand new spark plugs during your winterizing steps, they could get fouled with fogging oil when you first fire up your motor for the new year.

Cleaning and waxing your boat's gelcoat just prior to long-term storage helps to protect it from the elements.

Boat and Trailer Winterizing and Storage Steps

1 If you have any detachable electronics, a trolling motor, a kicker motor, fishing gear, flares, or inflatable PFD's onboard, remove and store them indoors.

2. If you live where snow accumulates, to protect your Bimini top from the weight of snow and ice, either remove and store it in your garage, or collapse it and zip the protective boot over it.

3. Disconnect and remove the batteries, and store in a cool (but not freezing), dry place. Check to make sure that your batteries are fully charged before storing.

4. Thoroughly clean your boat inside and out; including the bilge, baitwell, fish boxes, coolers, and the hull. Make sure all water drains out of all compartments and the bilge. Also clean the motor top-to-bottom. After cleaning the powerhead and letting it dry, spray it with corrosion inhibitor. This may sound like a lot of work, but it's a lot easier than waiting until after it's all been sitting for several months.

5. Double-check that your drain plug is removed, and also that there are no leaves or anything in the bilge that could cause your boat to fill up with water. If stored on a trailer, make sure that the trailer tongue is set high enough for your boat to drain without holding water in the bilge.

6. For best results, your boat should be either covered with a quality, well-vented boat cover, or professionally shrink-wrapped for any long-term or short-term storage – regardless of climate. There's simply no better way to protect your investment from the elements and contaminants. If you do cover your boat – before it's done – slightly prop open some of the compartment doors and hatches with pieces of foam to allow air circulation. Placing containers of moisture absorber in the boat can also help to prevent mildew.

7. If you store your boat on a trailer, consider slightly elevating the frame with plywood-supported jack stands to lift the tires just off the ground. Trailers parked idly on the ground for long periods can develop flat spots and sidewall dry-rot on the tires. Removing the wheels and storing them in your garage is another option, or if that's not doable then tire covers are the next-best thing if the tires are elevated.

> **This may sound like a lot of work, but it's easier than waiting until after it's all been sitting for several months.**

For long-term or winterizing boat storage, disconnect and remove the batteries. Store them in a cool – but not freezing, dry place.

Remember to put your drain plug back in.

Spring Start-up

Checklists help to avoid forgetting anything before your spring launch.

When you're ready to "wake" your boat up from its winter hibernation, it's helpful to use a couple of checklists, just to avoid forgetting anything important before your first launch of spring. The following checklist, along with the "USCG Required + Recommended Boat & Safety Gear Checklist" from Chapter 6, will help you get set for a full season of trouble-free boating and fishing.

1. Check your batteries, and if necessary, top off with distilled water and fully charge.

2. Top off your boat trailer's tire pressure, check the bearings, and check all of the lights.

3. After removing your boat cover or shrink-wrap, and putting everything back on and in your boat and trailer that you previously took off or out, use the boat and safety gear checklist from Chapter 6 to make sure you have everything on-board to be safe and legal out on the water. Check the date on your fire extinguisher too.

4. With your motor connected to a flusher and running hose, prime your fuel line's primer bulb, connect your kill switch, and start your motor. It will probably smoke profusely at first, but that's perfectly normal, assuming that you used fogging oil and ran fuel stabilizer through your motor during winterization.

5. While the motor is running, check for good water flow from the tell-tale. After letting it run for several minutes, if the motor idles smoothly and all seems well, then shut it off and disconnect the kill switch.

6. Give her a quick spring cleaning... your boat, that is. Check the bilge for any dirt or leaves that made their way in during storage, and make sure the bilge pump is working down there too.

7. PUT YOUR DRAIN PLUG BACK IN.

8. Launch your boat and run it out to check for: full power, smooth shifting in and out of forward and reverse gear, unrestricted throttle control, smooth and responsive steering control, working bilge pump, livewell pumps, gauges, electronics, lights, the horn, etc. Also check for leaks.

9. Once you've run the boat out and checked for anything that needs to be addressed, now it's time to go ahead and install new spark plugs and take care of any other annual maintenance items that you may have decided to hold off on until spring.

CHAPTER 15

Registration, Licensing, and Final Notes

If you're new to boating or have just recently decided to get back into it after years on dry land, you may be wondering what all of the current legal requirements are. Do I have to get a boating license? What are the age restrictions for kids to operate at boat? Do I need a fishing license? What about my boat, motor and trailer, I know that registrations are mandatory for boats and trailers, but do they all have to be titled too?

Generally speaking, in addition to the minimum federal requirements of the United States Coast Guard, vessel owners and operators are required to comply with the regulations and/or laws specific to their state. Laws and regulations vary by state, and also vary by vessel type and size, and by operator or licensee age. SB

Boating laws and regulations vary by state. They also vary by vessel type and size, and by operator or licensee age.

Fishing regulation laws and license fees help to fund the protection of many fish species, such as this healthy snook.

Boating Safety Education Laws

Most states have age-specific children's life jacket law requirements.

Each state has its own laws and regulations. Your state requirements are conveniently listed on one or more of these website pages:

- boat-ed.com
- americasboatingcourse.com/lawsbystate.cfm
- boaterexam.com/usa

All three of these websites provide state-approved online boating safety courses that are also NASBLA-approved; National Association of State Boating Law Administrators. Additionally, the first two of these websites post a clickable link to your state government's website for quick access to registration and titling requirements.For additional boating safety courses: uscgboating. org > Safety > Boating Safety Courses. (Note: not all jurisdictions accept online courses.) Whether required to or not, every boater should take a boating safety course, preferably from a NASBLA-approved course provider. The more you know the safer you, your passengers, your boat and everyone you share the waterways with will be.

U.S. Coast Guard Boater's Guide to Federal Requirements for Recreational Boats

Go to: uscgboating.org > REGULATIONS > Federal Requirements Brochure
Scroll down to the link: uscgboating.org/fedreqs/default.html
- Info on minimum federal safety equipment requirements for vessels.
- Vessel registration, numbering and documentation requirements.
- Navigation rules, operating procedures, USCG safety tips, etc.
- Marine emergency communications: satellite EPIRBs, DSC (Digital Selective Calling), VHF-FM marine radio channels, and radio regulations.
- Law enforcement issues: negligent operation, BUI (boating under the influence), termination of use, boat accident reporting requirements, and rendering assistance to other boaters.

Child Life Jacket Laws

Most states have children's life jacket law requirements. In states that don't, federal USCG rules require any child under 13 on a boat underway to wear a properly-fitting, USCG-approved life jacket or PFD. This USCG regulation does not change or supersede state laws.

Children's age and wearing requirements for life jackets for each state are conveniently listed at:
boatus.org/life-jacket-loaner/state-requirements

Boat and Trailer Registration

For easy access to your state government's website for the registration and titling requirements pertaining to boats, trailers, and in some states – outboard motors:
- americasboatingcourse.com/lawsbystate.cfm
- takemefishing.org/boating/register

Trailer Brake Laws

For a state-by-state list of laws regarding trailers brake requirements, go to:
drivinglaws.aaa.com/laws/trailer-brakes

Safety Checks

Get a FREE Vessel Safety Check – Offered by the U.S. Coast Guard Auxiliary and U.S. Power Squadrons. Here's the website to get started:
vdept.cgaux.org

State Fishing Licenses/Permits & Fishing Laws/Regulations

Have you ever wondered why you have to get and pay for a fishing license or permit? There are actually some excellent causes that the funds support, and they help to ensure that fishing will be enjoyed by our future generations. Fisheries, habitat and ecosystem development and protection, conservation education, endangered species programs, maps and publications, and other important programs – all benefit from the fees we contribute.

For your state's fishing licensing requirements and fishing regulations, and to pay for your license online, go to: takemefishing.org/fishing/license

Waterway law enforcement officer checks boaters for proper and current credentials.

Ever wonder why you have to get and pay for a fishing permit?

Remember to also be aware of your state's requirements for trailer brakes.

Boater Etiquette
...Things To Keep In Mind

There's always been a culture of camaraderie among fellow boaters.

1 Always be willing to lend a hand, knowing that you can usually expect the same in return. People new to boating are soon pleasantly surprised to find that most boaters are more than happy to go out of their way to offer assistance to other boaters. Give a little help whenever a boat is pulling into the dock, or having mechanical problems out on the water. There's always been a culture of camaraderie among fellow boat owners, and as long as we all continue to watch each other's backs, there always will be.

2. Help prevent Ramp Rage. Boat ramps have been the scene of countless cases of lost patience and flared tempers. It's usually provoked by boaters who are oblivious to the unwritten rules of the ramp, or are well aware, but are just plain inconsiderate. When launching or retrieving your boat, always be efficient about it by doing your pre-launch or post-launch prep work in the parking lot, out of the way. Unless you encounter a completely unexpected problem, the time that you occupy the ramp shouldn't be longer than 3 minutes. Wherever possible,

Glassy conditions greet the sunrise to start a beautiful day on the water.

Boats, bikinis and the beaches... it's no wonder boaters tend to be so friendly.

pull your boat over to a courtesy dock to board passengers.

3. Always mind your wake when passing by other boaters. This is obvious for No Wake zones. But everywhere else, keep in mind that slowing down just enough to come off plane actually produces a larger, more disruptive wake than

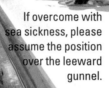

If overcome with sea sickness, please assume the position over the leeward gunnel.

continuing to cruise on plane at speed.

4. Respect the boaters around you at all times. Sound carries very well on the water, so keep your music volume at a reasonable level. If you have kids or dogs that tend to get loud, pick a hang-out spot that's distant and downwind from boaters who are fishing or clearly trying to relax in peace.

5. The same concept of consideration and respect for fellow boaters' time applies to fuel docks. Don't hog the middle of the fuel dock; always tie off where you'll leave room for other arriving boats. Always pump your gas as soon as a pump is available, and then immediately move your boat to take care of anything else.

6. Everyone knows littering is wrong. It's a fineable offense as well, so please never litter anywhere.

7. For fishing, always consider and respect anglers who have arrived at a fishing area before you; they have priority. Keep enough distance

Seasickness Advice

1. If you're prone to it, take non-drowsy motion sickness pills well before going to offshore. Prevention works better than treatment. Once you begin to feel queasy, it's too late for the pills.

2. Most people eventually get acclimated to being in a vessel at sea. If you're in the "not most people" category, but still love to go offshore fishing, ask your doctor about scopolamine patches, which can work better than pills and cause less side effects for some people. They're available by prescription only.

3. Avoid alcohol the night before going offshore, and get a good night's sleep. Being tired and hungover will predispose you to seasickness.

4. Eat a light, bland breakfast an hour prior to heading out. Most people find that an empty stomach is more sensitive. Include a protein such as a hard-boiled egg, energy bar, dry nuts or yogurt. Avoid greasy, acidic and spicy food and drinks. Fried eggs doused with hot sauce, a handful of bacon, and a tall glass of OJ are no way to start the day when you're gonna be dealing with rolling seas.

5. Keep hydrated throughout the day with plenty of non-alcoholic fluids.

6. When feeling seasick, keep your eyes on the horizon, facing the direction in which the boat is traveling. Avoid reading and focusing on things in the boat or close by. Stay topside in one spot close to the center of the boat. Also try to avoid any odors. If possible and appropriate, get into the water and submerge; this will often help you quickly feel better.

7. If you feel it coming on, don't try to fight it off... heave away. Prolonging the inevitable will only prolong your misery. But do it over the side on the leeward (downwind) rail of the boat, please. It'll make you feel better, quicker.

to allow them to continue fishing the same way that they were when you got there. Never troll or pole around fishing boats anchored, and never anchor in the midst of trollers or polers. Never leave a wake when passing by anglers working a shoreline or reef.

A Virtual Treasure Trove of Good Stuff – Just a Few Clicks Away

The amount and variety of information and resources available on the ever-expanding internet is pretty amazing. Virtually anything you could ever want to research or inquire about – including of course: boats, boating and fishing – can be found right online.

Boaters, soon-to-be boat owners, and anglers can save a lot of time and money by taking advantage of all the internet has to offer. There are websites aplenty for easy access to: state-required boater education and safety courses, boat and trailer registrations, boating and fishing licenses, and informative and helpful articles, blogs and tutorial videos.

Some of the best deals are found online for all kinds of boat and fishing-related products. Boat and outboard motor manufacturers' websites not only offer photos, descriptions, specifications and options for each of their product models, many of them also provide important and handy owner resources such as downloadable owner manual PDF's and warranty policies. And for the DIY maintenance and repair boat owners, outboard OEM parts catalogs are available too.

BEST BOAT Online
- floridasportsman.com/florida-sportsman-best-boat
- Florida Sportsman Forum Classifieds

On-Water Boat Towing Services and Insurance
- boatus.com/towing
- boatus.com/insurance
- seatow.com

Pre-owned Boats For Sale Listings
- boattrader.com
- boats.com
- boatstore.floridasportsman.com
- craigslist.org
- ebay.com
- nadaguides.com/boats (for used boat, motor and trailer values)

Free Online Owner's Manuals for Outboard Motors
- marine.honda.com/owners/manuals
- mercurymarine.com/service-and-support/storage-and-maintenance/engines/outboards
- nissanmarine.com
- tohatsu.com/tech_info/manuals.html
- yamahaoutboards.com/owner-resources/owners-manuals

Miscellaneous Organizations
- asafishing.org (American Sportfishing Association)
- blueocean.org (Blue Ocean Institute)
- coastalconservation.us (Center for Coastal Conservation)
- coralreef.noaa.gov (Coral Reef Conservation Program)
- joincca.org (Coastal Conservation Association)
- fishamerica.org (FishAmerica Foundation)
- fisheries.org (American Fisheries Society)
- futurefisherman.org (Future Fisherman Foundation)
- igfa.org (International Game Fish Association)
- oceana.org (Oceana Ocean Conservation)
- oceanconservancy.org (Ocean Conservancy)
- oneworldoneocean.com (One World One Ocean Campaign)
- takf.org (Take A Kid Fishing Foundation)
- thebasscollege.com/bassfishingclubs.htm (Bass Fishing Clubs)
- watersgeo.epa.gov/mywaterway (How's My Waterway – EPA's water condition site)

Miscellaneous Retailers
- amazon.com
- basspro.com
- cabelas.com
- dickssportinggoods.com
- gandermountain.com
- miamiboatshow.com
- reelsandtackle.com
- sportsauthority.com
- tackledirect.com
- tacklewarehouse.com
- westmarine.com

Families that play together, stay together... and what better way than by boating?

Boaters and anglers can save a lot of time and money by taking advantage of all the resources out there for bettering their knowledge.

Boat Anatomy and Terminology 101

Boater lingo is loaded with unique vocabulary, nautical terms and technical jargon rarely heard outside the field of boating. A review of the following definitions and diagrams will help you to better understand everything explained throughout this book, as well as help prepare you for your new life as a knowledgeable, savvy boat owner.

For those with a boating background, it's still a good idea to give this list the ol' once-over as a brief refresher course. You'll probably pick up a few new terms that you've heard of, but weren't quite sure about.

Aerator: an electric pump that forces oxygen into a baitwell or livewell to keep bait alive. (see Baitwell)

Aft: toward or at the stern of a vessel; the rear end. 34, 62, 94, 120, 181, 195

Aids to navigation: the system maintained by U.S. Coast Guard, consisting of visual, audible, and electronic signals or markers designed to assist mariners with navigation; devices specifically for assisting navigators in determining their position or safe course, or to warn of dangers or obstructions to navigation. 88, 166

Anchor light: a white safety light required for vessels while anchored at night, mounted above the boat's

Boat Overview

Terms and locations for some of the basic parts of a boat:

Bow Cleat · Starboard Side · Helm · Poling Platform · Bow · Deck · Gunwale · Stern · Port Side · Hull · Transom

Stern Diagram

Terms and locations for many of the boat parts and features common to outboard fishing boats:

Rocket Launchers

T-top

Cleat

Rod Holders

Motor Cowling

150 FOUR STROKE

T-BAG

Water Flow Indicator (Pilot Tube)

Motor Well

Stern Eye

Stern Eye

Livewell Drain

Scupper Drain

Trim Tab

Chine

Lower Unit

Deadrise

Transducer

Trim Anode

Prop

Raw Water Inlets

Bilge

Skeg

highest point for maximum, all-around visibility by other vessels. 117, 131, 162

Anchor line: the rope attached to an anchor. 124, 176

Anchor locker: a stowage compartment for the anchor, anchor chain and anchor line, usually located in the bow section. 177

Anode (aka **zinc anode** or **sacrificial anode**): an aluminum, zinc or magnesium alloy piece of hardware that is attached to a saltwater boat or its motor components in order to inhibit rapid, galvanic (dissimilar metal), saltwater corrosion; also used on freshwater boats that stay moored in the water for extended periods. 213, 245

Astern: at or toward the stern; moving a vessel backwards. 180, 187, 195

Attitude: the lengthwise angle of a boat as it rides on the water; in reference to planing, proper attitude is riding parallel to the water (on plane) with the bow level or just slightly raised by no more than 5 degrees. 61, 79, 93, 145

Baitwell (aka **livewell**): a built-in, covered water tank in a fishing boat, used to keep bait or fish alive with a raw water pump to recirculate the water and/or an aerator pump to provide oxygen. 98

Beam: the width of a boat at its widest point. 24, 64, 173

Bearing: the direction from your location to any distant point, given in degrees from north. 162

Bilge: the lowest or deepest section down inside of a vessel's hull where water collects. 45, 59, 62, 72, 117, 153, 181, 213

Bimini top: a canvas canopy for shade and partial rain protection, usually collapsible and situated mainly over a boat's helm section. 40, 186, 234

Boarding ladder (aka **swim ladder**): an attached or attachable ladder, accessible from the water for reboarding a boat. 41, 45, 49, 129

Boat Types:
Aluminum Jon Boat 30
Aluminum Utility Boat 31
Bass Boat 34
Bay Boat 38
Catamaran or Multihull 43
Center Console Boat or Open Fisherman 48
Deck Boat 42
Dual Console Boat 46
Fishing Skiff 33

Fish & Ski Boat 41
Flats Boat or Flats Skiff 36
Multi-Species or Walleye or All-purpose Fishing Boat 32
Pontoon Boat 44
Walkaround Boat or Express 50

Bow: the front or forward section of a vessel. 25, 30, 41, 46, 58, 93, 103, 120, 124, 138, 145, 153, 178, 188, 192, 196, 244

Bow eye: the U-bolt mounted through a boat's bow stem, used to secure tow lines or trailer winch hooks. 137, 140

Bow navigation light (aka **running lights**): the light(s) located on a vessel's bow, with red visible from the port side and green visible from the starboard side, required for nighttime running and low-visibility conditions. 101, 117, 118, 131, 162

Bow stop: the vee-shaped block or roller mounted on a boat trailer into which the boat's stem rests. 140

Brackish water (aka **inshore saltwater**): waters that are a mix of both freshwater and seawater or saltwater; contains a salinity of between .05percent and 3percent, (seawater has an average salinity of between 3.1percent and 3.8percent); estuaries are typically brackish. 28, 30, 33, 38, 41, 44, 176, 211

Breakaway lanyard: an emergency safety cable on a boat trailer that activates trailer brakes in the event the trailer becomes detached from the tow vehicle while towing. 137

Bunks: the lengthwise support boards on a boat trailer onto which the boat's hull rests. 56, 136, 140

Buoy: an anchored and distinctively marked float that serves as an aid to navigation. 166, 169, 181, 200

Capsize: to flip a vessel completely over or turned onto its side in the water. 63, 106, 120, 124, 153

Casting platform: a boat's elevated deck area or raised platform used for unobstructed casting while fishing, sometimes equipped with swiveling pedestal chairs. 37

Cathedral hull (aka **Tri-hull**): a monohull shape resembling an inverted "w" with a vee-hull centered between two smaller, vee-like sponsons; this hull design provides excellent lateral stability, quick planing and a shallow draft, however – in comparison to a deep-vee hull, isn't well-suited for choppy waters due to its relatively rough and wet ride in conditions exceeding moderate chop. 25, 26, 33, 42

Channel: the navigable route of a relatively shallow waterway, dredged and/or marked as the deepest, safest pathway to travel through the body of water; channels can be naturally occurring or man-made, and include both deep-dredged, ship-navigable lanes of an estuary or river leading to port facilities, and the smaller channels leading to facilities such as marinas or public boat ramps. 88, 121, 124, 128, 131, 147, 151, 157, 159, 162, 166, 168, 179

Chine: the portion of boat hull where the bottom and sides intersect, the shape of which contributes to the boat's lateral stability, as well as the hull's planing characteristics and ride quality. 24, 245

Chart: a navigational map. 88, 121, 157, 163, 165, 168, 179, 200

Chartplotter: an electronic marine navigation device that integrates GPS data with an electronic navigational chart (ENC), displays the ENC along with the position, heading and speed of a vessel for course plotting. 35, 49, 169

Cleat: a permanently mounted piece of hardware on a vessel or on a dock, to which dock lines are attached, designed to easily secure lines using a cleat hitch rather than a knot. 36, 178, 186, 194, 245

Cleat hitch: a particularly quick and easy method of securing a dock line onto a cleat, that is also quick and easy to untie, yet provides a remarkably strong hold if tied correctly. 180, 193

Console: the helm and control panel of a boat. 27, 30, 39, 46, 48

Course: the intended route to a destination. 121, 149, 153, 158, 165

Course bearing: the bearing to be followed to stay on a leg of a course. 162

Cruising speed: the speed or RPM at which a boat/motor gets optimal, high speed fuel economy by keeping the throttle at just above planing speed, can vary widely for different boats. 55, 58, 79, 130

Dead man's switch: see **Safety lanyard switch**.

Deadrise: the degree of V-shape, or angle in a boat's hull. 245

Deck: the top side of a vessel, generally refers to the areas that can be walked on. 17, 24, 57, 62, 65, 103, 117, 123, 244

Deep-vee: a vee-shaped hull, characterized by a sharp deadrise of more than 20 degrees, designed to cut through choppy waters or rough seas, and provide a smoother ride. 25, 26, 62

Depth sounder: an electronic device that measures and displays water depth below the boat, its alarm can be set to sound when in an area too shallow, intended to assist in verifying current depths, but not to be used as an aid to navigation, as it doesn't read approaching depths ahead. 35, 121, 169, 202

Dock line (aka **mooring line**): a relatively short rope with a looped end, used to tie a vessel to a dock or another object while in the water; can also be called a bow line, spring line or stern line – depending on which section of the vessel it is attached to. 118, 128, 186, 192, 194, 196, 229

Downrigger: gunnel-mounted, weighted line fishing gear, used for deep-water trolling. 33, 49, 95

Downwind: in the direction toward which the wind is blowing. 146, 196, 241

Draft (aka **draw**): the vertical distance between a vessel's waterline and the deepest part of the keel, however – for boats with an outboard motor, the draft is measured from the waterline to the bottom of the motor's skeg, with the motor tilted completely down; the minimum depth of water needed to float a particular vessel without any part of it touching bottom. 24, 64

Dry weight: the weight of a vessel without any fuel or water in its tanks.

Dry boat (aka **dry ride**): refers to a boat with a hull that is well-designed to deflect waves and spray down or out and away from the boat, rather than allowing water to spray upward from the sides and into the boat. 36, 55

DSC-VHF radio: Digital Selective Calling; with the touch of a button, instantly sends a distress alert to the USCG and other nearby vessels, (takes the search out of Search & Rescue); Very High Frequency; a bandwidth designation commonly used by marine two-way communication radios. 88, 119, 129, 133, 157

EPIRB: Emergency Positioning Indicating Radio Beacon; an electronic device used to alert search and rescue services in the event of an offshore emergency, transmits a distress signal with user registration data and positioning information to USCG satellites that assist in rescue operations. 129, 133, 238

Estuary (can be a **bay, harbor, lagoon, sound**): a partially enclosed coastal body of brackish water or saltwater with one or more rivers or streams flowing into it, with an open connection to the ocean;

although affected by winds and tides, estuaries are protected from the full force of ocean waves, winds, and storms by the reefs, barrier islands, or land fingers that delineate an estuary's seaward boundary; much of the **Intracoastal Waterway** is an estuary.

Estuarine species: oceanic finfish and shellfish that use estuaries during some or most stages of their life cycle.

Fender (aka **dock fender** or **dock bumper**): a cylindrical or round, heavy-duty vinyl cushion, used to protect the hull sides of a boat from damage or scratches while tied up to a dock or another boat. 186, 192

Fish finder: an electronic device that uses sonar to locate fish that are below or near the boat and display them on a monitor, most units also serve the same purpose as a depth sounder. 89, 95, 121, 202

Flats (aka **grass flats**): the shallowest, inshore or shoreline areas of a body of water; most commonly refers to saltwater shallows. 36, 92, 151, 203, 206

Float Plan: a form or list of detailed info pertaining to your boat trip - left with a person prior to departing who can be depended on to notify the USCG or local rescue if you don't check in or return as scheduled; it lists a detailed description of your boat, your departure point, your destination(s), stopover points, expected return time, all persons onboard + their emergency contact info + any medical conditions, a list of onboard safety equipment/electronics/provisions, home port details including vehicle and parking info, and emergency phone numbers for the USCG, local authorities and tow services; a very wise CYA precaution. 128, 133

Fore (aka **forward**): toward or at the bow (front) of a vessel. 34, 195

Fouled: obstructed / impeded; such as a propeller with a line caught in its blades, or a stuck anchor. 72, 173

Freeboard: the vertical distance from a boat's waterline to the lowest point of the gunnel. 24, 32, 180,

Gunwale (aka **gunnel**): the upper or top edge of the sides of a vessel. 28, 100, 244

GPH: Gallons Per Hour; measurement of a boat's fuel consumption, boats are not rated in MPG. 20

Hatch: a deck opening for access to a compartment; also: the cover over such an opening. 56, 59, 64

Head: the toilet facilities in a vessel. 47, 50

Heading: the compass direction toward which a vessel is pointing or traveling. 147, 162, 165, 201

Helm station: the captain's chair section of a vessel where the steering wheel, console and operational controls are located. 24, 27, 39, 41, 58, 199, 244

Hole shot: refers to the time it takes for a boat to accelerate "out of the hole" to get on plane from a dead stopped position in neutral. 84, 92, 150

Hp: horsepower; the power rating of a motor. 12, 16, 20, 59, 75, 79, 117

Hull: the structural and external body of a vessel's bottom and sides which provides buoyancy, the shape of a hull significantly affects the stability, power necessity, efficiency, ride quality, handling characteristics, top speed capability, and seaworthiness of a vessel. 14, 17, 24, 56, 59, 69, 80, 93, 144, 151, 229, 244

Idle: refers to the running of a motor while at rest and in neutral, and under no load; idling. 56, 73, 196, 213, 235

Idle speed (a classic oxymoron): refers to operating a vessel at the slowest possible speed necessary to maintain both forward motion and maneuverability; the low speed sustained when a vessel is put into forward gear without advancing the throttle, or with minimal forward throttle; proper idle speed produces little to no wake. 20, 121, 130, 162, 186

Inshore: see Estuary; also: on or near a coastal shore; or toward the shore. 29, 33, 38, 89, 133

Jack plate: a hydraulically or manually-adjustable mechanism, attached between a boat's transom and outboard motor, used to raise the vertical positioning of the motor in order to get up on plane in shallower water and to run shallower than with a standard mount; can also improve fuel economy if set correctly. 83, 92, 151

Keel: the lengthwise, structural centerline of a vessel hull; the backbone. 24, 56, 60, 77, 140

Kicker motor: a small auxiliary outboard motor, used in lieu of a boat's primary motor(s) for fuel- efficient, low-speed trolling or cruising, or as a spare backup motor. 32, 75, 77, 234

Kill switch: see **Safety lanyard switch**.

Knot: unit of measure for speed equal to 1 nautical mile per hour; approximately 1.15 mile per hour. 153, 173

Leaning post: a padded bolster mounted at the helm station, used to lean back against (instead of conventional boat seats), usually an option only in center

Power pole (aka **shallow water anchor**): a hydraulic anchoring device, mounted to the transom of a shallow water fishing boat; provides quiet, quick and easy anchoring in shallow waters, available in single units or pairs, and for up to 10 ft. depths; an upgrade option that prevents having to constantly wrestle with a standard anchor and line. 97, 206

Range: the distance that a vessel can travel (at cruising speed) on a full tank of fuel.

Rocket launcher: a set of rod holders on a fishing boat, designed to consolidate and vertically hold multiple fishing rods in a neatly stowed, yet readily accessible position; attached to the boat's T-top or tower, or to the captain's chair seatback frame, or the transom. 87, 245

Rod holder: a hardware device or a set of gunnel holes on a fishing boat, designed to vertically or horizontally hold fishing rods, to keep them neatly stowed, yet readily accessible. 94

Rub rail: the protective bumper attached around the perimeter of a vessel at its outermost points. 56, 59, 60

Safety lanyard switch (aka **kill switch** or **dead man's switch**): a important safety feature comprised of a short cord with a clip on one end that connects to a boat's safety/kill switch, and a clip on the other end that attaches to the boat operator's PFD or clothing, designed to pull out and disconnect the safety switch – instantly shutting off the motor if the operator falls away from the helm or falls overboard; as an added safety precaution, most are also designed to prevent the motor from starting at all unless the lanyard clip is connected. 117, 125, 128, 214

Scupper: a rudimentary device covering a drain hole in the hull, designed to allow rain or water in the boat to drain out by gravity, without allowing water to re-enter through the same drain, designed to act as a one-way valve, although some types or brands aren't completely reliable. 62, 153, 245

Seaworthy: a vessel that is designed, constructed and outfitted for safe voyage at sea; able to handle rough seas and weather. 25, 27, 43, 46

Self-bailing: a gravity-fed deck drainage system that allows rain and water to automatically drain out of the boat, without a pump. 58, 62

Shallow-vee: a semi-vee-shaped planing hull, designed to be a compromise between a flat bottom hull and a deep-vee hull. 25, 26, 34, 36

Sidle: the sideways motion of a vessel when slowing approaching a dock or other object; to dock a vessel by coasting in parallel to the dock. 186

Skeg: the fin-like projection at the bottom of the lower unit of an outboard or sterndrive motor, it assists in steering and control by serving as a rudder. 83, 245

Slip (aka **wet slip**): a berth between two piers or sets of pilings at a marina, designated for either short-term docking or long-term wet storage of vessels. 100, 183, 188, 195, 228, 231

Sponsons: the lengthwise, outer two portions of a cathedral or tri-hull, designed for lateral stability.

Spring line: a dock line tied off at or near the middle section of a vessel to control fore or aft movement while docked; or to apply opposing pull against another line to prevent dock contact. 192, 195, 229

Starboard: the right side of a vessel when facing forward to the bow. 120, 150, 159, 162, 167, 188, 244

Statute mile: a distance of 5,280 feet; the U.S. standard measure of distance on land and most inland waterways.

Stem: the forward, upright centerline of the hull that cuts through the water. 33

Stepped hull: a refined vee-hull design featuring lateral notches, or steps, in the keel and hull bottom; designed to reduce the hull surface area in contact with the water while on plane, in order to enhance lift, reduce drag and increase both speed and fuel efficiency, but can only provide these advantages at or above cruising speeds, and for some models – only when the boat is not loaded down to weight capacity. 17, 38, 48

Stern: the aft section of a vessel; the back or rear end. 25, 26, 70, 84, 124, 141, 146, 150, 186, 188, 195, 245

Sterndrive motor (aka **inboard/outboard motor** or **I/O**): a boat propulsion system that combines an inboard engine with outboard drive; the engine is mounted down inside the stern section of the hull, and connected through a sealed hole in the transom – to the outdrive, which is externally mounted to transom. 12, 70, 72, 117

Stow: to store and secure loose items such as gear and provisions into a compartment, locker or stowage area onboard a vessel, in order to keep them organized, out of the way, and prevent them from sliding or rolling around while underway. 45, 47, 64, 174, 177, 181

Strakes: sets of lengthwise, linear ridges molded into a boat hull, designed to improve planing lift and handling performance, and to provide a smoother, dryer ride. 23, 24

Swamp: to suddenly take on an excessive amount of water onboard a vessel; to fill or sink a vessel with water. 61, 120, 124,

Swim platform: a platform built into or attached to the stern of a boat, equipped with a boarding ladder to provide easy access into and out of the water. 38, 42, 49, 121

Tiller-steered outboard motor: a small, portable, low-hp outboard motor made primarily for small, light, basic vessels such as jon boats; uses a tiller handle fitted with motor controls to throttle and steer directly from the motor, rather than from a steering wheel or helm; also used as an auxiliary or kicker motor on boats larger in size. 30, 33

Tilt: refers to the angle position of an outboard motor when not underway; for boats equipped with a power trim and tilt system, the control switch is located at the helm, and on many outboards an additional tilt switch is located on the motor itself for ground access; the power tilt function is used to lower the motor down to the vertical running position, and to completely raise it to a horizontal position – which serves several key purposes. 56, 59, 71, 72, 83, 211, 221, 229, 230, 232

Transom: the vertical wall of a boat's stern; the structure to which outboard motors are attached. 17, 56, 72, 77, 90, 92, 101, 137, 146, 150, 206, 244

Trim: refers to the angle of the outboard motor in relation to the boat's hull while underway; trim angle directly affects a boat's planing attitude; for boats equipped with a power trim and tilt system, trim is adjusted using the same helm switch that controls power tilt. (In this context, attitude adjustment is quite literal.) 77, 79, 83, 92, 93, 140, 145, 150, 153

Trim tabs: a pair of hydraulically controlled, horizontal plates mounted to the transom where it meets the hull bottom, installed on boats that require maximum trim control, and to help offset a boat's unbalanced weight distribution while at cruising or high speeds. 49, 56, 93, 145, 146, 150, 153, 245

T-top: an aluminum-framed tower attached at the helm station of a center console boat or bay boat, with a flat, canvas or fiberglass overhead cover tall enough to stand under; it provides a solid handhold, as well as shade and partial rain protection for two or more people at the helm, and commonly features one or more built-in, weather-proof compartments designed to house electronic components and provide a dry-storage area; it usually has an attached set of rocket launchers and/or outriggers. 28, 38, 49, 87, 101, 245

USCG: United States Coast Guard. 108, 116, 118, 127, 238

Underway: refers to a vessel being in motion, or having begun to move or cruise. 92, 107, 109, 121, 144, 162

Ventilation: anomaly that occurs when air is drawn into a propeller's blades, causing it to push more air bubbles than water, which greatly reduces the load on the motor, allowing it to race and spin the prop at excessive RPM, resulting in cavitation, and generating little or no thrust until the prop slows enough for the air bubbles to subside; causes of ventilation can be a motor being tilted up too high, a motor that is mounted too high on the transom, or a damaged propeller. 77, 83

Vessel: a watercraft or ship of any type. 19, 43, 61, 108, 116, 118, 122, 127, 146, 158, 162, 173, 188, 236

Wake: the waves created by a moving vessel. 122, 126, 148, 187, 191, 241

Waterline: the intersection or line along the hull of a floating vessel where the surface of the water meets. 62, 72, 77, 178, 229

Waypoint: the GPS coordinates of a specific location. 88, 169, 198, 201, 204

Windlass: a winch – usually electric-powered - used to raise and lower a boat's anchor, if equipped. 49, 181

Windward: the direction from which the wind is blowing. 196

SPECIAL ACKNOWLEDGEMENTS:

A very grateful, big thanks to the following people and companies for photo opportunities, photo credits and/or general support:

Aaron Dumont
Abby & Sam White
Adam Eggers, PA1, U.S. Coast Guard
Bill Graham
Blair Wickstrom
Bryan Troy
Chris McCallister
Clark Howard
Coleen, Ed & Ian Nelson
David Conway
David & Reva Granati
Fred Sutton
Gary Whitehead
Gordon Clark
Jerry Butz
Joice Curry
Mark Lang, Officer, MPD Marine Patrol Unit
Matt Kerr
Mike Tarasavage
Nate Bowerman

Nick Telemachos
Nicole Tarasavage
Peter & Dixie Novaro
Richard Robinson
Ryan McKeone
Steven Terry
Tom Sanders Jr.

321 Boat Club, Melbourne, FL
Anchorage Yacht Basin, Melbourne, FL
Bass Pro Shops / Tracker Boats
Bennington Pontoon Boats
Best Food Town, Indian Harbour Beach, FL
Bluepoints Marina, Port Canaveral, FL
Boaters Exchange, Rockledge, FL
BoatUS
Boston Whaler
Carolina Skiff Boats
Day Brothers Boats, Plattsburgh, NY
Erik Wickstrom Photography
Firstwatch Gear
FormulaPropeller.com
G3 Boats
Grady-White Boats
Harbortown Marina, Merritt Island, FL
Hurricane Boats

Hutchinson Island Marriott Beach Resort
Lake Placid Marina, Lake Placid, NY
Lowe Boats
Lund Boats
NMMA/Progressive Ins. Miami Int. Boat Show
Polar Kraft Boats
Power Sports Storage of Corona
Reynolds Racing & Marine, Harriman, TN
Richter Anchors
Rinker Boats
Riverwatch Marina, Stuart
Robalo Boats
Rocna Anchors
Scout Boats
Sea Tow U.S. Stuart
Southeast U.S. Boat Show, Jacksonville, FL
Telemar Bay Marina, Indian Harbour Beach, FL
Tow Boat U.S. Stuart
Uncle Bob's Self Storage, Suntree, FL
United States Coast Guard
West Marine
WoodyBoater.com
World Cat Catamarans
Yamaha Communications, Heidi Weber

Information in this book is meant to supplement, not replace, a complete boating safety course. As with any activities involving mechanical equipment and power, speed, balance, coordination, and environmental factors, powerboating poses some inherent risk. The author advises readers to take full responsibility for their safety and know their limits. Before practicing the procedures, methods and skills described in this book, be sure that your boat, boat motor, boat trailer, and safety equipment are all well-maintained, and in good, reliable condition. Do not take risks beyond your level of experience, aptitude, training, and comfort level.

Much of this book is based on personal experience and anecdotal evidence. Although the authors have made every reasonable attempt to achieve complete accuracy of the content in this book, they assume no responsibility for errors or omissions. You should use this information as you see fit, and at your own risk. Your particular situation may not be exactly suited to the scenarios and examples explained herein; in fact, it is likely that they won't be the same, and you should adjust your use of the information and recommendations accordingly. Nothing in this book is intended to replace common sense, legal, medical or other professional advice. It is meant to inform and entertain the reader.

Portions of this book contain excerpts from the 2014 e-book publication BOATING SAVVY: What KNOT To Do™ – Often-overlooked & Lesser-known Keys to Safe & Smart Power Boating, 2nd Edition, also written by James Crounse.

"When I was 17, I read a quote that went something like: 'If you live each day as if it was your last, someday you'll most certainly be right.' It made an impression on me, and since then, for the past 33 years, I have looked in the mirror every morning and asked myself: 'If today were the last day of my life, would I want to do what I am about to do today?' And whenever the answer has been 'No' for too many days in a row, I know I need to change something."

~ Steve Jobs

BOATS DVD

The *Sportsman's Best: Boats* DVD brings the pages of the accompanying book to life. Join author Dave East as he explains everything a prospective boat buyer needs to know before purchasing a boat and all the basics of running and rigging that boat for fishing and family fun.

DVD CHAPTERS:

- ► THE APPEAL
- ► CHOOSING THE BEST BOAT FOR YOU
- ► OUTBOARD MOTORS
- ► RIGGING FOR FISHING
- ► TRAILERING, LAUNCHING
- ► BASIC DOCKING TECHNIQUE
- ► BOAT OPERATING, HANDLING
- ► ANCHORING
- ► BOAT MAINTENANCE

Enjoy your boat from the first day you purchase it with the help of this guide to boat ownership. Read this book, watch the DVD, the rest is up to you.

"Boats open a whole new world to anglers and families wanting to enjoy our rivers, lakes, bays, and oceans. After reading the book and watching the DVD, everyone in the market for a boat and every new boat owner will be better prepared to enjoy their boating adventures."

—*Blair Wickstrom, Publisher, Florida Sportsman*

DVD Executive Producers: Chris Collins & Scott Sanders